Woodworking for the Home
STORAGE PROJECTS
for All Around
the House

W9-BBE-199

PAUL ANTHONY

NIALL BARRETT

JEFF MILLER

The Taunton Press

The Taunton Press

Inspiration for hands-on living®

The Taunton Press, Inc., 63 South Main Street, PO Box 5506, Newtown, CT 06470-5506
e-mail: tp@taunton.com

LAYOUT: Cathy Cassidy
ILLUSTRATORS: Ron Carboni, Michael Gellatly, Melanie Powell, Rosalie Vaccaro
PHOTOGRAPHERS: Paul Anthony, Rich Bienkowski, Chris Holden, Tanya Tucka
COVER PHOTOGRAPHERS: (front cover) Chris Holden; (back cover, clockwise from top left) Rich
Bienkowski, Chris Holden, Tanya Tucka, Rich Bienkowski

LIBRARY OF CONGRESS CATALOGING-IN-PUBLICATION DATA:
Anthony, Paul, 1954-
  Woodworking for the home : storage projects : for all around the house / Paul Anthony, Niall Barrett, Jeff Miller.
     p. cm.
  ISBN 1-56158-801-6
  1. Cabinetwork--Amateurs' manuals. 2. Storage in the home--Amateurs' manuals. I. Barrett, Niall. II. Miller, Jeff,
1956- III. Title.
  TT197.A56 2005
  684.1'6--dc22
                         2005003429
Printed in the United States of America
10 9 8 7 6 5 4 3 2 1

The following manufacturers/names appearing in *Woodworking for the Home: Storage Projects* are trademarks: Festool®,
Lee Valley ™, Record®, Rockler℠, Stanley®, Watco™, Woodcraft®, Woodworker's Hardware℠

WORKING WITH WOOD IS INHERENTLY DANGEROUS. Using hand or power tools improperly
or ignoring safety practices can lead to permanent injury or even death. Don't try to perform
operations you learn about here (or elsewhere) unless you're certain they are safe for you. If
something about an operation doesn't feel right, don't do it. Look for another way. We want you
to enjoy the craft, so please keep safety foremost in your mind whenever you're in the shop.

To Niall, Jeff, and Paul, who put in the extra effort
to show other woodworkers how to build these projects

ACKNOWLEDGMENTS

THE PROJECTS IN THIS BOOK were drawn from four previously published Taunton books: *Classic Kitchen Projects* and *Building the Custom Home Office* by Niall Barrett, *Home Storage Projects* by Paul Anthony, and *Children's Furniture Projects* by Jeff Miller.

Photos for Niall's books were taken by Chris Holden, and for Jeff's book by Tanya Tucka. Paul Anthony took the photos for his book, with the exception of those taken by Richard Bienkowski and Greg Browning.

Thanks also to woodworkers Ken Burton, Denis Kissane, Adolph Schneider, Allen Spooner, and Peter Turner, who contributed projects.

CONTENTS

INTRODUCTION

S tuff. We humans are magnets for it. Everyday life seems to require a cornucopia of accessories—from bed linens, clothes, and food, to books, office supplies, and computer equipment. And that doesn't include all of the other collectibles that we're so fond of, including jewelry, music equipment, toys, and curios. The price of all this stuff, of course, is that it all has to live somewhere. And it needs to be accessible and organized or you'll waste hours of your life digging around for things buried in boxes or piled in corners.

But not to worry. Even if your home is beginning to resemble a frat house, there are plenty of good solutions for cleaning up the clutter. In this book you'll find cleverly designed projects for organizing and storing your belongings. And we're not talking closet shelving here; these are furniture-quality pieces that you'll be proud to display in your home as your own handiwork.

The projects in this book span a range of styles and draw upon the design expertise of some of the best woodworkers in the country. The designs range from simple to ambitious, and any of them can be modified to suit your particular needs. Some, like the plate display rack, can be built in a few hours. Others, like the hanging pot holder or CD cabinet, could probably be knocked out in a weekend. More involved projects such as the kitchen island or

mobile closet could take a week or more, depending on how fussy you are about construction and finish quality. In any case, all of the projects are well within the reach of any determined woodworker with a basic complement of tools.

In the process of building the projects, you'll also learn a lot about woodworking. Each chapter includes great information on techniques, tools, joinery, and finishing. You'll discover better ways to lay out and cut joints, fit drawers, and clamp up work. Never tried resawing or veneering? You'll find out how easy they can be. You'll also learn how to make clever jigs that will serve you in future woodworking projects.

Just as important, you'll learn how to design your own storage furniture. The first chapter walks you through the steps of assessing your particular storage problems and developing appropriate solutions. Among other things, it discusses sizing furniture to maximize storage, matching or complementing existing décor, tailoring a piece to suit its location, and making the most of available space.

So have at it. You'll enjoy making these pieces. They'll beautify your home and make your life more efficient and enjoyable. After all, the more organized your things are, the more space you'll create for comfort (or, of course, for more stuff!).

—Paul Anthony,
Author of *Home Storage Projects*

You can take the basic plan of any project and modify it to match your existing capacity needs and decor. This kitchen base cabinet is an upsize version of the small wine cabinet on p. 154.

DESIGNING AND BUILDING STORAGE PROJECTS

ESIGNING FOR STORAGE can be both a curse and a blessing. On the one hand, the immense design possibilities can seem overwhelming: You can make cabinets, boxes, bins, or benches and outfit them with dividers, shelves, drawers, doors, or racks. On the other hand, you often have the advantage of designing around items' specific sizes and shapes, which can give you a focus and a good running start. If you carefully consider the particular items to be stored and the space that the finished project will occupy, you've got half the battle won.

In this book, you'll find projects for use throughout the home—from the living room and office to the kitchen, bedroom, and bathroom. Some of the projects have been carefully designed to maximize storage for particular objects such as CDs, wine bottles, and office files. Other projects, such as the kitchen island, storage bed, printer stand, and toy chest, offer great versatility for general household and office storage.

Most of the pieces in this book should work great for you just as they are. However, you may want to customize some of them to suit your personal needs. In some cases, you'll want to change the size of a design to accommodate your specific collection of items. Sometimes, you'll want to modify the dimensions to suit a certain space in your house or apartment.

Planning and Customizing Designs

When it comes to designing, begin with what you know. Note the dimensions of the objects to be stored. If you are dealing with a standard size, as for file folders, design around that size to minimize wasted space. For example, a cabinet for CDs should accommodate the cases while leaving just enough space for finger access.

In some cases, you can't be sure what the finished project will hold. The kitchen island, for example, needs to be able to store a variety of things. In that case, it's wise to build in as much flexibility as possible, incorporating drawers and cabinets of different dimensions. Drawers provide great storage because they'll hold so many different items while keeping them clean and accessible, but out of sight. Cabinets are easy to build and can be used to display your collections if you don't install doors. When designing different size drawers and compartments in a single piece, it's aesthetically best if they graduate in size from the smallest at the top to the largest at the bottom.

Full-size drawings are a good way to get an idea of what your finished project will look like, especially in the details. They also help in the construction because all the dimensions are right there.

Also, don't forget to plan for transitional items, such as paperwork in process, or for temporary storage for items that will eventually be tossed or distributed.

Customizing the Size of Your Project

You can change the overall size of any project in this book to alter its storage capacity. Sometimes, you'll need to maintain certain compartment dimensions; but other than that, you've got a lot of room to play.

For example, the compact disc cabinet (p. 196) could easily be made wider or taller, as long as you maintain the height and depth of the individual compartments. Similarly, although the width of the drawers in the file cabinet (p. 273) must be maintained, you can build the drawers to the length of the drawer slides you choose. Or you can make the cabinet three or four drawers tall. If possible, create a full-size drawing of your project. The dimensions

will be close by for reference, and you'll have a realistic idea of the finished product.

Designing to fit a particular space

If you're building a piece to suit a particular space, you'll want to fit the space visually. But don't forget to consider the negative space in the whole picture. For example, if you're making a cabinet to stand against a particular section of wall, you may not want to span the entire width of the section, but instead leave a bit of room on either side and above to create a visual frame of sorts.

Often, you may want to match existing cabinetry, such as building the wine cabinet to serve as a dedicated base cabinet that matches the style of your kitchen. You can sometimes borrow design elements from a nearby piece of furniture, such as a particular edging profile or door frame treatment. And you can personalize your pieces further by "signing" them with your own custom wood pulls or faux finish.

Allowing for future expansion

Don't forget to plan ahead, especially if you have collectors in the family. You may *think* you'll never own 100 CDs. Uh huh. Your wife may *promise* to cut back on buying new baking supplies. Right. Years ago, I vowed never to maintain more than one file cabinet's worth of paperwork. Well, I'm up to five now. (But that's it!) In any case, incorporate some extra space from the start, but don't overdo it. You can usually just build more units when they're needed, but it's surprising how quickly you can run out of room in the original piece.

Materials

All of the projects in this book are made from a combination of solid wood and hardwood plywood. A few of them involve a bit of simple veneer work. Most of the projects incorporate some hardware, ranging from screws and hinges to locks and pulls. None of the materials is hard to find.

Solid wood is available from lumber suppliers, mills, home-supply centers, and mail-order sources. Hardwood plywood can be purchased at some home-supply centers and wood dealers. You may also be able to buy it from a friendly commercial cabinet shop. Veneer is harder to find and often needs to be purchased by mail order. All of the hardware is available at your local hardware store, at your local home-supply center, or through mail-order suppliers.

Solid wood

Wood is a beautiful material, but you have to understand a few things about its basic properties to work with it successfully. In solid form, it's a whole different animal than in its stable plywood form.

Solid wood moves. It always will, and you have to account for that fact or your project may self-destruct over time. If you restrain a solid-wood panel by gluing it into a frame, for example, the panel can crack or can explode the joints in the frame. If you glue a tabletop to its aprons, the top will almost certainly crack over time. If you don't allow

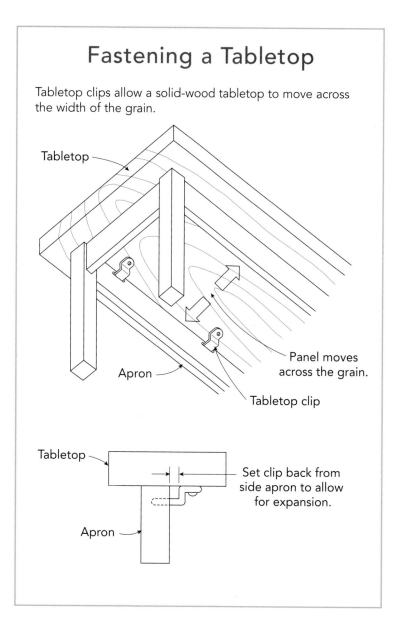

Fastening a Tabletop

Tabletop clips allow a solid-wood tabletop to move across the width of the grain.

Tabletop

Apron

Panel moves across the grain.

Tabletop clip

Tabletop

Apron

Set clip back from side apron to allow for expansion.

enough room for movement in a drawer front, it can swell and stick in its frame, causing possible damage to the pull when someone tugs heartily on it to open the drawer. But don't be discouraged, if you remember just a few rules of thumb, your projects will probably outlive you.

First, remember that wood expands and contracts *across* the grain. Movement *along* the grain is negligible and not really a concern in most furniture. What this means is that you can fit a panel in a frame fairly tightly at its ends, but you need to allow room at the sides. How much room depends on the season during which you're building.

Stability Is in the Cut

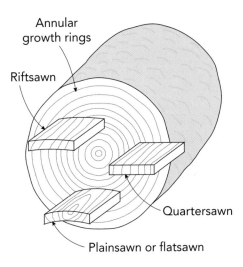

Annular growth rings

Riftsawn

Quartersawn

Plainsawn or flatsawn

The section of the log from which a board is cut largely determines how much it will shrink and warp. Quartersawn boards—evidenced by annular rings that run perpendicular to the face of the board—are the most stable. Riftsawn boards are moderately stable, whereas plainsawn boards are most prone to seasonal expansion and contraction, as well as warp.

When attaching a solid-wood tabletop to an apron, as in the kitchen island (p. 100), use tabletop clips that screw to the panel and insert into slots in the apron. Set the clips back from the side aprons a bit to allow the top to expand. When fitting solid-wood drawers, consider the season during which you're building. If working during the humid summer months, fit the drawers fairly snug in their openings. Come the dry winter months, they'll shrink a bit without leaving too big and unsightly a gap.

Of course, wood doesn't just move across the grain. It can also warp in many ways—cupping, bowing, and twisting. You can minimize warp by using properly dried lumber and letting it acclimate to your shop for at least a few days before cutting into it. Sometimes, you really need a stable piece of solid wood because you don't have any way

of restraining it within a frame, such as with the compartment door in the medicine cabinet (p. 128). In that case, use quartersawn wood, which is simply a piece of wood that has been cut from the log so that the annular rings run perpendicular to the face of the board. The next best cut is riftsawn. Try to avoid using plainsawn lumber for unrestrained panels.

Hardwood plywood

Plywood has certain advantages over solid wood, the primary one being that it is stable, so you don't have to worry about accommodating wood movement. You can fit plywood panels snugly into frames or drawer side grooves without worry. Because of its stability, it's ideal for panels that must fit tightly between legs. Hardwood plywood also makes a great substrate for veneering.

Hardwood plywood isn't cheap, but on a square foot basis it's typically less expensive than solid wood. Stay away from construction plywood, particularly as a veneer substrate. It's often full of voids and prone to warpage and delamination.

Hardwood plywood does have its disadvantages, of course. Because the face veneer is so thin, it's subject to damage that's not easy to repair. Also, whenever the panel edges will be exposed, they'll need to be covered with solid wood. Alternatively, you can cover the edges with commercial veneer tape, but I generally shy away from veneer tape because of potential delamination problems. I've seen it happen too often.

Veneer

Veneer provides the opportunity to really dress up a project relatively inexpensively. In fact, many fancy woods are available only in veneer form these days. Plus, some cuts would be troublesome to use in solid-wood form because of potential warpage problems. Veneering also allows you to match an exposed back panel to its case wood without having to buy an entire piece of expensive hardwood plywood.

To those who haven't tried it, veneering may seem daunting. However, the simple veneering you'll find in this book isn't difficult at all. Just follow the step-by-step instructions and you'll be amazed that you ever thought it was hard to do. One caveat: Don't use contact cement for veneering. It may be the easiest way to attach the veneer, but most experienced woodworkers have learned not to trust the longevity of the bond.

Hardware

Hinges, pulls, catches, drawer slides, locks, screws, and other hardware are essential parts of many projects. They contribute not only to the proper operation of doors, drawers, and lids but to the overall personality of the piece. There is a universe of different hardware out there, and you have a lot of options when it comes its design, quality, and cost. I recommend, though, that you don't skimp in this area. After putting all that work into constructing a fine piece, why sully it with cheap, poorly made hardware?

The sad truth is, it's difficult to find good hardware at your local hardware store or home-supply center. To get good-quality extruded hinges, brass ball catches, cupboard locks, and the like, you'll probably need to purchase them by mail order. In the cut list for every project, we've also listed a supplier and part number for the specific hardware used.

Perhaps the most ubiquitous hardware found in cabinetry is the common screw. Common as they are, screws are often installed incorrectly. One typical mistake is not drilling a shank clearance hole for a screw when fastening two workpieces together. The clearance hole, drilled in the "upper" workpiece, allows the screw to pass freely though it, drawing the two pieces fully together. In addition, a pilot hole often needs to be drilled to allow the screw threads to penetrate the wood without having the screw head snap off. In softwoods, the pilot hole

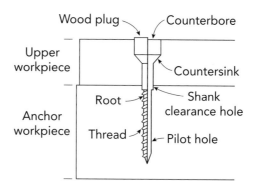

Installing a Screw

To fasten workpieces with a screw, a shank clearance hole in the upper piece allows the screw to draw the two boards fully together. A pilot hole allows the screw threads to penetrate the wood without having the screw head snap off. Flat-head screws need to be countersunk, and wood plugs require a counterbore.

should match the diameter of the screw's root. In hardwoods, the pilot hole should be slightly less than the thread diameter.

If installing a flat-head screw, you'll need to countersink the workpiece to accept the tapered bottom of the screw head. Many types of countersinks are available, some of which incorporate a pilot bit for quicker work. If you're going to hide the screws with plugs, as in the printer stand (p. 261), you'll need to drill counterbores to accept the plugs.

Small brass screws are often used for installing brass hinges, catches, and other hardware. Always drill a pilot hole to prevent the soft brass heads from snapping off. It's also wise to prethread the pilot hole using a steel screw of the same size as the brass screw. If you want to lubricate a screw for easier driving, use wax. Don't use soap, as it attracts water and thus corrosion. Use a

Shelf supports come in a wide variety of styles and materials.

Dado, Groove, and Rabbet Joints

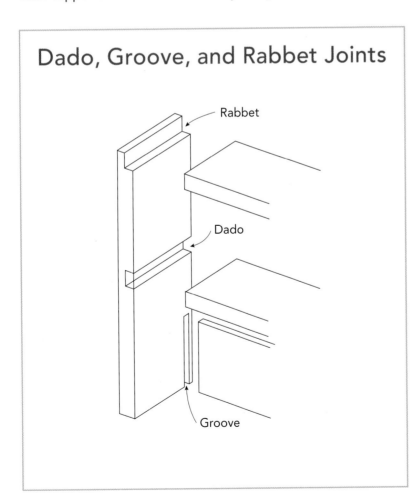

Rabbet

Dado

Groove

screwdriver that fits snugly into the screw slot without slop. I never power-drive small brass screws because they're so easy to snap.

Another type of hardware that's commonly used in these projects is the shelf support. You have a lot of choices here, so you can pick whatever type you like.

Joinery

The joinery in these projects can all be done with common woodworking tools, as explained in the step-by-step text. You also have the option of altering the joinery to suit your particular tools. For example, if you don't own a biscuit joiner, you can often attach parts with dowels or splines instead. Sometimes you can use biscuits instead of tenons, but don't expect the same strength. Whatever joint you choose as a substitute, make sure it's appropriate for the application. Here's an overview of the joints used for the projects in this book.

Dado, groove, and rabbet joints

Dadoes, grooves, and rabbets are among the simplest of joints to make. One half of each joint is simply the squarely cut edge of one of the workpieces. In the case of dadoes and grooves, the edge is housed between two shoulders on the mating piece. With a rabbet joint, the workpiece sits against a single shoulder. The only difference between a dado and a groove is that a dado runs cross-grain whereas a groove runs with the grain.

Dado joints are often used to join shelves and dividers to case sides, tops, and bottoms. One of the most common uses for grooves is to hold a drawer bottom in place. Rabbets are frequently used to house case backs.

Rabbet-and-dado joints

One common joint is the rabbet-and-dado joint, which is often used to attach pieces at right angles, such as in case and drawer corners. But it can also be used to join shelves to case sides, because it's a little simpler than cutting tenons on the ends of the shelves. This is a fairly strong joint if fit and glued properly. When using it to join shelves to case sides, orient the tongue downward for better strength.

Mortise-and-tenon joints

The mortise-and-tenon joint is a time-honored method of joining pieces of wood at an angle. The joint is very strong and reliable. Although you can cut tenons with a handsaw and then drill and chop the mortises, the quickest way to make the joint is with machines. Tenons are typically cut on the tablesaw, as described in the step-by-step project instructions, and the mortises are routed out. The mortises are always cut first, and the tenons are sawn to fit them.

A perfectly viable alternative to the traditional mortise-and-tenon joint is the loose, or "floating," tenon joint. Rather than incorporating the tenon as an integral part of one of the workpieces, the joint consists of two mating mortises that accept an independent tenon. Loose-tenon joinery is used in the file cabinet project (p. 273).

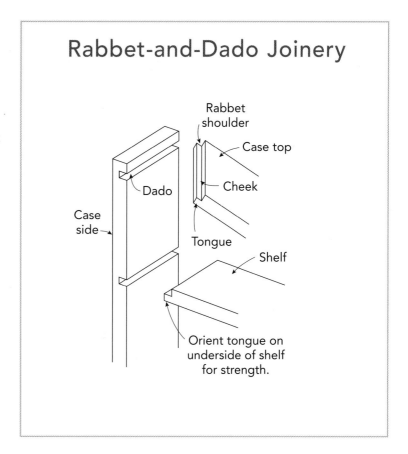

Rabbet-and-Dado Joinery

Rabbet shoulder

Case top

Cheek

Dado

Tongue

Case side

Shelf

Orient tongue on underside of shelf for strength.

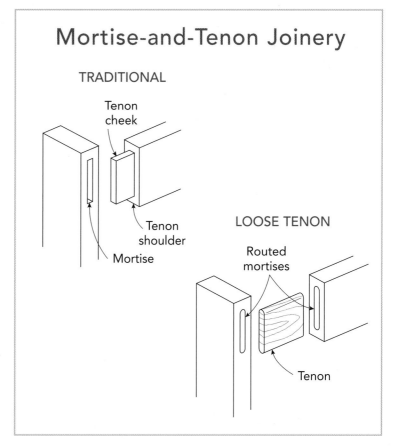

Mortise-and-Tenon Joinery

TRADITIONAL

Tenon cheek

Tenon shoulder

Mortise

LOOSE TENON

Routed mortises

Tenon

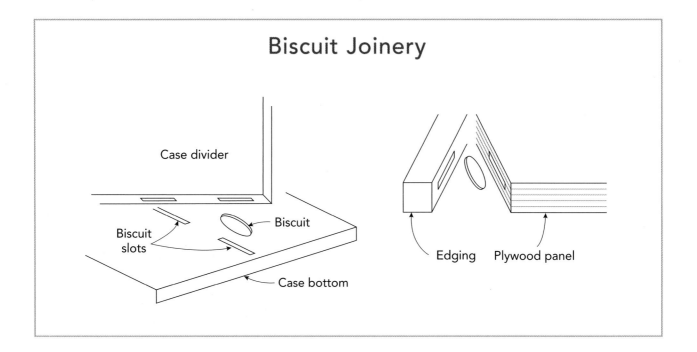

Biscuit Joinery

Case divider

Biscuit slots

Biscuit

Case bottom

Edging   Plywood panel

Biscuit joints

A relatively new development in joinery, the biscuit, or "plate," joint employs compressed, laminated, football-shaped splines that are glued into mating slots in the workpieces. Biscuits make for fairly strong joints and allow some lateral movement for aligning the workpieces. The compressed wood biscuits swell in their slots after glue is applied. Biscuits are a particularly convenient way to join case pieces at right angles. This joint also aligns and attaches edging and miter joints.

Spline joints

If you don't own a biscuit joiner or if you want absolute maximum strength and alignment all along the joint, you can use spline joinery. I'm particularly fond of using splines to join case miters, as used in the

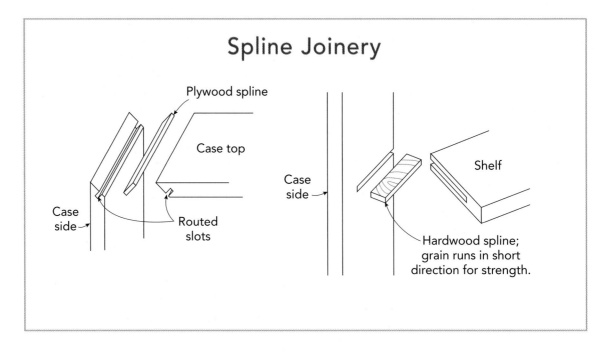

Spline Joinery

Plywood spline

Case top

Case side

Routed slots

Case side

Shelf

Hardwood spline; grain runs in short direction for strength.

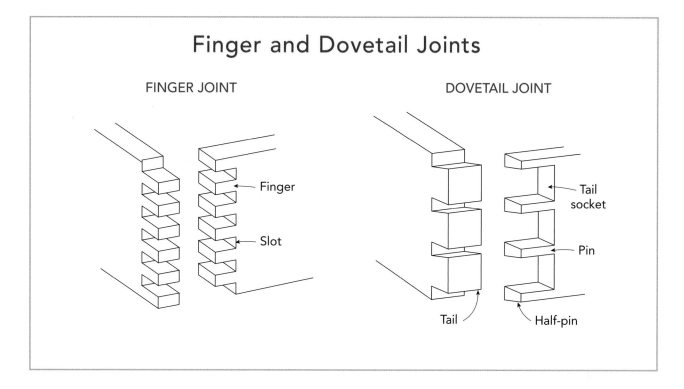

Finger and Dovetail Joints

FINGER JOINT

Finger

Slot

DOVETAIL JOINT

Tail socket

Pin

Tail

Half-pin

wine cabinet (p. 154). To make the joint, you simply rout identical grooves in the mating pieces and then glue a wooden spline into them.

Finger joints and dovetails

Finger joints and dovetails are two of the strongest methods for attaching workpieces at an angle. Finger joints, also called box joints, are most often used to connect drawer corners. Dovetails are also commonly used for drawer joinery but are seen joining case sides to case tops and bottoms, too. Finger joints are easy to make on the tablesaw, as explained in the directions for the spice drawer/shelf on pp. 58–59. Dovetails are easy to make using one of the many commercial jigs available. But you can also cut them by hand, as shown in the storage bed (p. 184). If you've got only a drawer or two to dove-tail, you can often cut them by hand quicker than you can set up a jig.

Tools

All of the projects in this book were built using a basic complement of small-shop tools and equipment. In this section, we'll take a look at some of them and discuss alternative ways to go about a technique if you're lacking certain tools or machines.

Layout tools

Good work depends on accurate layout and measurement. You don't need an awful lot of layout tools, but the ones you have should be accurate and useful. You need at least a few squares of different sizes, a ruler and tape measure, a marking gauge, a bevel gauge, a sharp marking knife, and an awl. If you're buying layout tools, don't skimp on the quality. You can't cut correctly unless you can mark and measure correctly. For example, get a good steel rafter square instead of a framing square, as the former is often better made and more accurate.

Cutting tools

Among the cutting tools that you'll need are good drill bits, sawblades, and router bits. Woodworking requires a lot of drilling, so

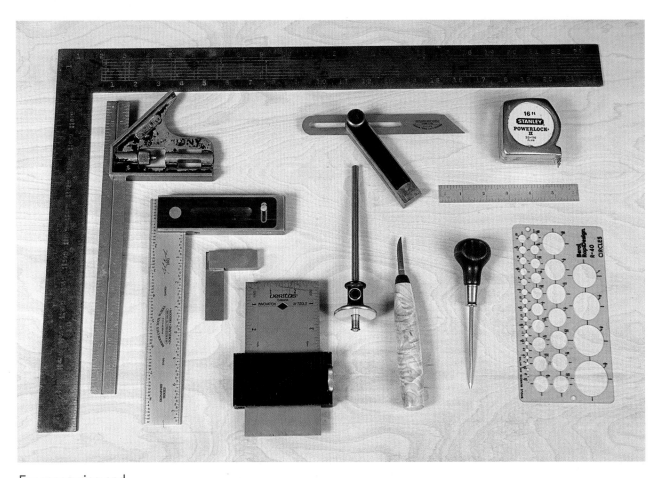

For measuring and marking, you need a basic complement of accurate tools. *From left:* rafter square, combination square, large and small try squares, "sliding" square, bevel gauge, marking gauge, tape measure, marking knife, 6-in. ruler, awl, and circle template.

use good bits. Standard twist drills are actually designed for cutting metal. For woodworking, you want bits that will neatly shear the wood fibers as they cut, so use the right tools for the job.

Good-quality circular sawblades are also important because the majority of the workpieces are cut on the tablesaw. I use a high-quality carbide combination blade that does the work of both ripping and crosscutting with very little tearout, even in plywood. I paid nearly $100 for it, but it's worth every penny. Good-quality dado heads are even more expensive, but necessary for cleanly cut dadoes, rabbets, tenons, and grooves. When it comes to sawblades, you generally get what you pay for. Check tool reviews in woodworking magazines and online message boards to get suggestions for good blades.

You'll also need a few good router bits, including a couple of straight or spiral bits for cutting mortises, a flush-trimming bit

for routing edging, and a slot-cutting bit for routing grooves. If you don't already have these bits, they'll be a great addition to your arsenal. Buy carbide bits; steel bits burn out far too quickly to be worth the initial cost savings.

As for hand tools for cutting, you probably already have a set of chisels and a few handplanes. Just make sure they're good and sharp for use. One other tool I highly recommend is a cabinet scraper. Basically just a steel card with a turned edge, it's hard to beat a scraper when it comes to smoothing wood. There's plenty of information to be found in magazines and books on the subjects of sharpening chisels, planes, and scrapers.

Equipment and accessories

Depending on the projects you want to make, you'll need some basic woodworking equipment. The machines used include a

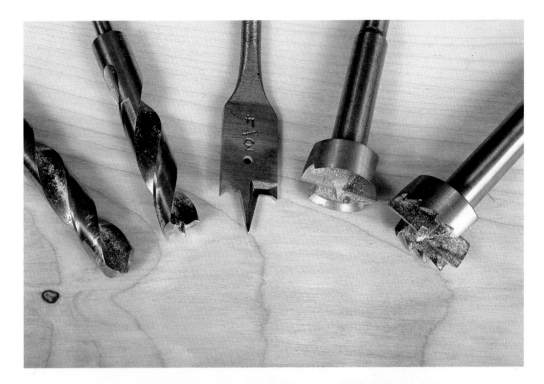

Standard twist drills (far left) are designed for drilling metal, not wood. Instead, use bits designed to shear the wood fibers as they drill. *From right:* multi-spur bit, Forstner bit, spade bit with shearing tips, brad-point bit.

A good dado head will cleanly cut a variety of joints. To set up this stack dado, mount the appropriate-width chippers between the two outer blades, shimming between the chippers and blades to fine-tune the width of the dado head for a specific cut.

A crosscut sled is invaluable for cutting panels as well as for general crosscutting purposes. Its long fence and double runners make it much more accurate than a standard miter gauge, particularly for cutting 90-degree angles. For cutting miters, you can screw a temporary fence to the sled panel.

tablesaw, jointer, thickness planer, drill press, bandsaw, lathe, and biscuit joiner, as well as, of course, a router or two. It would be hard to get by without a tablesaw, but you could probably find alternatives to the other machines.

If you don't have a jointer or thickness planer, you could use handplanes. You could use a hand drill instead of a drill press. If you don't have a bandsaw, you may be able to get by with a jigsaw for scroll work, or by thickness planing stock instead of resawing it. No lathe? Borrow time on a friend's, or ask him to do the turning. If you don't have a biscuit joiner, you could use dowels or splines instead. If you don't have a router (imagine *that*!), you could drill and chop mortises by hand.

Helpful accessories to have on hand include a good router edge guide and a crosscut sled for the tablesaw.

General Tips and Techniques

For each project, we've provided step-by-step instructions particular to that piece. Here, I'll discuss certain general woodworking procedures that apply to just about every project you make.

Laying out and stock preparation

Reading cut lists The dimensions in the cut lists are presented in order of thickness, then width, and finally length. Note that the length dimension always follows the grain direction of lumber or the face grain of plywood. Although finished sizes are given in the cut list, it's best to take your workpiece measurement directly from an opening or frame when appropriate, such as when fitting backs, drawer bottoms, or inset doors and drawer fronts.

Laying out Along with the actual shape of a project, the grain patterns on the individual pieces largely determine the beauty of the finished furniture. Haphazard grain lines can ruin an otherwise graceful design. It's best to use straight grain for rails, aprons, stiles, legs, and other narrow frame members. Save the wilder grain for the center of door and case panels and for drawer fronts. If you have a run of side-by-side drawers, cut the drawer fronts from the same board, maintaining the same grain continuity on the finished piece.

It's usually wise to mill extra stock for tool setups at the same time you mill your project stock. That way, you can be assured the test pieces will be the same dimensions as the project stock.

When laying out plywood, I always inspect it first for flaws using a strong, glancing sidelight in a darkened shop. I sweep the light both along and across the grain. Remember that plywood often varies in thickness from piece to piece. Thus dado joints and rabbet joints will fit better if all

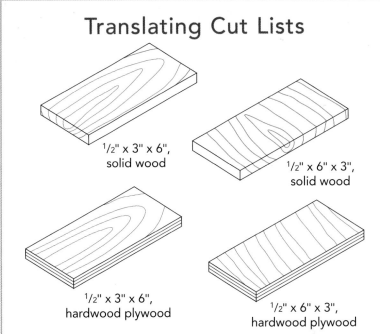

Translating Cut Lists

$1/2$" x 3" x 6",
solid wood

$1/2$" x 6" x 3",
solid wood

$1/2$" x 3" x 6",
hardwood plywood

$1/2$" x 6" x 3",
hardwood plywood

Cut list dimensions are listed in order of thickness, then width, and then length. The length dimension always follows the grain direction of lumber or the face grain of plywood. Although the pieces shown here are all the same size, their cut list dimensions are listed differently.

Grain Layout

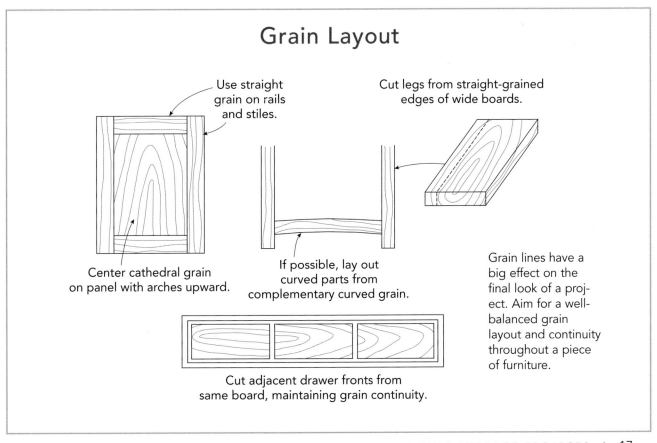

Use straight grain on rails and stiles.

Cut legs from straight-grained edges of wide boards.

Center cathedral grain on panel with arches upward.

If possible, lay out curved parts from complementary curved grain.

Grain lines have a big effect on the final look of a project. Aim for a well-balanced grain layout and continuity throughout a piece of furniture.

Cut adjacent drawer fronts from same board, maintaining grain continuity.

Triangle Marking System

Using triangles to orient your workpieces provides a quick reference for machining and assembly. As you can see here, a triangle immediately identifies the top, bottom, left side, and right side of an assembly.

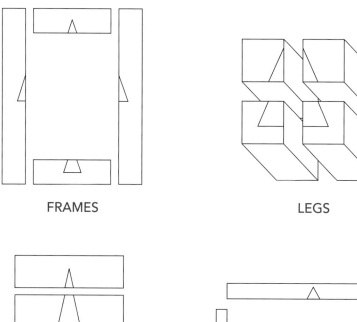

FRAMES

LEGS

PANELS OR DRAWER FRONTS

APRONS OR DRAWER BOXES

of the parts that slip into those joints are cut from the same piece of plywood.

For orienting individual parts, I use the triangle marking system, which tells me at a glance how a part relates to its mates.

Assembly tips

✦ I typically apply glue to both mating surfaces, except when applying edging. For that, I apply a thick coat just to the plywood edge. An ink roller works well for spreading a thin, even coat of glue. For brushing glue onto tenons and tongues and into mortises, I use a solder

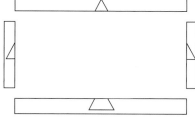

flux brush. A small artists brush is good for getting into small holes and grooves.

✦ When gluing up, work on a flat surface. If a piece isn't lying flat, you won't be able to check it accurately for square.

✦ Use contact cement to attach thick leather pads to pipe-clamp jaws, preventing damage to workpieces.

✦ Use cauls to distribute clamping pressure, centering them over the joint. To span long joints, use crowned cauls. On smaller pieces, it's easier to use cauls that almost cover the entire piece being clamped.

- If a piece isn't square under clamping pressure, try shifting the angle of the clamps on the joints to bring it into square.
- Always do a dry clamp-up to rehearse your clamping procedure. While a cabinet is dry-clamped, fit its back snugly into its rabbets so you'll be able to insert it unglued to hold the case square while the glue cures.
- To clean up excess glue, use a clean rag and clean water, replenishing the water as necessary to prevent wiping diluted glue into wood grain and jeopardizing the finish. Alternatively, wait until the glue has cured to a rubbery consistency and then pare it away with a very sharp chisel.

A favorite finish

I've used a lot of different finishes over the years, including tung oil, various Danish oils, homemade oil-and-varnish mixes, nitrocellulose lacquer, and polyurethane. There's one finish that I'm particularly fond of that yields a beautiful, soft luster without a thick build sitting on top of the workpiece. It's a mixture of oil and varnish that's heavy on the latter and is called a "wiping varnish" by some finishing experts. It is resistant to water, alcohol, and abrasion and is easy to repair. The smooth, soft luster is largely a result of the method of application, which I'll describe here. Several manufacturers make a version of this finish, which is sometimes sold under the names "tung oil finish" and "Danish oil finish."

Begin by sanding the surfaces through 220-grit; then thoroughly brush off the sanding dust. Check for glue splotches by inspecting the pieces under a strong side-light in a darkened shop or by wiping suspect surfaces with mineral spirits or naphtha. It's a good idea to prepare your finish rags ahead of time: Tear cotton sheeting into pieces about 20-in. square.

The product I use comes in two different mixes: a sealer and a top coat. The sealer

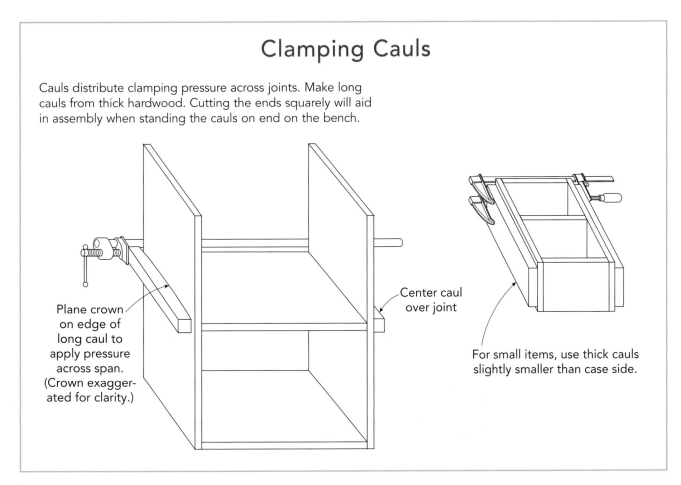

Clamping Cauls

Cauls distribute clamping pressure across joints. Make long cauls from thick hardwood. Cutting the ends squarely will aid in assembly when standing the cauls on end on the bench.

Plane crown on edge of long caul to apply pressure across span. (Crown exaggerated for clarity.)

Center caul over joint

For small items, use thick cauls slightly smaller than case side.

Flood the initial sealer coat onto the workpieces. For absorbent woods, the author uses a brush. For most hardwoods, application with a rag is more efficient and wastes less finish.

mixture is relatively thin and soaks well into the wood. Use it for the first coat. On absorbent woods, use a brush to flood the sealer into the wood, because it soaks up so quickly. On harder woods, use a rag, applying it more sparingly so as not to waste a lot of finish when wiping off the excess. Use a small artist's brush to work the finish into shelf support holes or small notches. Let the sealer coat soak in and apply more finish to "dry" spots as needed. Some softwoods seem to never quit soaking in the finish. No matter. Just make sure you get a lot of finish into the wood. When the wood no longer seems hungry, wipe off the excess finish thoroughly and let it dry overnight.

The next day, sand the finished wood fairly vigorously with 400-grit wet/dry silicon carbide paper, lubricating the paper and

the surface with mineral spirits. Wipe off the excess spirits afterward.

Next, apply the second coat of finish, using the top coat mixture. This is thicker than the sealer and sets up tack more quickly, so you'll need to work smaller areas at a time. To put on this coat and all subsequent top coats, use a rag formed into a "bob" by crumpling the edges of the rag backward into the center to create a small bag. Lightly dip the face of the bob into the finish and wipe it onto the workpiece. (Avoid soaking the rag, as you'll be using it to wipe off the excess finish.) Repeat this application procedure until you've covered an area the size of which you'll be able to handle before the finish tacks up too much. Experiment by working fairly small areas for starters.

When the finish starts to tack up, which is pretty quickly with this top coat, start wiping off the excess. Use the same rag, undoing the bob and crumpling the rag to disperse the residual finish throughout. Wipe the surface thoroughly, rubbing it vigorously and quickly. If the finish becomes too tacky to wipe, simply apply fresh finish to soften it. As you wipe, the rag should become about as tacky as a commercial tack cloth used to remove dust. Perfect. This will leave a very thin coat of finish on the surface. When the rag becomes wet, replace it with a fresh one. Avoid soft cloths, such as old T-shirts, because they're too absorbent. When you've coated all the surfaces, let the work dry overnight.

For the third coat, begin by wet sanding with 600-grit wet/dry sandpaper. Then repeat the above procedures. You'll find that every new top coat dries more quickly and leaves the work a bit shinier. After the third coat dries, dry scrub it with 0000 steel wool, carefully brushing off the residue and blowing off the workpieces with compressed air.

Wipe on one last coat in the same manner as before. I find that these four coats are usually sufficient to impart a wonderful luster to the project, but I'll generally apply one more coat to tabletops and other surfaces that can expect more than their fair share of liquids and abrasion.

WARNING

♦ ♦ ♦

When finishing, work in a well-ventilated area and dispose of rags properly. To prevent the spontaneous combustion of the rags, lay or hang them out flat to dry or submerge them in water.

Apply the top coats using a rag formed into a "bob": Crumple the edges of the rag backward into the center.

PART ONE
Kitchens and Baths

ADJUSTABLE SHELVES

Niall Barrett

I HAD BEEN TRYING TO WORK out a really simple (read "fast") way to make an elegant wooden version of the old standby, metal standards and brackets. Although I have seen many commercial versions of wall-hung shelving systems built of wood, I wanted something cleverly uncomplicated (if you know what I mean). The problem was always the shelf support brackets. What I needed was a way to hold up the shelves that didn't rely on brackets.

Luckily, I got this flash of insight. Why not just make couple of uprights with matching notches in them and stick the shelves into the notches? As long as the shelves fit the notches just right and weren't too deep or heavily loaded, it should be fine.

The physics of it seem to work: The notches support the shelves and hold quite a lot of weight. The first time I made it, however, installing it on the wall proved somewhat difficult. Once you cut notches in the uprights, they become more flexible. When you screw these flexible pieces of wood to a not-so-flat wall, the notches either spread open or pinch closed just enough to make the shelves either too loose or too tight in their slots. When open, the shelves slide easily from side to side.

In keeping with the original spirit of this project, the solution to these issues turned out to be simple. A spline inserted into the back of each upright stiffens them so they do not bend, and matching notches in the backs of the shelves keep them from moving side to side. The arrangement also has the added benefit of being rigid enough that the whole unit can be hung from just two points at the tops of the uprights. So, with several refinements, I present you with amazingly simple adjustable shelves!

ADJUSTABLE SHELVES

The shelves fit into notches in the uprights and are cantilevered.
There are no brackets or other hardware to hold the shelves in place.

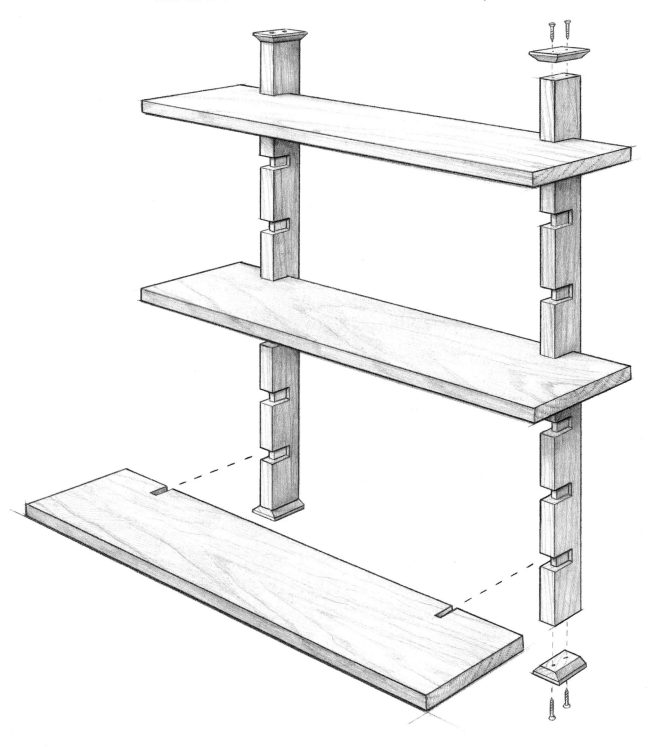

Front and Side Views

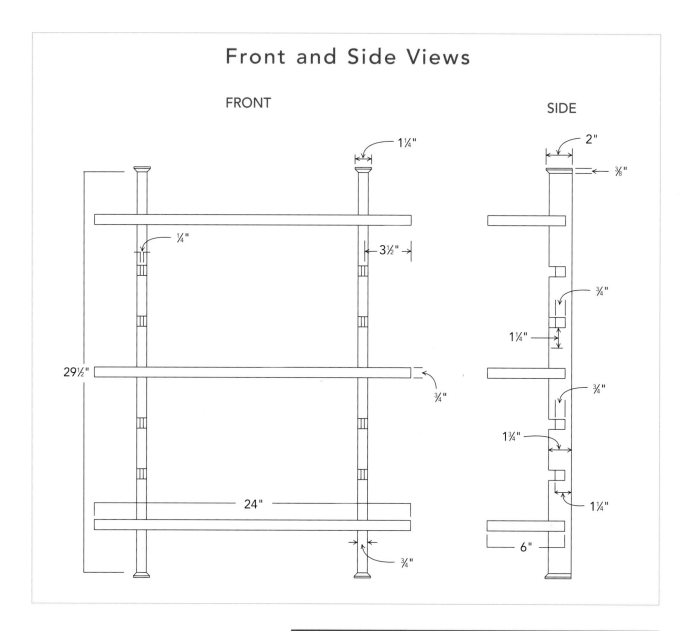

FRONT

SIDE

Stock Preparation

ALL THE PARTS SHOULD first be milled to size and then shaped accordingly. I find it's more efficient to do the bulk of the jointing, planing, ripping, and crosscutting work at the same time.

1. Mill the uprights to their finished size.

2. Cut the shelves to width and length, but leave them a little thicker than ¾ in. for now.

3. Mill the spline material, again leaving each piece a little thick, wide, and long.

CUT LIST FOR ADJUSTABLE SHELVES			
2	Uprights	1¾" x 29½" x ¾"	solid oak
3	Shelves	6" x 24" x ¾"	solid oak
4	Caps	1¼" x 2" x ⅜"	solid oak
2	Splines	1¼" x 29½" x ¼"	solid oak

Other materials

2	Keyhole hangers and screws
8	#8 x ¾" brass screws (to attach caps)

Notch Layout in Uprights

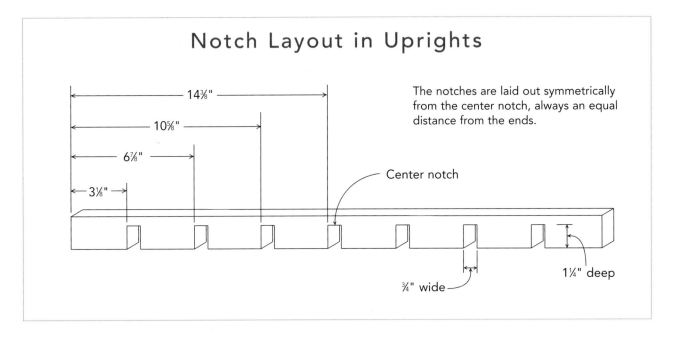

14⅜"

10⅝"

6⅞"

3⅛"

The notches are laid out symmetrically from the center notch, always an equal distance from the ends.

Center notch

1¼" deep

¾" wide

PHOTO A: Cut the shelf notches in the uprights with a dado blade on the table saw.

1. Clamp the uprights together to cut notches in them simultaneously. This will ensure that the joints line up with each other and the shelves are parallel.

2. Cut the notches an equal distance from either end of the uprights. This makes it possible to cut a notch in each end of the uprights for each setup. I used a flip stop on my miter gauge to register each series of cuts, but you can also use the tablesaw fence for registration (see **photo A**).

3. Cut the last notch in the center of the uprights.

Splines

1. Install a ¼-in.-wide dado blade in your tablesaw; set it to the same 1¼-in. height as in the previous setup.

2. Position the fence to make a cut down the center of the back edge of the uprights.

3. Cut the groove for the splines in each upright.

4. Plane the spline material until it's easily pressed by hand into this groove. Don't make the spline too thick because the glue will swell it slightly and it will grab as you insert the spline.

4. Make one long piece 1¼ in. wide and ⅜ in. thick for the caps. Make enough stock to cut four caps plus a couple of extras.

The Uprights

To cut ¾-in.-wide by 1¼-in.-deep notches for the shelves in the uprights, use a dado blade on your tablesaw and a miter gauge (see "Notch Layout in Uprights").

5. Insert the dry splines about halfway into the grooves.

6. Spread glue on both sides of the part of each spline that remains exposed. It is important to apply the glue in this manner. The splines do not need much to keep them in place; if you put too much glue into these joints it will only end up squeezing out in the dadoes and around the visible portions of the splines, which will be extremely difficult to clean up!

7. Tap the spline in the rest of the way until it bottoms out in the cut (see **photo B**). You may have to put it in a vise or use some clamps to get it in all the way.

8. Once the splines are fully seated, place some clamps along the joint to make sure it remains tight until the glue dries.

9. Once the glue is dry, trim the excess off the splines. A sharp handsaw for the ends and a block plane for the back will make short work of this.

Shelves

1. Shim the ¼-in. dado blade so it will make a cut just a little wider than the slot the spline fits into. This will allow the notches you will cut in the shelves to fit easily over the splines.

2. Lower the blade to cut ¾ in. deep and set the tablesaw fence 3½ in. from the blade.

3. Using a miter gauge with a tall auxiliary face attached to support the shelves, cut a notch in each end of the back of all the shelves (see **photo C** on p. 30).

4. Take these still slightly thick shelves and plane them down until they fit easily into the notches of the uprights. They should slide in easily but not be too loose.

Remember that these shelves still need to be sanded and that it doesn't take much for these shelves to be too loose (see "Shelf Connection Detail" on p. 30).

PHOTO C: With a ¼-in. dado blade, notch the backs of the shelves to fit over the splines. Use the rip fence to ensure the notches are an equal distance from the ends of all the shelves.

Shelf Connection Detail

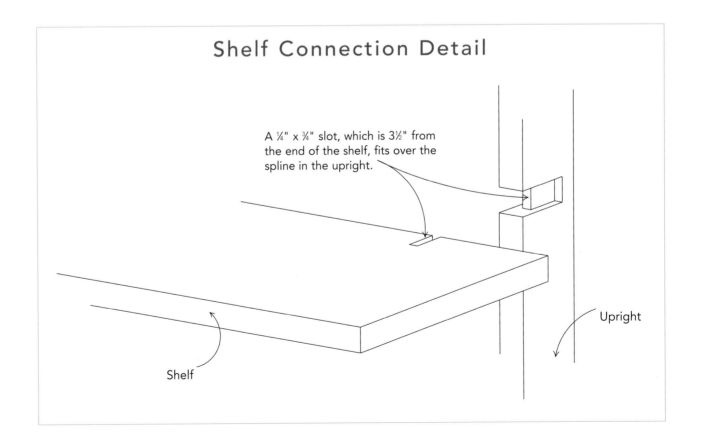

A ¼" x ¾" slot, which is 3½" from the end of the shelf, fits over the spline in the upright.

Upright

Shelf

PHOTO D: Install hanger hardware flush with the back side of the uprights.

Hangers

The next step is to install some metal hangers in the top back of each upright. There are several types of hangers available from woodworking suppliers, and the exact installation method will depend on the type you choose. You will need to choose a flush hanger, however, to allow the shelves to hang flat against the wall. A typical installation requires you to mortise the hanger into the workpiece.

1. With a sharp marking knife, trace the outline of the hanger onto the top back of each upright.

2. Using a sharp chisel, remove enough material to allow the hangers to be installed flush.

3. Drill a hole inside each mortise deep and large enough to allow each hanger to fit over a screw head.

4. Screw the hangers in place (see **photo D**).

Decorative Caps

1. Bevel both long edges of the cap stock on your tablesaw with the blade tilted 45 degrees. This bevel should leave the narrow side of the stock $^{13}/_{16}$ in. wide (just slightly wider than the uprights). It should also leave a right angle flat along each long edge $^{1}/_{8}$ in. wide.

2. With the blade still tilted, transfer the workpiece to your miter gauge set at 90 degrees and cut a matching bevel on each end (see "Making the Caps" on p. 32).

Making the Caps

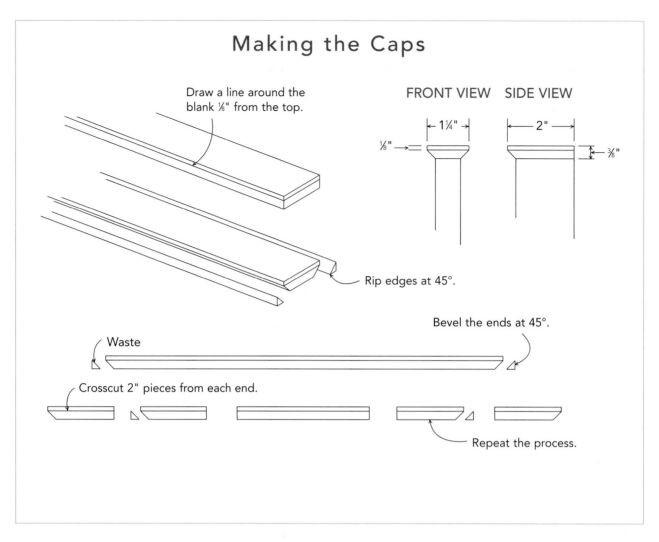

Draw a line around the blank ⅛" from the top.

FRONT VIEW   SIDE VIEW

⅛"   ← 1¼" →   ← 2" →   ⅜"

Rip edges at 45°.

Bevel the ends at 45°.

Waste

Crosscut 2" pieces from each end.

Repeat the process.

PHOTO E: Install the top and bottom end caps with two brass screws.

DESIGN OPTION: LARGE OR SMALL?

The shelves in this chapter are relatively small, but I have built several different sizes of this kind of shelving, including some quite large (see the photo).

You can certainly make a unit as tall as your ceiling height will allow, but shelves deeper than 9 in. should be avoided. You could possibly make them a little deeper by making the uprights larger and deeper (the ones in the photo are 2½ in. deep and 1½ in. wide), but I think the scale would look wrong.

A shelf length of 48 in. is the maximum for a unit with two uprights—as long as you keep 30 in. between upright centers and 9 in. on each side. If you want a wider unit, you will have to use more uprights. All of this is assuming ¾-in.-thick shelves. You can use thicker shelves, but you really gain very little since the thicker shelves are heavier. I also think the lighter look of ¾-in. shelves is more in keeping with the simple, open spirit of the piece.

A much larger version of the adjustable-shelf project, used to hold this antique-radio collection. It isn't a good idea to make this type of shelf much larger than this.

3. Crosscut a 2-in. piece off of each end and repeat the process until you have enough caps for the project and a couple of extras. I recommend cutting extra because it only takes a few moments to do, and these little pieces can sometimes split when you drill holes for the attachment screws.

4. Drill two countersunk holes for some small brass screws and some mating pilot holes into the ends of the uprights, and attach the caps (see **photo E**).

Sanding and Finishing

Sand all the parts to at least 150 grit. You might find it easier to temporarily remove the caps for sanding and even finishing, and you should definitely remove the hangers for finishing. I finished my shelves with a satin spray lacquer, but as with many of the projects in this book, a good-quality oil finish or even a carefully applied brush-on water-based polyurethane would also work well.

SERVING TRAY

Niall Barrett

WHO HAS NOT RELISHED the idea of being served breakfast or at least afternoon tea? Imagine a tray bearing delicious things to eat, freshly squeezed fruit juices, and maybe even the clichéd single rose in a vase.

Serving trays, such as the one presented here, carry an air of luxury and a refined sense of convenience about them. Unlike times past, most of us do our own serving these days, but the ritual remains the same. In addition, these trays are useful when entertaining. Carrying a pot of tea and cups to the living room, or even clearing plates after dinner, is made a lot easier with a serving tray such as this. The handle openings on the side of the tray make for a comfortable hold when transporting fragile items. And after

building a project like this rather than buying a cheap, temporary one, you can feel good about the quality, knowing it will last generations.

As projects go, this one is deceptively simple. While it won't take very much time to make, it will present a certain amount of technical difficulty. The tray requires some precision cutting for the joinery, and it's a bit tricky to clamp up. But by learning how to make glue-up blocks, the process will go much more smoothly, and you can apply the technique when you build other projects that contain box joints.

The good news is that I have already made most of the mistakes there are to make on this project, and my warnings should help you avoid them. After all, that's what I am here for!

SERVING TRAY

This elegant serving tray uses a variation on the box joint, with routed handle openings on the sides.

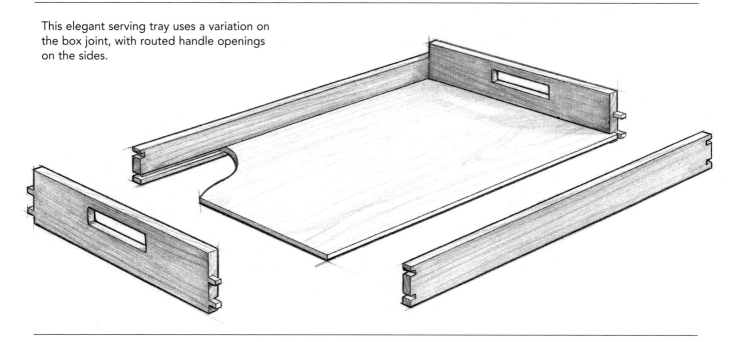

Side, Top, and End Views

SIDE

½"

3"

2"

END

⅝"

1"

¼"

¼"

¼"

4"

¼"

¼"

12"

TOP

20"

½"

11½"

12"

Bottom Panel

19½"

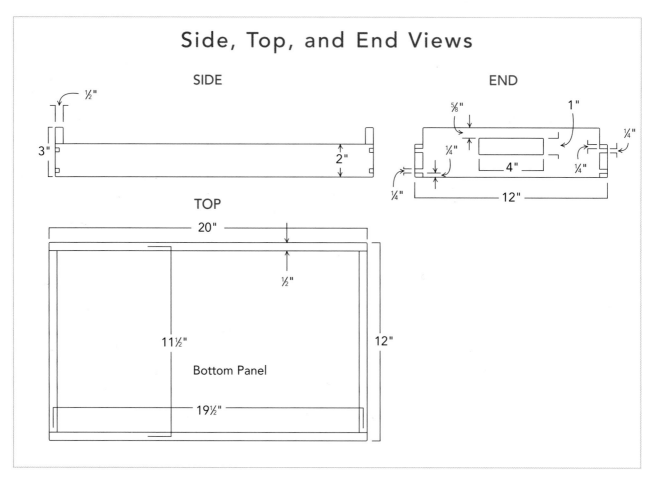

CUT LIST FOR SERVING TRAY			
2	Long tray sides	20" x 2" x ½"	solid mahogany
2	Short tray sides	12" x 3" x ½"	solid mahogany
1	Tray bottom	11½" x 19½" x ¼"	mahogany plywood

Construction and Assembly

I MADE THIS TRAY OUT OF mahogany because I like this wood and I had a piece of ¼-in. mahogany plywood left over from another job. It may not be the easiest material to find, especially the relatively small piece you will need for the bottom of this tray. There is certainly no reason why you can't use a wood more to your liking and perhaps one that's easier to obtain.

Cutting a Groove for the Bottom

1. Mill the solid-wood parts for the sides to the dimensions stated in the cut list.

2. Cut a piece of ¼-in. plywood for the bottom to the dimensions stated in the cut list. You will need to have the material for the bottom on hand to check the size of the groove it fits into.

3. Install a ¼-in. dado blade on your tablesaw and set it to cut a groove ¼ in. deep, ¼ in. from the bottom of the workpiece.

4. Make a test cut in a piece of scrap wood to make sure the setup is correct. Check the fit of your plywood bottom panel in this test groove. It should be snug without needing to be forced. If it's too tight, you may have to shim your dado blade.

5. Once you are certain the setup is correct, cut a groove in the bottom inside face of each of the sides.

6. Leave the tablesaw as is. The setup for grooving the sides is the same for the first step in the joint sequence.

Cutting the Joints for the Long Sides

1. Build a jig or carrier that will hold the frame parts on end while you cut the corner joints (see "Carrier Jig" on p. 38). The jig is nothing more than a right angle of plywood with a support behind the face, which also acts as a handle to push the workpiece and jig through the tablesaw blade while keeping your hand in a safe place.

Be sure to locate the screws that hold the jig together so that they will not be in the path of the blade when the jig is in use.

2. Without changing the tablesaw dado setup, place the carrier jig against the rip fence.

PHOTO A: A simple carrier jig supports the long tray sides when notching the ends with a dado blade.

Carrier Jig

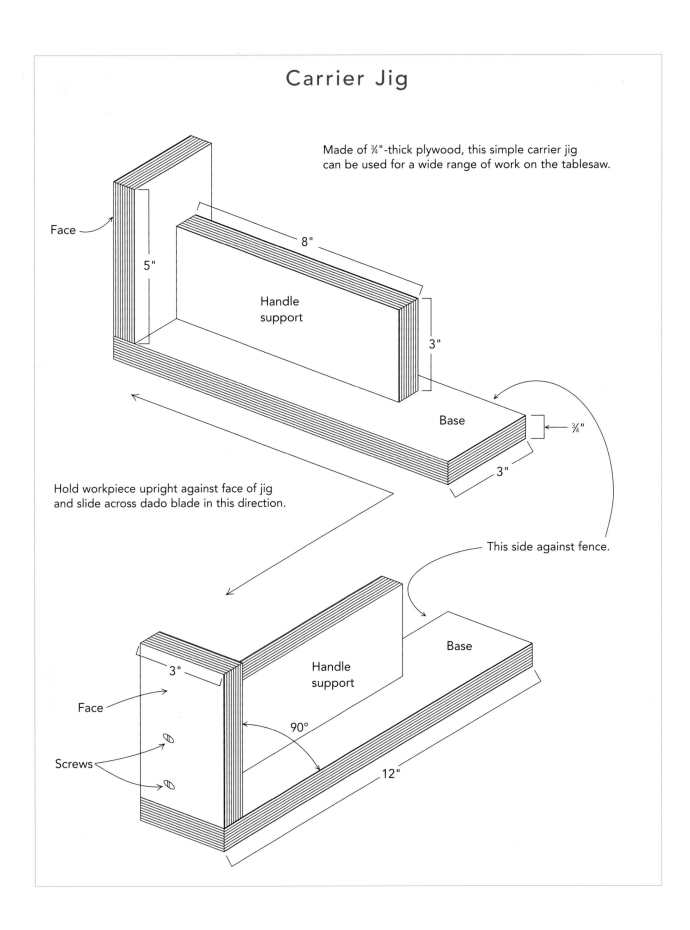

Made of ¾"-thick plywood, this simple carrier jig can be used for a wide range of work on the tablesaw.

Face

5"

8"

Handle support

3"

Base

¾"

3"

Hold workpiece upright against face of jig and slide across dado blade in this direction.

This side against fence.

3"

Face

Screws

Handle support

90°

Base

12"

3. Position one of the long tray sides on end, flat against the face of the jig with the bottom-groove side against the fence. The groove will line up with the dado blade, and the slot you will cut here will be filled with a pin on the mating part of the joint, hiding the groove.

4. Holding the workpiece in place, slide the jig across the dado blade (see **photo A** on p. 37).

5. Flip the workpiece so that the groove side is away from the fence and repeat the cut.

6. Do the same for the other end of the workpiece and for both ends of the other long tray side. You'll end up with two notches in each end of the long sides, one in the same location as the groove for the bottom. This completes the joint work on these pieces.

Cutting the Joints for the Short Sides

The next step is to create pins on the ends of the short tray sides that fit the slots you made in the long tray sides. You will need to make five cuts in each end of the short pieces, but the saw settings are very simple.

1. With the same dado setup, and using your miter gauge set to 90 degrees, lay a short tray side inside face down with a long edge against the miter gauge.

2. Run the piece across the blade, nibbling away at the waste until the end meets the fence. This creates a ¼-in. by ½-in. rabbet in the end of the piece (see **photo B**).

3. Spin the piece around and cut a rabbet in the other end.

4. Repeat this procedure for the other short tray side.

5. Using the long sides as a template, mark the location of the pins with a sharp pencil or (better yet) a marking knife.

6. Raise your dado blade to ½ in. high. Using the marks you made on these parts as a reference, set your fence so that the dado blade is on one side of one pin and, using your carrier jig, make a cut in each end of

PHOTO B: With the same dado-blade setting, cut rabbets on the ends of the short tray sides.

PHOTO C: Cut away the waste around the marked pins with the dado blade at the same setting as the last step.

PHOTO D: Crosscut the waste on the sides with the workpiece on edge. This leaves a cleaner finish on the ends.

each short tray side. Repeat this procedure to define the pins, then nibble away the waste between the pins (see **photo C** on p. 39).

7. Cut away the waste on the short ends to define what will be the handle portion of the tray ends (see **photo D** on p. 39). I do this work by crosscutting with the miter gauge rather than nibbling it away because this method leaves a better finish. (The end shows on the finished tray.) Raise the dado blade until it is just high enough to remove this waste, and set the fence so that it is just slightly more than ½ in. away from the outside of the blade.

It's a lot better to cut the shoulder just slightly smaller than exactly right. The slight reveal this creates is hardly noticeable, but it will assure that there is nothing in the way when you glue up the frame.

8. Make any adjustments necessary to fit the joints together. Remember, the pins are fragile, so don't force them.

Routing the Handle Opening

The handle opening is routed with a template and a plunge router fitted with a guide bushing and a straight plunge bit. The size of the template opening is determined by the diameter of the bit-and-bushing combination you use. Remember, the smaller the bit and bushing you use, the smaller the radius in the corners of the cutout will be. I used a ⅛-in. bit with a ⁵⁄₁₆-in. bushing because I wanted as nearly square a cutout as possible.

1. Make the template (see "Handle-Routing Template").

2. Plunge and rout the hole in about three steps, going a little deeper each time. The tray sides are only ½ in. thick, but it is still a good idea. This is especially important if you are using a small-diameter bit, since these are fragile (see **photo E**).

PHOTO E: Plunge rout the handle hole in the sides with a template and collar guide.

Handle-Routing Template

The template is made of a frame that captures the workpiece, so no aligning is necessary from piece to piece. The workpiece is fitted into the template and the template is screwed workpiece-side down to a piece of plywood clamped to the bench. This keeps the clamps out of the way of the routing operation.

SECTION THROUGH SIDE

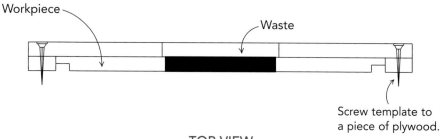

Workpiece

Waste

Screw template to a piece of plywood.

TOP VIEW

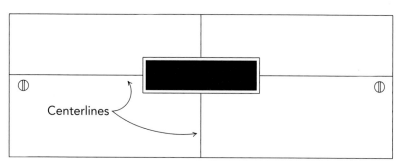

Centerlines

BOTTOM VIEW

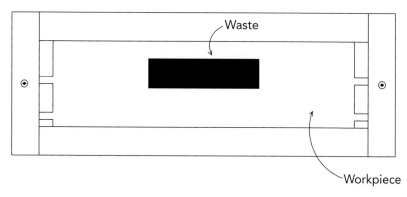

Waste

Workpiece

SECTION END VIEW

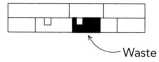

Waste

CUSTOM GLUE BLOCKS FOR CORNER JOINTS

Clamping corner joints such as dovetails and box joints can be tricky. Blocks on either side can prevent the joint from closing completely. The only other option is to clamp just to the side of the joint, which can distort the sides and leave the joints not quite bottomed out.

Instead, make some glue-up blocks or cauls that put pressure only where you want it. You'll need two different types of cauls. One will apply pressure to the pins and the other will straddle the pins and apply pressure to the side.

Once you have the glue-up blocks prepared, try them out on the dry-assembled tray with some clamps, making sure all the joints close tightly. One last thing—you don't want the cauls to become glued to the joints. During clamp-up, cover their faces with some adhesive tape to keep them from sticking to the joints.

Similar blocks will work for dovetails and other types of box joints.

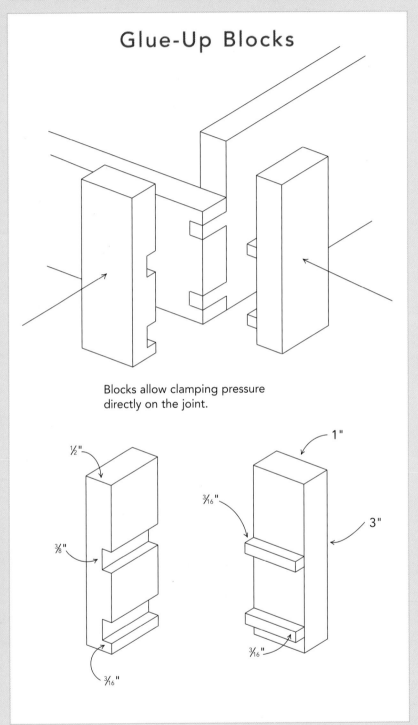

Glue-Up Blocks

Blocks allow clamping pressure directly on the joint.

½"

⅜"

³⁄₁₆"

1"

³⁄₁₆"

3"

³⁄₁₆"

PHOTO F: Clamp up the tray using blocks that put pressure only on the parts of the joints that need it.

Glue-Up

1. Cut the bottom so that it fits comfortably in the grooves between the sides. It should be large enough that it doesn't move around but not so large that it interferes with closing the joints. This is a plywood bottom, so wood movement will not be a problem.

2. Finish-sand both sides of the bottom and the insides of the tray sides to 150 grit, and dry-fit all the parts just to make sure everything goes together easily. You don't want to have any surprises during actual glue-up.

3. Make glue blocks for clamping that put pressure only on the parts of the joints that need it (see "Custom Glue Blocks for Corner Joints").

4. Disassemble the tray and apply glue to all mating surfaces. Leave a small amount of glue in the corners of the grooves for the bottom so that it will help reinforce the tray

corners. Be as neat as possible when applying the glue; the less squeeze-out you have on the inside of the tray, the better. It's difficult to do a good job of cleaning glue out of the corners of a finished piece.

5. Carefully assemble and clamp the piece, making sure that it remains square while clamping (see **photo F**).

Finishing

When the glue is dry, remove the clamps, finish-sand the outside of the tray to 150 grit, and finish your tray. Don't forget to sand the insides of the handle openings. I finished my tray with satin spray lacquer for durability. If you don't have the ability to spray, you can certainly use an oil finish. I suggest a polymerized tung oil, since it is the most durable of the oil finishes I have used.

SPICE AND TEA SHELF

Niall Barrett

WHEN COLLECTING PROJECTS for this book, I just had to include this shelf. There has been an almost identical one in my kitchen for many years, and I wouldn't think of doing without it. I happened upon it before I became a woodworker, in a gift store, hanging on a wall and filled with mugs. I'm not sure exactly why I was so attracted to it, but I just had to have it. When I asked about it, the store owner informed me that it was only part of the display. Not one to be put off when I want something, I pushed the issue and was rewarded: The manager ordered one for me. Unfortunately, I had no good use for it.

As it turns out, the shelf has been one of the most useful kitchen storage items I've ever had. At the time, I lived in a tiny apartment in Brooklyn, New York, which had almost no free wall space. By default, the shelf ended up on a small sliver of wall space next to the stove. Slowly but surely, the shelf filled with the things I used near the stove (what a surprise!): spices, condiments, containers of tea and coffee, etc. Unlike other so-called spice racks, this shelf holds a fair amount of stuff. When I moved to another apartment with no similar wall space near the stove, I discovered that this shelf works just as well horizontally.

Made of stained pine stapled together, the original shelf was unremarkable, except for its long and seemingly thin proportions. The shape makes this piece both pleasing to the eye and useful in the kitchen. The version in this chapter is slightly longer, wider, and deeper than the one I bought close to 30 years ago. The larger size more easily accommodates items such as tea boxes and larger spice containers. I made it from walnut rather than the original pine.

SPICE AND TEA SHELF

This long, thin shelf provides valuable open storage in a kitchen—perfect for tea, coffee, spices, and other sundries.

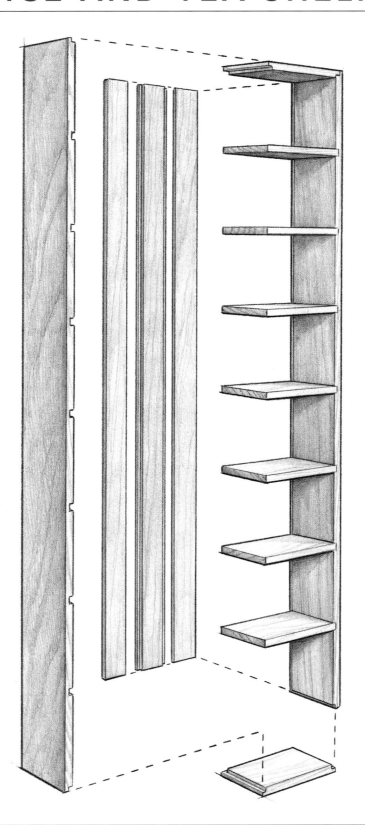

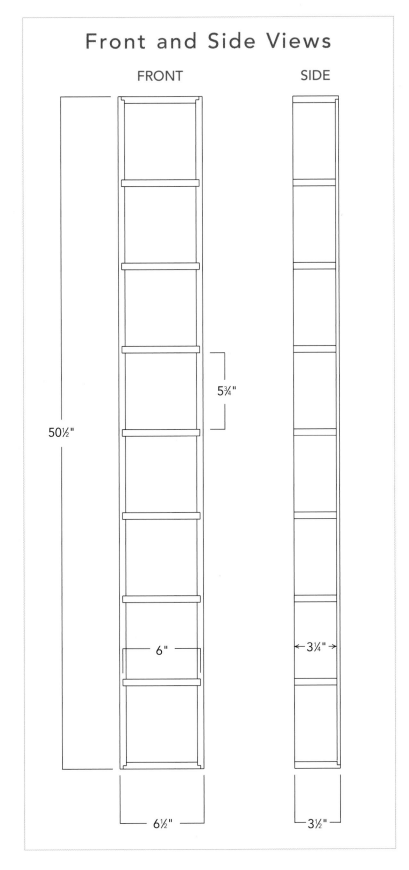

Front and Side Views

FRONT   SIDE

50½"

5¾"

6"   3¼"

6½"   3½"

Construction and Assembly

I CHOSE WALNUT FOR THIS PROJECT because I thought that a hardwood would be a better choice than soft pine. The walnut also most closely matches the dark stain of the old shelf, which proved to be a good choice for a kitchen environment. The joinery is very simple and so is the setup. Once you have the pieces milled to size, the rest of the work is on the tablesaw. It's important that all the parts are the same thickness (except the back) to ensure that the joints are tight.

1. Mill the shelves, sides, and top and bottom to precisely ½ in. thick.

2. Cut them to their finished size according to the dimensions in the cut list. Keep the cutoffs to use later for test pieces.

Cutting the Joinery

All of the joinery is easily cut on the tablesaw, with the same ½-in. dado blade installed for all steps. Adding a simple auxiliary fence makes it possible to use the same blade for different-width cuts without changing the setup or cutting into your rip fence.

Rabbets for the sides, back, and top

The rabbets along the back edges of the sides, top, and bottom capture the back. The rabbets on the ends of these pieces make up the corner joints of the case.

1. Install a ½-in.-wide dado blade in the tablesaw.

2. Make and attach a piece of medium-density fiberboard (MDF) or scrap plywood, at least ¾ in. thick, to the face of the rip fence. This will serve as an auxiliary fence.

3. With the blade below the table surface, set the auxiliary fence ⅜ in. over the blade. Turn the saw on, and slowly raise the blade into the fence until the blade is ¼ in. high.

4. Set the fence to cut a ¼-in.-wide rabbet.

CUT LIST FOR SPICE AND TEA SHELF

2	Sides	50½" x 3½" x ½"	solid walnut
2	Top and bottom	6" x 3½" x ½"	solid walnut
7	Shelves	6" x 3¼" x ½"	solid walnut
1	Back	50" x 2⅛" x ¼"	solid walnut
2	Backs	50" x 2¹⁄₁₆" x ¼"	solid walnut

Other materials

25	Brass screws	#4 x ⅝"

Cutting the shelf dadoes in the sides

1. Without changing the height of the blade, reposition the rip fence 6¼ in. away from the dado blade.

2. With the end of the workpiece registering against the rip fence and guiding the workpiece with the miter gauge, cut a dado on the inside face.

3. Spin the workpiece end for end and repeat the process on the other end. Do this for both side pieces.

4. Cut the other shelf dadoes in the same way, repositioning the rip fence to make the dadoes evenly spaced (see "Dado Spacing").

5. The last dadoes you cut have to be in the very center of their respective sides. If they aren't, they won't line up (see **photo B**).

5. Rabbet the ends of the sides, top, and bottom, guiding them with the miter gauge, registering the ends against the auxiliary fence (see **photo A**).

6. Rabbet the back edge of the sides, top, and bottom by running them along the rip fence.

PHOTO A: Use both the rip fence and miter gauge to guide the rabbet cuts on the ends of the sides, top, and bottom.

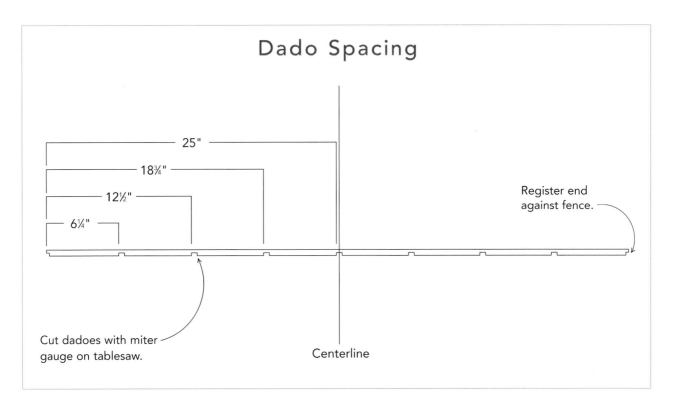

Dado Spacing

25"

18¾"

12½"

6¼"

Register end against fence.

Cut dadoes with miter gauge on tablesaw.

Centerline

PHOTO B: Cut the center dadoes of both sides last. Register the same end of each side against the rip fence to ensure the dadoes are aligned.

Assembling the Sides and Shelves

1. Sand all the parts to 150 grit. I recommend sanding by hand with a block. If you sand the shelves too much, they won't fit their dadoes.

2. Test-fit and match the shelves to dadoes for the best fit. Then label the shelves so they're easy to locate during glue-up.

3. Test-assemble the case. Make any minor adjustments necessary.

4. Apply glue in the dadoes with a brush, covering the bottoms and the walls. Applying glue only in the dadoes will greatly reduce squeeze-out, which would be difficult to clean up.

5. Clamp up the shelf to a flat surface, such as a benchtop. Under clamping pressure, the thin wood can distort easily, making the fit of the dadoes either too loose or too tight, bowing the finished shelf. Make sure to apply clamping pressure across the length of each joint.

6. Check frequently for square as you apply clamps, and skew them as necessary to bring the joints square.

7. Clamp the top and bottom in place last, both to the bench and across the length of the shelf.

Attaching the Back

While the carcase dries, work on the back. You could make the back out of plywood; however, since I didn't have a piece of ¼-in. walnut plywood, I made a three-piece, shiplapped, solid-wood back. This configuration accommodates seasonal wood movement (see **photo C**).

1. Mill and size the three back pieces to finished dimensions (see "Thin Stock Options"). The piece in the center is a little wider.

2. Lower the dado blade to ⅛ in. high, then reset the rip fence to make a ³⁄₁₆-in.-wide cut.

3. Cut the rabbets in the back pieces. The center piece is rabbeted along both edges.

PHOTO C: The pieces for the back are shiplapped to accommodate seasonal wood movement.

THIN STOCK OPTIONS

Small projects often call for stock thinner than standard ¾ in. The thinner stock can give the piece a lighter look and rarely compromises strength. While you can certainly plane down 4/4 stock to ½ in. thick, you'll end up wasting 50 percent of the board feet you just bought. Alternatively, you can buy thin stock from some mail-order catalogs, but you are limited in size, selection, and species.

A better alternative is to resaw your own stock. The bandsaw is the very best tool for resawing. The thin blade wastes very little wood, and the throat capacity of even a small bandsaw is enough to make average widths of lumber. The tablesaw can also be used to resaw but is limited by the cutting height, and the wider blade wastes more stock. In my opinion, it's also risky to resaw on the tablesaw.

Resawn on the bandsaw, lumber that's about 1 in. thick will yield two ⅜-in.-thick boards. To get ½-in.-thick lumber through resawing, you need to start with pieces at least 1¼ in. thick. Resawing often releases tensions in the wood, causing it to distort. The extra thickness is needed to straighten out the boards and obtain ½-in.-thick finished pieces.

Resawing is also the way to achieve book-matched boards. Glued together, they can make distinctive panels for cabinets and doors.

The two other pieces are rabbeted only along the inside edge (see "Detail of Back" on p. 52).

4. Finish-sand the pieces to 150 grit.

5. Fit one of the side back pieces tight into the back of the case. Use a clamp if necessary.

6. Drill and countersink pilot holes along the edge and screw into the rabbet on the sides. Place the screws midway between each shelf. Make sure you properly size the pilot holes. The hole should be slightly bigger than the width of the screw shank. Brass is very soft, and it's easy to break the screws when the holes are too small.

7. Repeat the process for the other side back piece. Note that there isn't much to screw into. Use small #4 brass screws, and angle the pilot hole very slightly.

8. Fit the center piece, spaced evenly between the two side pieces. Drill and countersink pilot holes into the center of the back of each shelf, as well as the top and bottom into the rabbet (see **photo D**).

PHOTO D: Screw the center back panel into the shelves. Treat the brass screws gently, as they break off easily.

Detail of Back

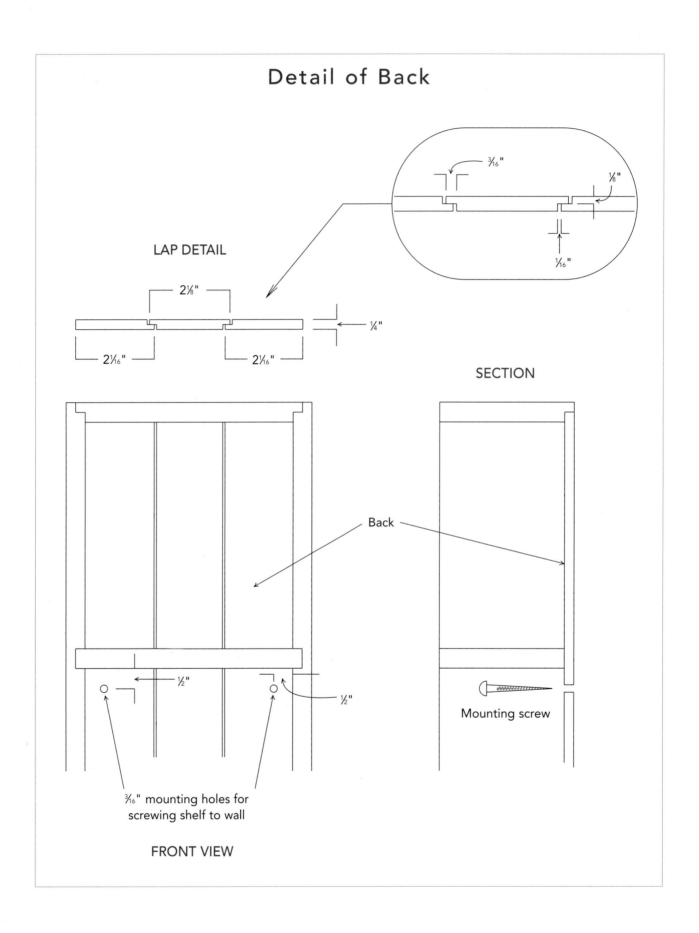

LAP DETAIL

2⅛"

2¹⁄₁₆"

2¹⁄₁₆"

¼"

³⁄₁₆"

⅛"

¹⁄₁₆"

SECTION

Back

Mounting screw

½"

½"

³⁄₁₆" mounting holes for
screwing shelf to wall

FRONT VIEW

DESIGN OPTION: HORIZONTAL SPICE SHELF

At over 4 ft. tall, this shelf can be difficult to place in a kitchen. There might not be a vertical space tall enough in your kitchen to accommodate it. The shelf works just fine, though, when hung horizontally.

The shelves become dividers, and the side on the top becomes a second shelf space. Also, you can make shorter (or taller) versions of this shelf, as you like.

Horizontally, the shelf offers two levels of storage space—in the shelves and on top.

Finishing Up

1. Drill four ³⁄₁₆-in. holes—two at each end—through the back at the locations shown (see "Detail of Back"). Only two on one end are necessary to hang the shelf vertically. The other two make it possible to hang the shelf in either a vertical orientation or a horizontal one (see "Design Option: Horizontal Spice Shelf").

2. Finish-sand the outside of the carcase to 150 grit.
3. Apply an oil finish. I used Watco™ Danish Oil, but any high-quality oil finish will work just fine. As not all oil finishes work in the same way, I recommend following the manufacturer's directions. I've never gone wrong this way.

SPICE DRAWER/SHELF

Niall Barrett

THIS PROJECT WAS INSPIRED by the rows of small drawers I have seen in many European kitchens, usually placed under a wall cabinet adjacent to the stove. They are called spice drawers because at one time they were indeed used to store loose spices. These days, they are more often used to store other items, but the name hangs on. Although these drawers are useful enough by themselves, I chose to add a shelf to make it a little more practical and to give more options for placement in the kitchen. It is just the right size to either hold its own on a large piece of wall or be slipped between a couple of cabinets.

This is one of those pieces that cries out for small-scale, visible joinery as well as thinner than usual materials. I chose ¼-in. finger joints (sometimes called box joints), which I think fit the scale of this piece perfectly. Repetitive joinery, such as finger joints, is a product of the machine age and was often used for packing and shipping containers and crates. These joints would be difficult to cut by hand, mostly because of the sheer number and (usually) diminutive size of the joints. They are, however, easily cut on the tablesaw with a simple jig. The setup is a little fussy and usually requires making a number of test pieces, but after that, you can cut these joints all day long!

SPICE DRAWER/SHELF

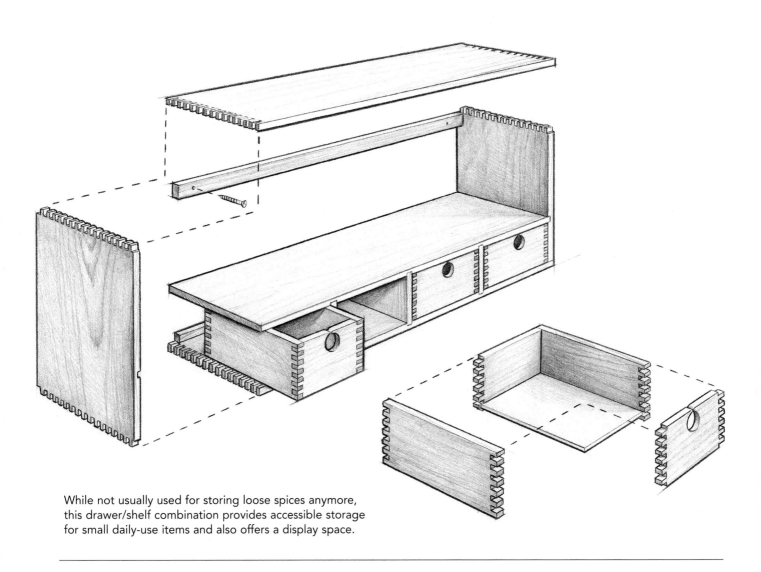

While not usually used for storing loose spices anymore, this drawer/shelf combination provides accessible storage for small daily-use items and also offers a display space.

Construction and Assembly

I CHOSE CHERRY FOR THIS PIECE, but you could certainly use another wood. I would, however, try to stay away from the more splintery woods, such as oak or ash, since the tiny joints might tend to break out.

Milling Parts

1. Mill the top and sides of the case and the front, back, and sides of the drawers to the dimensions in the cut list. These parts will all have finger joints. To mill stock this thin, you have several options, including planing down thicker stock or resawing.

2. Mill several extra 8-in.-wide pieces for testing the finger joints.

Top, Front, and Side Views

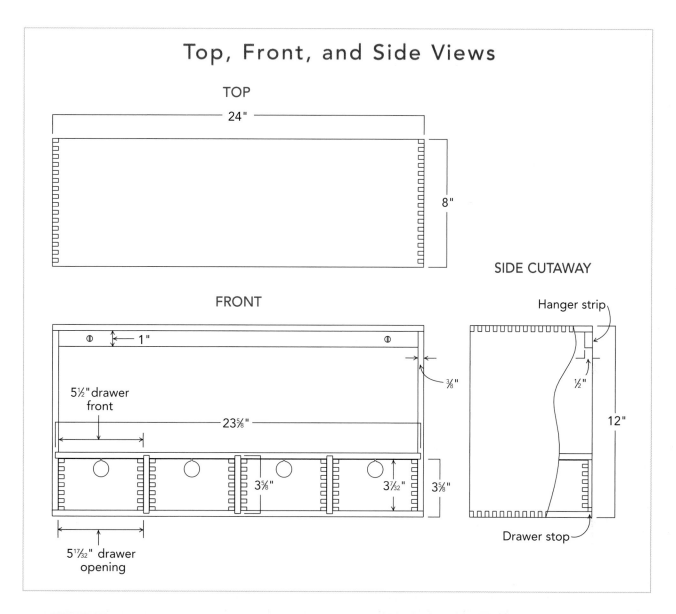

TOP

24"

8"

SIDE CUTAWAY

FRONT

Hanger strip

1"

3/8"

5½" drawer front

23⅝"

½"

12"

3⅝"

3 7/32"

3⅝"

5 17/32" drawer opening

Drawer stop

	CUT LIST FOR SPICE DRAWER/SHELF		
2	Top and bottom	24" x 8" x ⅜"	solid cherry
1	Shelf	23⅝" x 8" x ⅜"	solid cherry
2	Sides	12" x 8" x ⅜"	solid cherry
3	Drawer dividers	3⅝" x 8" x ⅜"	solid cherry
1	Hanger strip	23¼" x 1" x ½"	solid cherry
8	Drawer sides	3¼" x 7¾" x ⅜"	solid cherry
8	Drawer fronts and backs	3¼" x 5½" x ⅜"	solid cherry
4	Drawer bottoms	5⅛" x 7⅜" x ¼"	solid cherry
4	Drawer stops	5 17/32" x ¼" x ¼"	solid cherry

3. Mill the shelf, dividers, drawer bottoms, hanger strip, and stock for the drawer stops to dimension. Leave the drawer-stop stock long for the moment. You'll fit it later to the actual openings.

Dadoing for the Dividers and Shelf

The shelf fits into dadoes in the case sides, and the drawer dividers fit into dadoes in the bottom of the shelf and the top of the bottom of the case. You want four evenly spaced drawer openings in the completed case.

1. The dadoes for the shelf are located 3⅝ in. up from the bottom edge of the piece.

2. On the bottom of the case, the two outside dadoes for the drawer dividers are located 5²⁹⁄₃₂ in. from the ends. The third dado is in the center.

3. On the shelf, the two outside dadoes are 5²³⁄₃₂ in. from the ends of the board. The third dado is also centered.

4. Cut the dadoes on the tablesaw, using a ⅜-in.-wide dado blade, set to cut ³⁄₁₆ in. deep.

Use the rip fence to locate the cut and the miter gauge to guide the piece in the cut. (See the spice and tea shelf, pp. 44–53, for detailed information on dadoing.)

Cutting the Finger Joints

The drawers and case sides are held together with finger joints. To cut consistently sized fingers, you'll first need to make a jig (see "Finger-Jointing Jig").

Joining the drawers

I cut the drawers so that the fronts and backs have end-grain pins showing at the top and bottom.

1. Cut the front and back pieces first. Make the first cut by placing a ¼-in. by ¼-in. spacer between the workpiece and the pin. (The leftover pin stock for the jig works well for this.) This makes the first cut at the very edge of the board (see **photo A**), so that the front and sides join with their edges flush.

PHOTO A: With a finger-jointing jig on the table-saw, cut the fingers on the fronts and backs, making the first cut using a spacer block the thickness of the fingers.

PHOTO B: Make subsequent cuts in the fronts and backs, always positioning the registration pin in the previous kerf.

FINGER-JOINTING JIG

A simple plywood auxiliary fence attached to the miter gauge makes an excellent jig for cutting finger joints. It should not take you more than a few minutes to make, and it's the only reasonable way to cut the joints.

1. Clamp an auxiliary plywood fence to your tablesaw's miter gauge, with several inches stretching across the line of cut.

2. Install a ¼-in.-wide dado cutter in your tablesaw and raise it to cut a ⅜-in.-deep cut.

3. Run the auxiliary fence over the dado blade, cutting a notch in the bottom edge.

4. Mill a foot length of ¼-in. by ¼-in. pin stock.

5. Remove the auxiliary fence and glue a 1½-in. length of the pin stock in the slot, flush with the back and bottom edges of the auxiliary fence. The workpiece will register against this pin. Put the rest of the pin stock to one side for the moment.

6. Reattach the auxiliary fence to the miter-gauge head so that the dado blade will cut a notch exactly ¼ in. to the left of the pin.

7. Cut two test pieces to ensure the jig works properly and cuts ¼-in. slots spaced exactly ¼ in. apart. The test pieces should slide together easily, with light hand pressure.

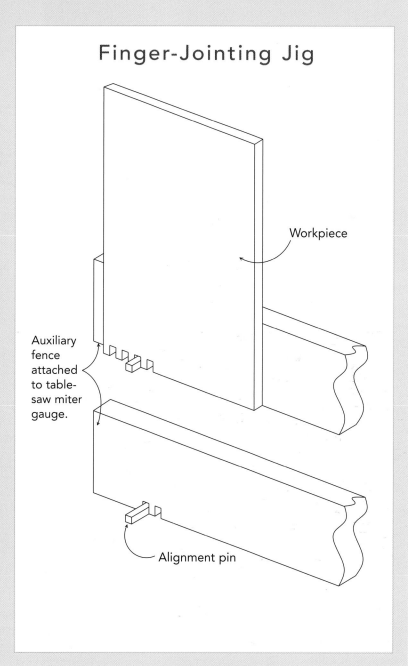

Finger-Jointing Jig

Workpiece

Auxiliary fence attached to table-saw miter gauge.

Alignment pin

PHOTO C: To cut the sides that mate with the fronts and backs, make the first cut with the side of the workpiece (without the spacer) butting against the registration pin. This will start a complementary pattern of kerfs and fingers.

PHOTO D: Locate the groove for the drawer along the bottom edge of the drawer sides, aligned with the second finger/kerf pair.

2. Remove the spacer, lift the workpiece up, position the slot you just cut on the pin, and make the next cut.

3. The subsequent cuts follow the same pattern, moving the workpiece from left to right (see **photo B** on p. 58).

4. For the pins in the side pieces, place the workpiece against the registration pin (without the spacer) and cut the first slot (see **photo C**).

5. All the subsequent cuts are the same as for the front and back.

Joining the case

1. Cut the joints in the top and bottom of the case, following the same technique used for cutting the sides of the drawers.

2. Cut the joints in the sides of the case, following the same technique used for cutting the fronts and backs of the drawers, using the spacer for the first cut.

Grooving for the Drawer Bottoms

In the sides of the drawers, the groove will line up with the first notch. In the fronts, the groove will line up precisely with the first pin, removing half of the pin and leaving a void that you'll fill in a later step.

1. Set the rip fence on your tablesaw ¼ in. from the dado blade. Set the blade to cut ³⁄₁₆ in. deep.

2. Cut a ¼-in.-wide by ³⁄₁₆-in.-deep groove in the bottom inside edge of all drawer parts (see **photo D**).

3. Cut drawer bottoms to fit these grooves.

Making the Drawer Pulls

1. Drill a 1-in.-dia. hole in the drawer fronts, centered ⅝ in. down from the top edge. Use a Forstner bit on a drill press, with a piece of scrap backing up the workpiece so that the wood doesn't break out on the bottom side.

2. Using a small handsaw, cut a thin slot through the top edge of the drawer front into the hole (see "Making the Drawer Pull").

PHOTO E: Soften the edges of the handle detail with fine sandpaper, being careful not to reshape the kerf or file cuts.

3. File a slight V in the top and bottom of the kerf using a small triangular file.

4. Round all the edges slightly with sand-paper (see **photo E**).

Assembling the Drawers

1. Dry-fit all the drawers and adjust the fit as necessary, making sure the drawer bottom has at least 1/16 in. of room side to side to allow for seasonal wood movement.

2. Finish-sand the drawer parts to 150 grit.

3. Make clamping cauls to put even pressure across the joints. Put packing tape on the inside faces of the cauls to keep them from adhering to the drawers.

4. Brush glue on all the joint faces of one drawer but not on the drawer bottom or grooves.

5. Assemble and clamp the drawer, checking and adjusting for square. Repeat the process for the other three drawers.

6. When the glue has set, make 1/4-in. by 3/16-in. pegs and plug the holes in the sides left from cutting the drawer-bottom grooves (see **photo F**).

Making the Drawer Pull

5/8" 1" dia.

Step 1: Drill 1"-dia. hole centered 5/8" from top edge of drawer front.

Step 2: Make saw kerf.

Step 3: Shape kerf with small triangular file.

PHOTO F: After you assemble the drawers, fill the holes in the sides left from routing the drawer grooves.

PHOTO G: Assemble the case from the bottom up, fitting the drawer dividers, bottom, and shelf together first, then the sides, and last the top.

Drawer Details

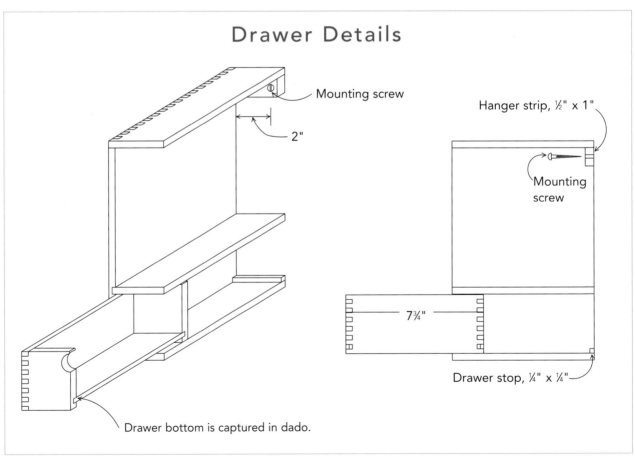

Mounting screw

2"

Drawer bottom is captured in dado.

Hanger strip, ½" x 1"

Mounting screw

7¾"

Drawer stop, ¼" x ¼"

Assembling and Finishing the Case

1. Glue and clamp the case together, starting with the bottom, drawer dividers, and shelf (see **photo G**). Next, glue and clamp the sides, followed by the top.

2. After the glue has set, remove the clamps and install ¼-in. by ¼-in. drawer stops at the back of the case. These keep the fronts of the drawers flush with the front of the case.

Building them this way allows some front-to-back adjustment, if necessary, by changing the size of the stops.

3. Glue and clamp in place a ½-in. by 1-in. by 23¼-in. hanger strip in the inside top back edge of the piece. Be sure to drill holes for the screws you will be hanging it with before you glue it in place (see "Drawer Details").

4. Finish the case with oil and wax, or however you prefer.

DESIGN OPTION: DRAWERS ALONE

I designed this project to work well in any number of locations in your kitchen. However, the one location in which it would not work well is under an upper cabinet because the piece is rather tall. It's ironic, since this is the traditional location of the small drawers that were the inspiration for this project.

However, if this style and location is more to your taste, then it is a simple matter to omit the shelf portion. You can also add or subtract drawers to better fit your chosen location.

To build this version, you'll simply need to put ¼-in. hanger strips behind the two outer drawers along the top inside edge of the case.

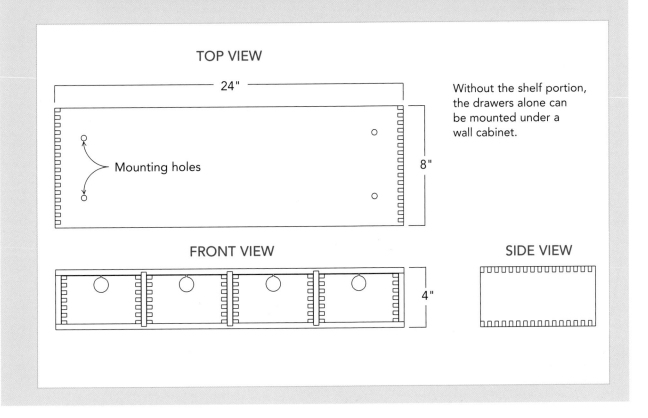

TOP VIEW

24"

Mounting holes

8"

Without the shelf portion, the drawers alone can be mounted under a wall cabinet.

FRONT VIEW

4"

SIDE VIEW

PANTRY DOOR SHELVES

ONE EXCELLENT AREA for storage is on the inside of a pantry door—a space that's often wasted. Here's a very simple set of shelves that you can screw to the door to hold everything from spices and canned goods to sandwich bags and aluminum foil.

What is ingenious about this design—presented to me by professional cabinetmaker Adolph Schneider—is the system of shelf stops. Each stop is simply a ¼-in.-diameter dowel that you bend to spring into its holes after assembling the unit. Schneider installs one dowel at the front of each shelf, but I decided to make a row of holes for each dowel so the stop can

be moved in or out to accommodate larger or smaller items. When placed in the outermost holes, the stop will allow space for a typical 4-in.-diameter can. When placed in the other holes, the stop will prevent smaller canned goods or spice jars from shifting when the pantry door is opened.

The shelf cabinet is made of ½-in.-thick hardwood plywood edged with solid wood. The top and bottom fit into rabbets cut in the cabinet sides, and the shelves fit into dadoes. Solid-wood strips hide the edges of the plywood. Of course, you can size the cabinet to fit any door.

PANTRY DOOR SHELVES

The sides and top are made of ½"-thick hardwood plywood with solid-wood edging. The back is ¼"-thick hardwood plywood. The ¼"-diameter dowels are bent and sprung into their holes after the case is assembled.

Back
Top
Shelf
Side
Edging
Dowel
Bottom
Rabbet

DESIGN OPTIONS

✦ Design the shelf dimensions and spacing to suit your particular storage needs.

✦ Apply veneer tape after assembly instead of solid-wood edging. (But be aware that the tape can tear away if snagged.)

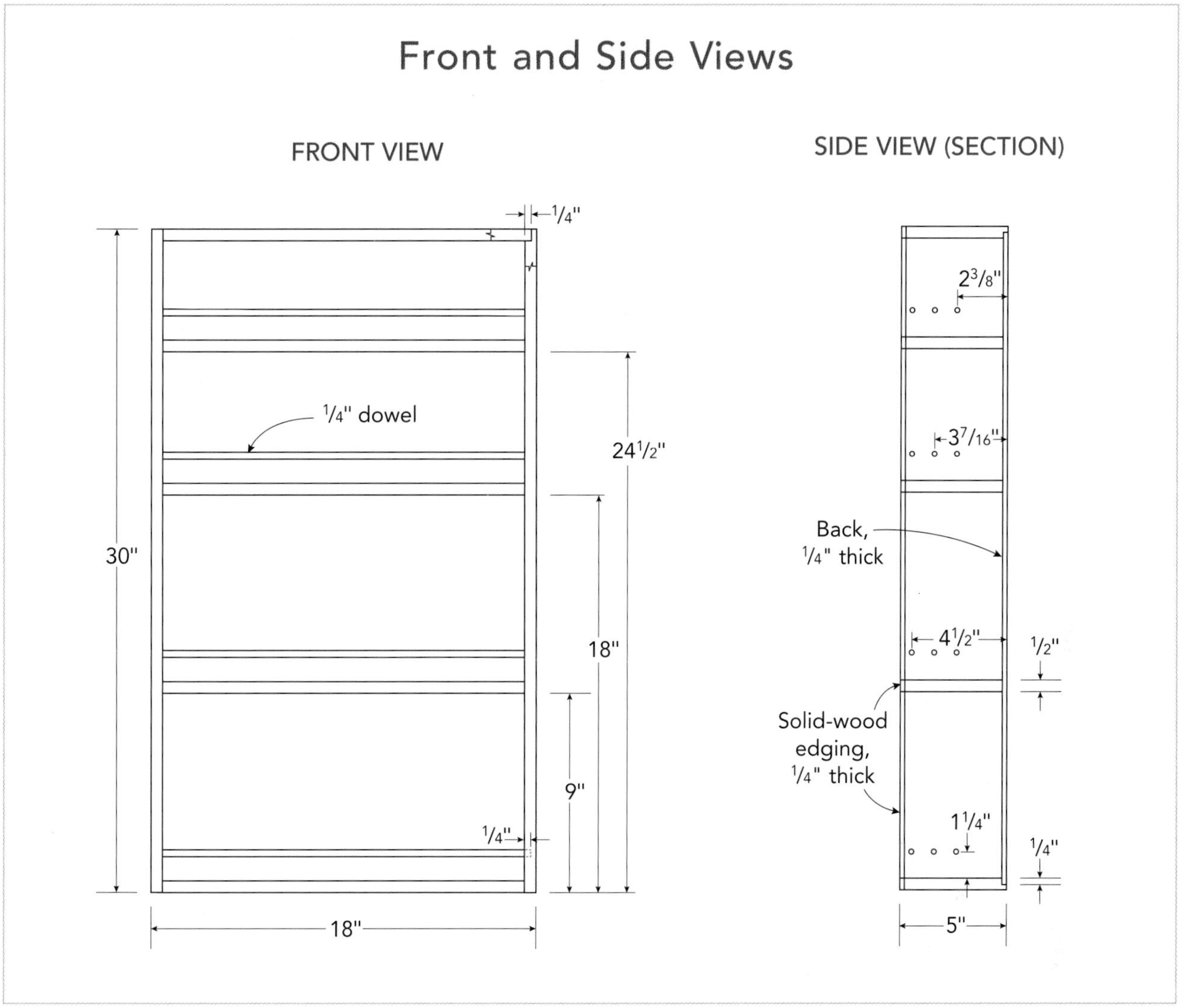
Front and Side Views
FRONT VIEW
SIDE VIEW (SECTION)
1/4"
1/4" dowel
24 1/2"
30"
18"
9"
1/4"
18"
2 3/8"
3 7/16"
Back, 1/4" thick
4 1/2"
1/2"
Solid-wood edging, 1/4" thick
1 1/4"
1/4"
5"

YOU'LL BEGIN BY MAKING the parts and cutting the joints. After attaching the edging and drilling the dowel holes, you'll notch the ends of the top, bottom, and shelf edging and then assemble the case. After that, a quick sanding and a few coats of finish will complete the job.

Preparing the Parts and Joinery

Make the parts

1. Lay out the plywood and saw the sides, top, bottom, and shelves to size. Use a good-quality blade that won't tear the veneers when crosscutting and make sure to cut away any factory edges.

CUT LIST FOR PANTRY DOOR SHELVES

2	Sides	½" x 4¾" x 30"	hardwood plywood
2	Top and bottom	½" x 4¾" x 17½"	hardwood plywood
3	Shelves	½" x 4½" x 17½"	hardwood plywood
1	Back	¼" x 17½" x 29½"	hardwood plywood
4	Dowels	¼" dia. x 17⅜"	solid wood
2	Edging strips	¼" x 9⁄16" x 30"	solid wood
5	Edging strips	¼" x 9⁄16" x 17¼"	solid wood

PHOTO A:
Sandwich the
solid-wood edg-
ing between its
mating case
pieces. Raise
the case pieces
on thin shims so
the edging can
overlap on both
sides. Scrap strips
protect the thin
rear edges from
clamp damage.

2. Make the ¼-in.-thick edging strips. I rip them from a board that I've planed to ⁵⁄₁₆ in. thick. I trim the overlap flush to the ½-in.-thick plywood after attaching the edging.

3. Saw the back, but leave it slightly oversize in length and width. You'll trim it for a perfect fit to its rabbets later.

Cut the joints

1. Lay out the dadoes for the shelves (see the drawing on p. 66). You'll probably want to customize the spacing to suit the size of your particular shelf cabinet, as well as the size of the items you plan to store in it. For aesthetic purposes, the sections should graduate from the largest at the bottom to the smallest at the top.

2. Mount a dado blade on your saw and shim it out to match the thickness of your plywood. Clamp an auxiliary fence to the rip fence; then saw the rabbets on the ends of the case sides. Alternatively, you could rout the rabbets as well as the shelf dadoes.

3. Using the rip fence as a stop, saw the dadoes to accept the shelves. Use a miter gauge with a long fence to guide the workpieces over the blade.

4. Saw or rout the ¼-in. by ¼-in. rabbets in the rear edges of the sides, top, and bottom, as shown in the drawing on p. 66.

Completing the Unit

Attach the edging and drill the holes

This cabinet has a lot of edging, which needs to be cut flush to the plywood pieces. Although you could apply the edging after assembling the case, routing or scraping it flush at the corners afterward can be difficult. As I'll show you here, you can attach the edging first; then notch it on the ends of the horizontal pieces, allowing them to tuck into the dadoes in the case sides.

1. Glue the edging onto all of the pieces, centering it across the thickness of the plywood. The shelf edging should extend to within about ⅛ in. of the end of the shelf. For efficiency, clamp two shelves together at once, keeping the edging in between (see **photo A**).

2. After the glue cures, plane the edging flush with the plywood. Alternatively, you could rout the edging flush using a flush-trimming bit first. Then plane or scrape it afterward.

3. Lay out the vertical spacing for the rows of ¼-in.-diameter by ¼-in.-deep dowel holes; then drill them on the drill press using a brad-point bit to prevent tearout. Use a fence to register each column of holes to the correct distance from the long edge of the workpiece.

4. Sand the pieces using a flat sanding block. Again, be careful not to round over the inside edges of the case pieces.

Notch the shelves and assemble the case

1. Trim the shelf edging to allow the ends of the top, bottom, and shelves to seat fully in the case dadoes. Using the tablesaw rip fence as a stop, feed each shelf on edge, with the blade raised just shy of the plywood edge (see **photo B**).

2. Use a sharp chisel to remove any remaining glue or wood residue from the edge of the plywood at the notched section.

3. Dry-clamp the case to make sure that the joints all draw up tightly and that there are no gaps between the case and shelf edging. Make any necessary adjustments by trimming the shelves or edging.

4. With the case still dry-clamped, trim the back for a very snug fit in its rabbets.

5. Glue up the case, using cauls to distribute pressure evenly across the joints (see "Clamping Cauls" on p. 19). Insert the back unglued to help hold the case square, but check to make sure that the front edges are also square while under clamp pressure. Wipe away any excess glue immediately using a clean rag and clean water.

6. After the glue cures, re-sand as necessary to smooth any grain that was raised by clean-up water.

7. Glue and nail or glue and staple the back into its rabbets and let the glue cure thoroughly, as the back will be holding the cabinet to the pantry door.

Finishing Up

1. Sand the entire case through 220 grit, gently rounding the corners and front and rear edges.

PHOTO B: After gluing on the slightly long shelf edging, nip it off ¼ in. from the end. Use the rip fence as a stop.

PHOTO C: Spring the dowels into place by bending them enough to insert them into their holes.

2. Cut and sand the ¼-in.-diameter dowels and test-fit them in their holes (see **photo C**). The dowels should be about ⁷⁄₁₆ in. longer than the distance between the inner faces of the case sides.

3. Apply a finish. This cabinet has several coats of an oil-varnish blend wiped on. (No need to get too fussy here; after all, it's inside a pantry most of the time.)

4. Hang the cabinet by screwing through the back in several places. If installing it on a hollow-core door, use molly or toggle bolts.

CUTTING BOARD AND KNIFE RACK

Niall Barrett

T HESE TWO PROJECTS GO hand-in-hand. After all, to cut and chop food you need both knives and a cutting board. Nevertheless, they are independent projects and may be built separately.

If you buy a "butcher block" cutting board these days, chances are what you'll get is a board with lengthwise strips of wood glued together. If you have ever seen a real butcher block, as in one really used by butchers, you may have noticed that it is rather different. A true butcher block is constructed of many pieces of wood arranged so that the grain of the wood runs vertically (up and down).

End grain is a superior cutting surface because it is able to "heal" itself. When the knife strikes this type of surface during cutting, the grain of the wood actually separates and then closes when the knife is removed. The wood itself is not cut; instead, you are cutting between the fibers. This ensures that knives keep their edge and that knife scars heal to maintain a clean working surface.

In contrast, "butcher blocks" made with the grain running lengthwise don't last. When drawing a knife across this surface, the wood fibers are cut slightly, creating a permanent wound. Over time, with thousands of cuts on the surface, the block will scar substantially, giving food places to lodge, and will deteriorate rather badly over the years.

Having said all this, it is quite a bit more work to produce a true butcher block. However, I thought it would be worth doing on a smaller scale. The construction process is interesting, and the surface created is extremely attractive. Think of this cutting board as a butcher block for your counter.

CUTTING BOARD

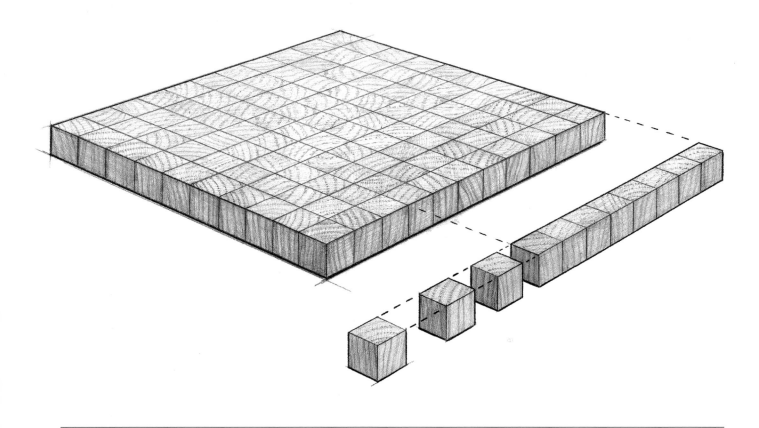

Making the Plank

THE FIRST STEP IN MAKING this cutting board is to build a conventional plank with edge-grain construction. Make sure that the strips are straight, flat, and square so that the glued-up top will be also. You might be tempted to use biscuits or dowels to align the pieces, but

don't. You will be recutting this top and reassembling it; any biscuits or dowels would show.

1. Rip 8/4 flatsawn stock into 11 strips, approximately 2 in. wide and 24 in. long.

2. Joint and thickness-plane the strips to $1^{13}\!/_{16}$ in. by $1^{13}\!/_{16}$ in.

3. Glue them together to produce a quartersawn top 20 in. wide, $1^{13}\!/_{16}$ in. thick, and 24 in. long. (By "quartersawn," I mean that all the end grain should run perpendicular to the face of the assembled butcher block.) You will have less trouble if you glue up these pieces a couple at a time until you have the top completed.

4. When the top is complete and the glue is dry, clean the top and flatten any minor irregularities with a belt sander or (preferably) a handplane. Be very careful with all

CUT LIST FOR CUTTING BOARD			
121	Blocks	$1^{13}\!/_{16}$" x $1^{13}\!/_{16}$" x 2"	solid cherry
Other materials			
Mineral oil			

Top and Side Views

The handsome end-grain cutting surface of this board
doesn't show knife marks and will last a lifetime.

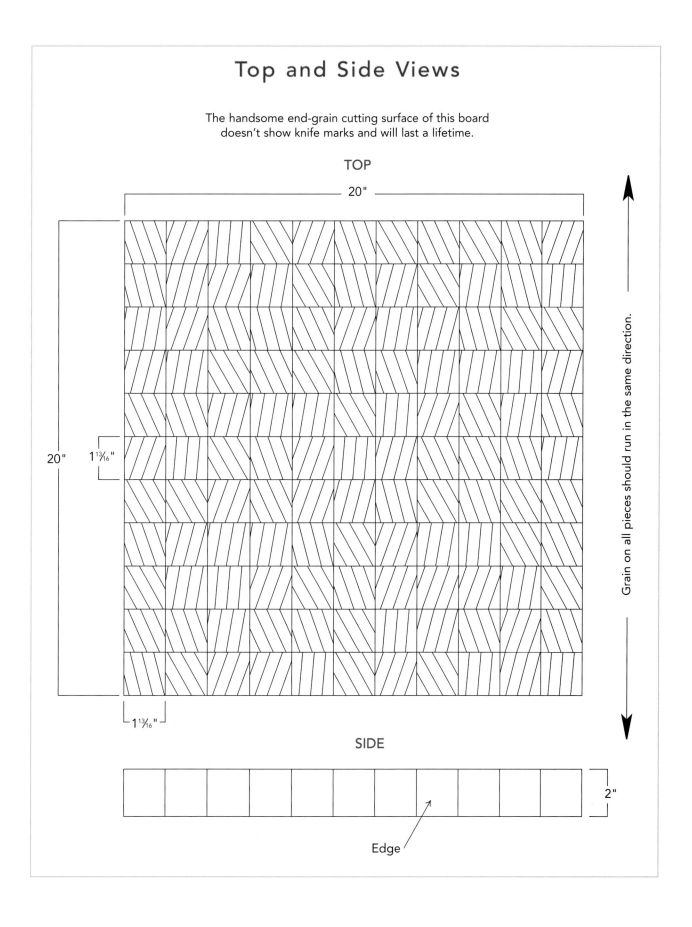

TOP

20"

20"

1¹³⁄₁₆"

1¹³⁄₁₆"

Grain on all pieces should run in the same direction.

SIDE

2"

Edge

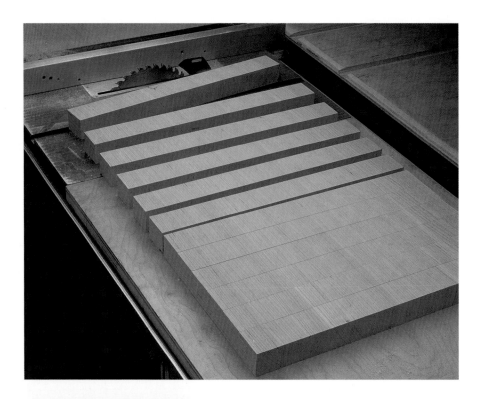

PHOTO B: Turn the strips on edge and arrange them until the grain patterns are pleasing.

this; it's crucial that the top and bottom surfaces be flat and parallel for the next step. If you have access to a wide belt sander or a planer wide enough to handle this piece, then by all means take advantage of it.

5. Square up one end of this perfect plank.

6. Crosscut the plank into 2-in.-wide pieces (see **photo A**).

7. Take these pieces and turn them so that their end grain is facing up.

8. Rearrange them to form a 20-in. by 20-in. by 2-in. square. I think it looks better if the end-grain squares look randomly placed, so move the parts around until you get a pleasing arrangement. When you are satisfied with how your block looks, glue the parts together, as in step 3 (see **photo B**).

Flattening the Top

Once your cutting board is assembled and the glue is dry, it's time to flatten and smooth the top and bottom surfaces. The hardest way to do this is also the most satisfying, since it leaves an absolutely exquisite surface. I'm talking, of course, about hand-

POLYURETHANE GLUE

Polyurethane glue is useful to glue up butcher-block tops for a number of reasons:

• Polyurethane is waterproof. Cutting boards will probably be cleaned and wiped down often with water.

• It's a single-part glue. There are other waterproof glues available, but most require mixing two parts. With polyurethane glue, there's no mixing involved.

• It has a reasonable open time. When you're rushing to put clamps on before the glue sets, you'll appreciate this feature.

• It's easy to spread; in fact, it acts as something of a lubricant in bringing joints together. It doesn't grab like a polyvinyl acetate (PVA) glue, so you can easily and more accurately line up and position the parts.

• You only have to spread polyurethane on one of the mating surfaces (something you will appreciate when gluing up this top!).

• As it cures, the glue expands into the wood fibers, strengthening the bond.

• It needs only minimum clamping pressure, requiring only that the parts be firmly held together. In fact, if you use too much clamping pressure you'll starve the joint and get a poor bond.

• Dried polyurethane is extremely easy to work; it won't clog your sandpaper or dull your cutting tools.

• On the down side, it doesn't clean up with water. Keep a rag and a can of acetone handy to wipe away glue squeeze-out and, if necessary, to clean your hands and clothes.

To ensure a good bond with polyurethane glue, remember that it cures in the presence of moisture. If the wood and/or the environment is particularly dry, try spraying a small amount of water onto the mating portion of the joint before clamping.

Polyurethane glues also like a little "tooth" or roughness to the joint. As the glue expands, it gets into and around this tooth and forms a mechanical bond. If your wood is glass smooth, the glue can't penetrate well and you could get a joint failure. For a piece that has been through the planer, a light scuffing of the surface with a piece of 80-grit sandpaper will give you enough tooth. Parts directly off the tablesaw are perfect just as they are.

---

planing! It takes a sharp plane, some time, and a lot of elbow grease, but nothing else will produce as nice a finish. A handplaned finish on side grain is a sweet thing, but a well-executed handplaned finish on end grain leaves the cherry feeling and looking like polished stone. It is quite astounding!

1. Set a smooth plane to take very thin shavings. I use a Record® #4½ (Stanley® makes an almost identical version). This is a slightly larger version of the #4 smooth plane. It is 10½ in. long and 2⅜ in. wide. The extra weight and size coupled with a wider-than-normal blade make it a good choice for this type of work, where you have a large, difficult surface to plane. The extra blade width makes it a little harder to push, but in this case you will be taking very light shavings. Regardless of your plane choice, it has to be extremely sharp and well tuned; you will probably have to hone it a couple of times during the work.

2. Always work toward the center of the piece to avoid breaking out the edges. Then just work the piece bit by bit until it is smooth and beautiful (see **photo C**).

Just so you don't think that I'm a hand-plane nut, I'll tell you how to get a really nice finish with less work: Just sand it (though it's still not as easy as it sounds!).

PHOTO C: The time and effort necessary to handplane end grain pay off with a glass-smooth finish.

1. With a belt sander, flatten the surface with 80 grit sandpaper.

2. Work your way up to 120 grit with the belt sander.

3. Switch to a finish sander, preferably a random orbit.

4. Go back to 100 grit and get rid of all the belt-sander marks. Then work your way up to 320 grit (or 400 grit, if you can stand it), at which point you will have a good approximation of the planed finish.

For those of you who think that this is all crazy—seeing that this is a cutting board after all and will be chopped and hacked daily—I have a third option for you: Just stop sanding when the board is flat and reasonably smooth.

Finishing

I finished this cutting board with some mineral oil, which is food-safe and attractive. There are a number of other food-safe finishes on the market, but mineral oil is inexpensive and easily available. This is important, since you will have to reoil your block fairly often if you use it a lot.

MAINTAINING A WOOD TOP IN THE KITCHEN

Hardwood cutting surfaces are very attractive and durable, but are wooden surfaces sanitary or difficult to maintain? Although there is some controversy as to whether wooden cutting boards are sanitary compared to plastic ones, wood ones are safe enough if taken care of properly.

Simple use of normal hygiene (soap and water) when cleaning any cutting surface is certainly in order. I also periodically use a weak solution of bleach (10 parts water to 1 part bleach). The solution won't harm the wood, and it helps keep the bacteria under control.

If your cutting board appears a bit dull after repeated use and cleaning, a simple reapplication of mineral oil (which is sanitary and food-safe) will brighten the finish and nourish the surface.

One last point: If and when your board gets to the point where you feel it is too unsightly, you can just turn it over and use the other surface. When that side needs to be spruced up, simply resurface it. Since it's 2 in. thick, you will be able to do this many times.

KNIFE RACK

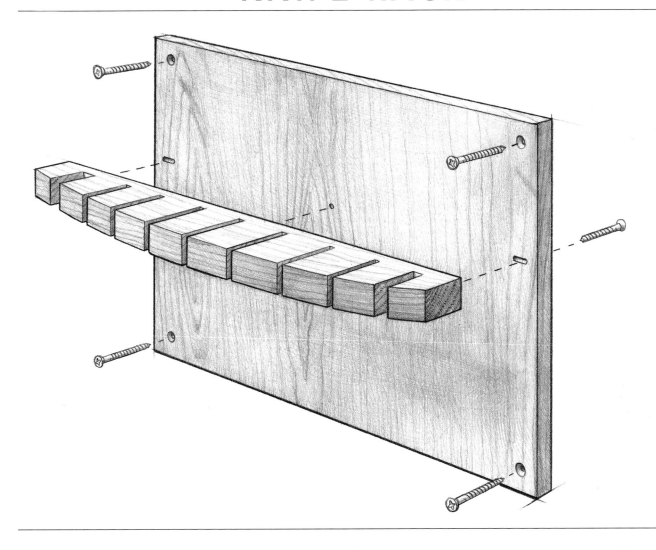

Construction and Assembly

I HAVE ALWAYS LIKED THE NOTION of a knife rack: a special place to keep kitchen knives safe, sharp, and accessible. Good knives are expensive, and the idea of just throwing them into a drawer seems disrespectful at best.

The problem is that most knife racks or holders either take up counter space (as in your common knife block) or hide the blades of the knives (clearly a safety measure), forcing you to identify a knife by its

CUT LIST FOR KNIFE RACK			
1	Back	¾" x 18" x 20"	solid cherry
1	Knife holder	19¾" x 1½" x 3½"	solid cherry

Other materials

	Polymerized tung oil	
2	Wood screws	#8 x 2"
1	Wood screw	#8 x 1"
4	Brass panhead screws with washers	#8 x 2"

Top, Elevation, and Side Views

This rack keeps knives safe but within reach. The blades are visible to help you pick out the right knife. It can accommodate knives of any size, plus two sharpening steels.

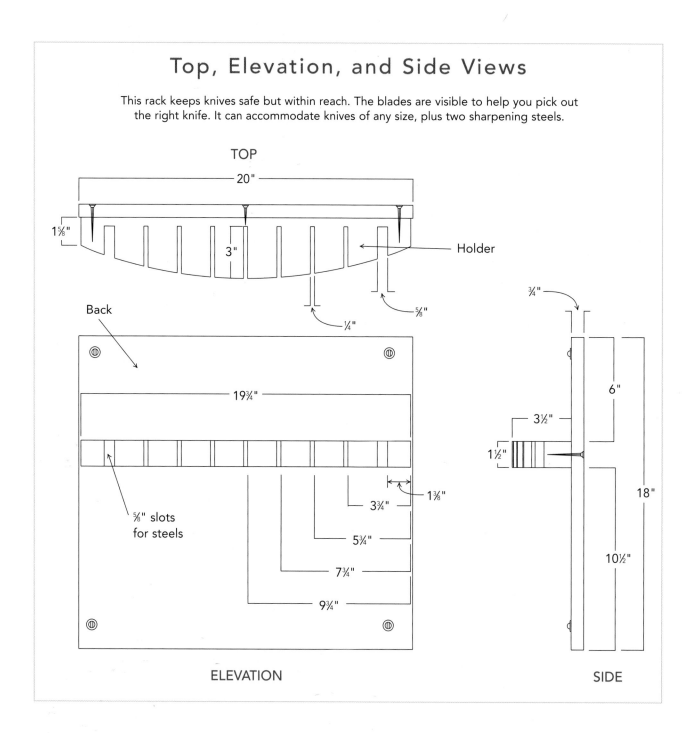

TOP

20"

1⅝"

3"

Holder

¼"

⅝"

Back

19¾"

⅝" slots
for steels

1⅞"

3¾"

5¾"

7¾"

9¾"

ELEVATION

¾"

6"

3½"

1½"

18"

10½"

SIDE

handle. To overcome these issues, I designed a rack that mounts on the backsplash under the cabinets at the back of the counter. This location reduces clutter on the counter and keeps knives within arm's reach but out of the reach of small children; with the blades visible, it is easy to identify the knife you wish to use.

Knife Holder

1. Joint and plane a piece of cherry to 3½ in. by 1½ in. by 19¾ in.

2. Place a ¼-in. dado blade in your tablesaw, set to a height of 3 in.

3. Set your tablesaw fence to the largest of the slot-position dimensions. This will be the center slot.

4. Place the workpiece against your miter gauge, set at 90 degrees, with the end against the fence, and make the first slot cut. Make sure you place a piece of scrap wood behind the workpiece to avoid tearout when the sawblade exits the workpiece.

5. Reposition the fence to the next smallest dimension and make the next cut.

6. Without changing the position of the fence, rotate the workpiece so that the opposite end is against the fence and make a cut.

7. Repeat this sequence until you get to the smallest dimension. The procedure is the same for these cuts, but you will need to change to a ⅜-in. dado blade. The ⅜-in. slots are designed to hold sharpening steels but will hold other items as well, such as a carving fork (see **photo D**).

8. Lay out the curve on the front of the piece that goes from the center of the front of the piece to 1⅝ in. from the back at each end.

9. Carefully cut about ¹⁄₁₆ in. from the line using a bandsaw (see **photo E**). A jigsaw or a coping saw will also work.

10. Sand to the line, and continue to finish-sand the entire piece to 150 grit.

PHOTO E: Guide the workpiece smoothly through the bandsaw to ensure an even curve on the front edge.

DESIGN OPTIONS: SMALLER HOLDER AND ALTERNATE HOLDER

Smaller Holder

It occurred to me while building the knife holder that by simply making the back of this holder smaller you can put it other places in the kitchen. You could still place it where I have suggested, but with a smaller back you could move it to another wall-mounted location without it looking out of place, as it would with the full back. The full back does provide some extra wall protection, but otherwise it should work the same (see photo).

Alternate Holder

I spent a great deal of time determining the best layout of slots to hold the most different kinds and sizes of knives. While I settled on the one presented in this chapter, it was by no means the only configuration I came up with. One other slot configuration I particularly liked is shown here (see "Optional Knife Holder").

I ended up not using this holder because it requires the knives be lifted clear rather than just pulled forward from the slots. This would

not have worked for the location I chose, but would be a good choice for a closed box holder or a straight counter insert. You would have to make a template for routing the slots. Alternatively, you could drill a hole at the ends of the slots, carefully cut them out with a jigsaw, then file and sand to the lines. This holder accommodates nine knives, one cleaver, and two sharpening steels.

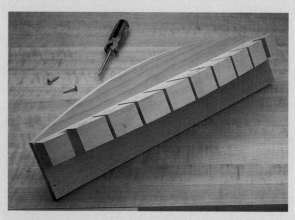

A shorter back works as well as a full back and offers a different look, though it provides less wall protection.

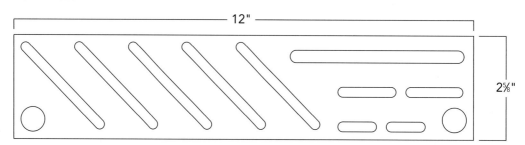

Optional Knife Holder

TOP VIEW

12"

2⅝"

This holder is 1¼" thick and can accommodate five slots 3" x ¼", two slots 1½" x ¼", two slots 1" x ¼", one slot 4½" x ⁵⁄₁₆", and two holes for sharpening steels ⅝" dia.

Back

The back is nothing more than a piece of cherry 20 in. wide by 18 in. long by ¾ in. thick. You can adjust the length to suit the space you have available, but make sure you have enough height for the longest knife you wish to store. I placed the top of the holder 6 in. down from the top of the back, which works for my knives. You may have to adjust this slightly up or down.

The knife holder is attached to the back with three screws, through the back and into the holder. You may have noticed that the holder is ¼ in. shorter than the back is wide. This is to allow the back to move seasonally and not have the holder stick out past the edge of the back if the back shrinks.

1. Joint, plane, and edge-glue enough cherry stock to produce a blank big enough for the back.

2. Trim the blank to size and finish-sand it.

3. Drill and countersink a hole for a center screw. Use a shorter screw, so as not to invade the center slot.

4. In order for the back to be able to move freely with seasonal wood movement, horizontally elongate the two outer attachment screw holes. Drill and countersink two overlapping holes for the screws on the ends (see **photo F**).

Finishing

I finished this piece with a polymerized tung oil, but any quality furniture oil will do. You don't need a food-safe oil, since you will not be preparing food on your knife rack. You do, however, want an oil that will wear well. You don't want to have to take this rack down too often to re-oil it.

Attach the rack to the wall using four decorative brass panhead screws with washers, one in each corner. Be sure to elongate the screw holes before to allow for movement. The washers will cover the holes.

PHOTO F: Cut elongated screw slots at the ends of the back to allow for seasonal wood movement.

HANGING POT RACK

Niall Barrett

POTS AND PANS PRESENT ONE of the more difficult and frustrating storage problems in the kitchen. Since they are often the largest kitchen utensils, even a small set can take up a considerable amount of space. We often end up stacking pans one inside the other in an effort to save space. This can lead to scratched and damaged pots. And inevitably the one we need is always on the bottom. The most common place that pots and pans end up is inside a base cabinet. In this location, finding the right pot often requires crawling, or at least kneeling, on the floor.

Commercial kitchens solve these problems by hanging pots and pans overhead on racks designed for this purpose. Usually made from metal and quite large, these racks can be ungainly. They can look out of place it some kitchens. Also, it can be difficult to safely hang these racks from a residential ceiling, since they can be quite heavy by themselves, before ever adding a pot!

The rack presented here is an elegant and practical solution to storing your cookware. It has the warmth of wood construction, and it is sized to fit the scale of a normal kitchen. In a kitchen with an average ceiling height (approximately 8 ft.), a pot rack should hang 16 in. down from the ceiling. This would put the top of the rack at 80 in. off the floor, about the height of the average doorway. This can, of course, be varied according to personal taste. Just remember that they shouldn't be hung so high that you need a stool to reach everything or so low that the pots hang in your way. Often they are hung over an island so they are centrally located and close to the action but away from the worst of the cooking grease and out of forehead-striking distance.

HANGING POT RACK

This wood rack can give any kitchen the convenience of professional pot storage. Blocks with hooks ride in channels formed by rabbets in the crosspieces. The frame is attached to the ceiling with metal chains.

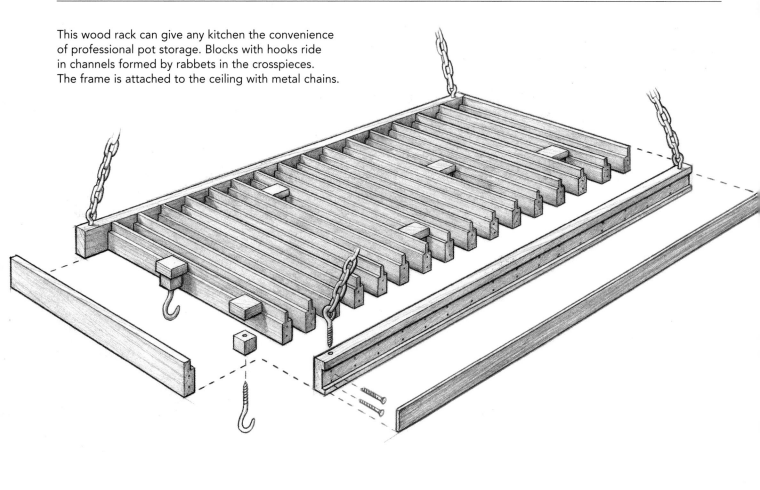

Construction and Assembly

THE RACK IS EASY TO MAKE. The pots hang from hooks set into blocks, which rest on the top edge of the rabbets in the crosspieces. The one trick, however, is that the crosspieces must be evenly spaced so that the hook plates ride freely on them but don't fall through. You want to be able to fit the hooks into any space.

Dimensioning the Parts

1. Mill the rails, stiles, and crosspieces from solid butternut to the dimensions in the cut list.

2. To mill the strips that cover the screw holes, you can either plane down thicker stock or resaw a 4/4 board on the bandsaw, then plane it to thickness. Mill the stock slightly larger in all three dimensions, so you can fit the pieces to their respective grooves.

3. Mill stock for the hook blocks. To make six blocks, you'll need either 6/4 lumber or two layers of ⅝-in.-thick stock glued face to face. The 1¼-in.-thick blank should be 10 in. long by 1⅜ in. wide.

Side, Top, and End Views

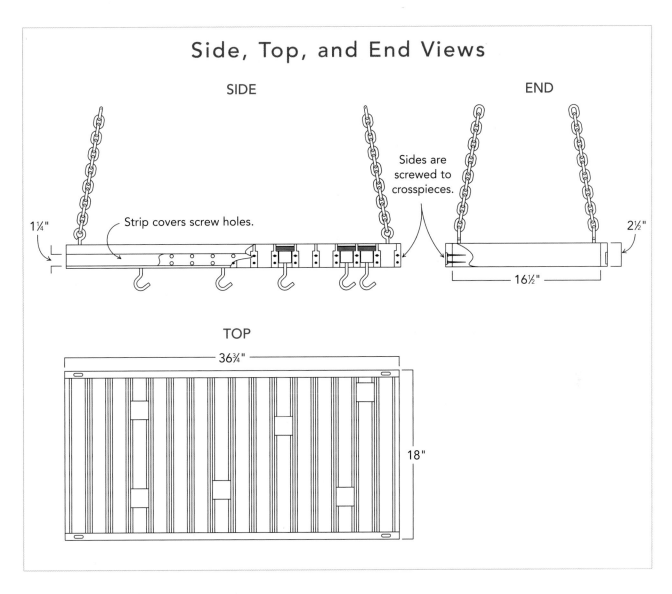

SIDE

END

Sides are screwed to crosspieces.

1¼"

Strip covers screw holes.

2½"

16½"

TOP

36¾"

18"

CUT LIST FOR HANGING POT RACK			
15	Crosspieces	16½" x 2½" x ¾"	solid butternut
2	Rails	16½" x 2½" x ¾"	solid butternut
2	Stiles	36¾" x 2½" x ¾"	solid butternut
2	Strips to cover screws	36¾" x 1¼" x ³⁄₁₆"	solid butternut
6	Hook blocks	1⅜" x 1⅜" x 1¼"	solid butternut
6	Hook plates	2" x 2" x ½"	Baltic birch plywood

Other materials

92	Wood screws	#8 x 1½"
6+	Chrome hooks	4⅞" x ⁵⁄₁₆"
4	Eyebolts	sized for the chain

Chain, as necessary

4. For the hook plates, cut 2-in. squares of ½-in.-thick plywood. I used Baltic birch, but since the plates don't show, it doesn't much matter what type of plywood you use.

Machining and Assembly

The joinery is very straightforward; the crosspieces are simply screwed to the frame. The whole assembly is stronger than it needs to be because of all the parts. The only substantial work is in cutting the rabbets on the tops of the crosspieces, which I did on the router table.

1. Fit a ¾-in.-wide straight bit, at least 1 in. long, in your router table.

2. Set the height of the bit to ¾ in.

3. Taking multiple passes, cut the rabbet ¼ in. deep on both sides of the top edge of the crosspieces and on the inside top edge of the rails of the frame (see **photo A**).

4. Make 32 spacers, 1½ in. wide by 2½ in. tall, from scrap plywood or solid wood. Make them as close to 1½ in. wide as possible. Small variations in width will be multiplied 32 times.

5. Trial-fit the frame and crosspieces together, fitting the spacers between each crosspiece to keep their spacing consistent. It's a bit of a juggling trick with all the pieces and clamps involved.

6. Adjust the width of the spacers, if necessary, to ensure that the rails meet the stiles and all of the crosspieces are equally spaced.

7. Finish-sand all the pieces to 150 grit.

8. Apply a small line of glue on the end of each rail, keeping it away from the inside edge, and clamp up the entire assembly with

Hook Block Detail

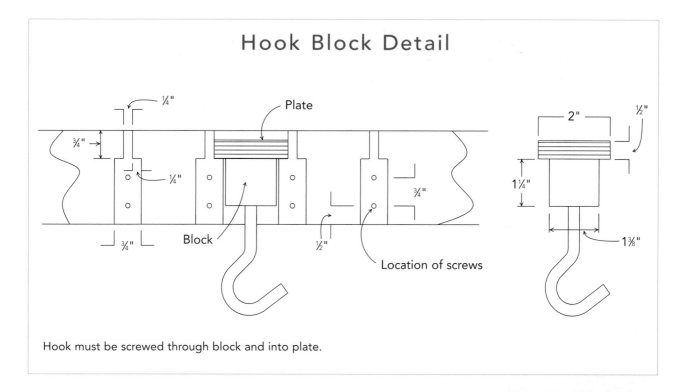

Plate

¼"

¾"

¼"

Block

¾"

½"

Location of screws

¾"

2"

½"

1¼"

1⅜"

Hook must be screwed through block and into plate.

the spacers in place. You need to avoid glue squeeze-out to ensure that you don't glue the spacers in place. The crosspieces don't need glue.

9. Drill pilot holes for screws through the stiles, centered on the crosspieces and rails (for screw location, see "Hook Block Detail"). Countersink the holes deeply so that the screw heads sit at least ¼ in. below the surface of the stiles (see **photo B**).

Covering the Screw Holes

To cover the screw heads, you'll need to rout a groove on the stiles and fit strips to cover the holes.

1. Lower the ¾-in.-wide straight bit in the router table to cut 3⁄16 in. deep.

2. Check that no screw heads are shallower than ¼ in. You don't want to hit a screw with the router bit.

3. In two overlapping passes, cut a 1¼-in.-wide groove across the screw holes on the stiles (see **photo C** on p. 88).

PHOTO B: Screw the crosspieces to the stiles using spacer blocks between each to align them. Countersink the holes so that the heads sit at least ¼ in. below the face of the stile.

PHOTO C: Cut wide grooves on the faces of the stiles with overlapping cuts on the router table. Be sure to cut over both rows of screw heads.

PHOTO D: Make and fit solid-wood strips to fill the grooves. They effectively hide the screws joining the piece.

4. Fit the strips you milled earlier into the grooves by trimming them to width. Leave the thickness and length oversize for now.

5. Glue and clamp the strips in place (see **photo D**).

6. When the glue has set, sand the strips flush with the stiles and trim the ends flush with the rails.

Assembling the Hook Blocks

You need to make blocks and plates that fit and slide freely between the crosspieces but that are wide enough to be secure (see "Hook Block Detail" on p. 87).

1. Lay out an X from corner to corner on the underside of each plywood hook plate. You'll use these to center the blocks on the plates.

2. Apply a light film of glue to the blocks and clamp them to the plates.

3. When the glue dries, drill pilot holes, sized to the hooks in the blocks, all the way through both pieces.

4. Finish-sand the blocks to 150 grit.

5. Screw the hooks into the blocks and plates so that the threads capture both pieces. You really want the hook hanging from the plate rather than the block.

Finishing and Hanging

1. Apply an oil finish to the frame, cross-pieces, and blocks. You can also choose not to finish this piece at all. The butternut will age beautifully on its own.

2. Size four pieces of chain to whatever length will make the frame hang at the height you need it.

3. Drill pilot holes for and attach eyebolts to the top four corners of the frame. You may need to open the eyebolt in a vise to capture the chain.

4. Set hooks in the ceiling above where you wish to hang the rack. Where and how you set the hooks depends on what type of ceiling you have and what's behind it. You must find something solid to connect to, because the frame and several pots and pans add up to a lot of weight. If you're uncomfortable finding a solid attachment in your ceiling, hire a professional to set the hooks for you.

5. Put the hook blocks into the frame from above (see **photo E**).

6. Hang the frame from the ceiling with the help of a friend or two.

DISH-DRYING RACK

Niall Barrett

I HAVE ALWAYS LIKED THE NOTION of dish racks. Traditionally hung over a sink, they not only provide storage space for your dishes but a place for them to drip dry. This makes it possible to put them away without bothering to wipe them. I have unfortunately never had a kitchen that allowed this use. The sinks in my kitchens have always been located in front of windows or beneath cabinets. Luckily, these racks are handsome enough to double as display racks to showcase your dinnerware, no matter where they are located.

When designing this piece I wanted to accomplish two things. I wanted it to have as large a holding capacity as possible and still fit comfortably between or next to upper cabinets. I also wanted it to be able to fit into any style kitchen, from contemporary to traditional.

At first glance, this dish rack may appear complicated and difficult to build. In reality, it is nothing more than three identically built frames screwed together, with two curved side supports screwed on last. Fabricating the laminated supports is relatively easy, once you have built the form. If you've never done this type of work before, this project will give you an extremely useful skill for other projects down the road.

The clean, vertical lines of this ash dish-drying rack will easily make it a welcome fixture in your kitchen. It will allow you dry or store up to 14 full-size dinner plates on the lower tier and an equal number of dessert plates or a mixture of cups and saucers or mugs on the upper tier.

DISH-DRYING RACK

This updated version of a drying rack will blend well in both modern and traditional kitchens. Three frames connect together and are supported by two curved arms.

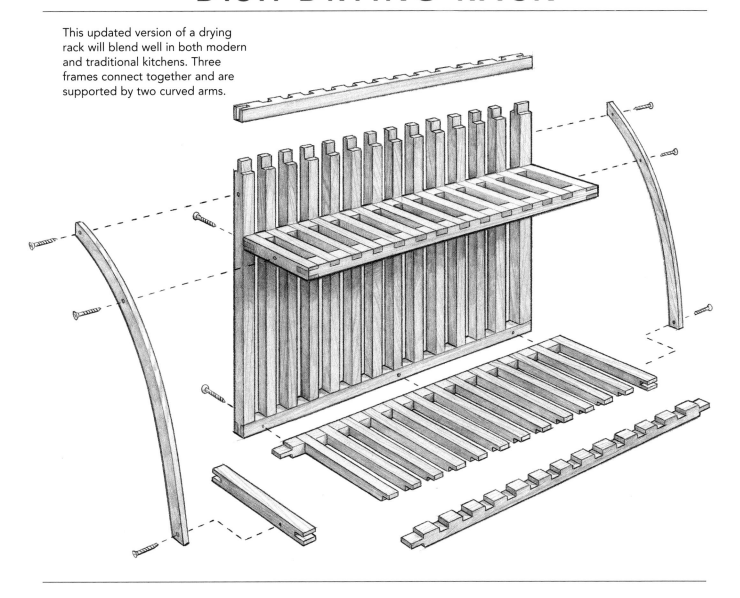

Milling the Straight Parts

DUE TO THE REPETITION OF joinery, the smart route is to cut joinery (rabbets and dadoes) in large boards, then rip them to size. Try to pick straight-grained, dry lumber. The less straightening you have to do to the individual parts (a total of 51), the better.

1. For the frame rails, mill a board at least 6 in. wide, ¾ in. thick, and 28¾ in. long.

2. For the slats and stiles, mill nine boards ¾ in. thick by 5 in. to 6 in. wide, at three different lengths: three boards 22 in. long, three 9 in. long, and three 6 in. long.

3. Rip two pieces ¾ in. wide off one of each board length. You want two pieces 22 in. long, two pieces 9 in. long, and two pieces 6 in. long. Set them to one side. These will become the stiles for the frame.

Front, Back, and Side Views

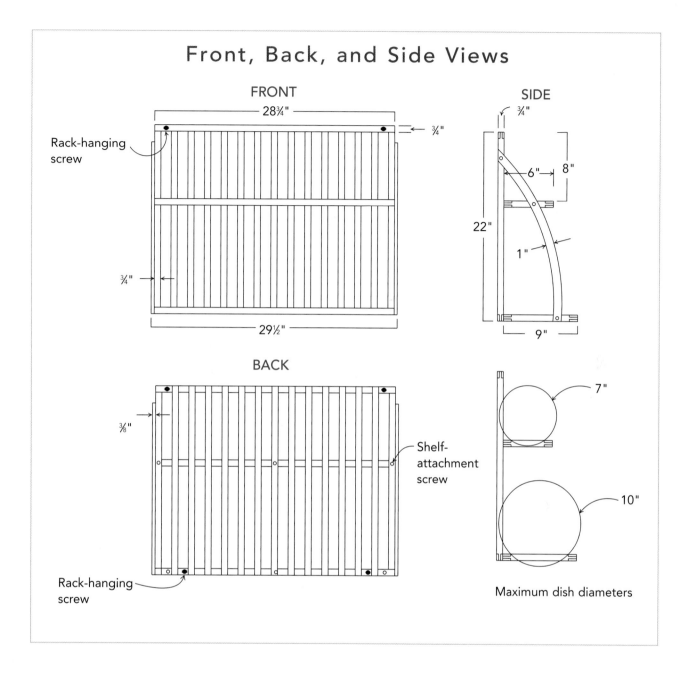

FRONT

28¾"

¾"

Rack-hanging screw

¾"

29½"

SIDE

¾"

6" → 8"

22"

1"

9"

BACK

⅜"

Shelf-attachment screw

Rack-hanging screw

7"

10"

Maximum dish diameters

Cutting the Dadoes in the Rail Blank

1. Install a ¾-in.-wide dado blade in the tablesaw.

2. Position the rip fence 2 in. from the dado blade and set the blade exactly ½ in. high.

3. Guiding the rail blank with the miter gauge, and with the end of the workpiece registering against the rip fence, cut a dado.

4. Spin the workpiece end for end and repeat the process.

5. Reposition the rip fence 3¼ in. away from the blade and cut the next set of dadoes.

6. Repeat this process, repositioning the fence away from the dado blade in 2-in. increments until you've cut dadoes across the whole face of the board.

Cutting the Rabbets on the Slat Blanks

1. Make and add a ¾-in.-thick auxiliary fence to your tablesaw's rip fence. A piece of plywood or other scrap is fine. The auxiliary

CUT LIST FOR DISH-DRYING RACK

6	Rails	¾" x ¾" x 28¾"	solid ash
2	Stiles, large frame	¾" x ¾" x 22"	solid ash
2	Stiles, lower shelf	¾" x ¾" x 9"	solid ash
2	Stiles, upper shelf	¾" x ¾" x 6"	solid ash
13	Slats, large frame	¾" x ¾" x 22"	solid ash
13	Slats, lower shelf	¾" x ¾" x 9"	solid ash
13	Slats, upper shelf	¾" x ¾" x 6"	solid ash
8	Laminate strips	1" x ⅛" x 36"	ash

Other materials

6	Brass screws	#6 x ¾"
6	Wood screws	#6 x 1½"
4	Rubber bumpers, clear	⅛" thick

fence keeps your dado blade from cutting into your rip fence.

2. Position the rip fence so that it just barely touches the dado blade. You want the rabbet just ¾ in. wide.

3. Cut the ½-in.-deep rabbet on both ends of the nine slat blanks (see **photo A**).

Ripping the Rails and Slats to Size

You'll want to rip the rail and slat pieces a bit wide so that the saw marks will be easy to clean up. Also, if the pieces warp a little, you can straighten them out without milling them undersize.

PHOTO A: Cut the rabbets in the ends of the slat blanks, using the miter gauge to guide the piece and the rip fence to set the width of the cut. Use the same method to dado the rails.

PHOTO B: Rip the dadoed rail and slat blanks at the same time and to the same width (¹³⁄₁₆ in.).

1. Remove the dado blade from the saw and install a rip blade.

2. Rip the nine slat and rail blanks into ¹³⁄₁₆-in.-wide pieces (see **photo B**).

3. Joint and then plane the sawn faces to a finished width of ¾ in., exactly the width of the dadoes in the rails. It's fine if some pieces have a little warp.

Cutting the Bridle Joints for the Frame

You should cut the mortise members in the rails first, because it's easier to fit the tenons to the mortises than the other way around (see "Joinery Details").

1. Cut the open mortises, ¾ in. deep and ¼ in. wide, centered on the ends of the rails. I use a simple shopmade jig for this work (see **photo C**), which supports the workpiece vertically on the tablesaw.

PHOTO C: Using a tablesaw and jig, cut the bridle joints. Either a shopmade or a commercial jig will work fine.

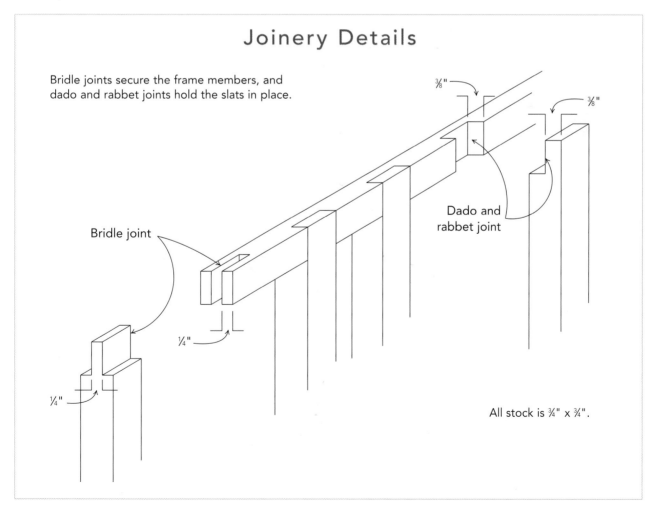

Joinery Details

Bridle joints secure the frame members, and dado and rabbet joints hold the slats in place.

Bridle joint

Dado and rabbet joint

¾"

¾"

¼"

¼"

All stock is ¾" x ¾".

PHOTO D: Cut the tenon shoulders on the tablesaw, using the miter gauge to guide the workpiece through the cut and a stopped auxiliary fence to make the shoulder locations consistent. The auxiliary fence should end before the blade cuts into the workpiece.

PHOTO E: Glue and clamp the frames together, making sure the bridle joints are snug. Then add slats as many at a time as you have clamps.

2. Cut the tenon faces, ¾ in. deep, in the ends of the stiles, using the same jig on the tablesaw (see **photo C** on p. 95).

3. Cut the tenon shoulders using the miter gauge to guide the workpiece (see **photo D**).

Assembling Three Frames

1. Assemble the rails and stiles of the three frames, gluing and clamping the bridle joints.

2. Clamp the joints across the width and length of the frame to bring the shoulders of the joints together. Clamp as near to the joint as possible without interfering with the joint closing.

3. Clamp the joints across their faces. At this point you can remove the other clamps. Wait until the glue has set before going on to the next step (installing the slats).

4. For the first slat, brush a little glue on the bottom and sides of the dadoes in the rails. This should be enough to hold it in place without a lot of glue squeeze-out, which would be hard to clean out between the slats.

5. One by one, install each slat and clamp it in place. You don't have to install all of them at once, since it takes 26 clamps for all the slats in each frame (see **photo E**).

6. When the glue has cured, clean up the frames and finish-sand them to 150 grit.

Making the Curved Support Arms

The curved support arms are bent laminations. It's a relatively simple process, though you'll need to build a jig.

1. Build a laminating jig, made from two layers of ¾-in. plywood (see "Bent Lamination Form").

2. Rip eight ⅛-in.-thick pieces 1 in. wide and 36 in. long. Ripping such thin pieces on

BENT LAMINATION FORM

The bent lamination form is made very simply from two sheets of plywood, with a 1-in. curved groove routed in the first layer.

1. Screw together two 9-in. by 34-in.-pieces of ¾-in. plywood, face to face. Place the screws in the locations indicated on the drawing to prevent routing through a screw later.

2. Set up a router trammel jig, either commercial or shopmade will work equally well, and fit your router with a ¾-in. straight plunge bit.

3. Rout the 23½-in. outside radius, ¾ in. deep. Make several light passes at partial depth so as to not strain the bit.

4. Rout the inside radius at 22½ in. Be careful to move the router in the direction that makes the bit rotate into the cut. If you move the router in the opposite direction, the bit may self-feed and pull the router out of your hands.

5. Remove the screws and separate the parts of the jig.

6. Apply clear packing tape to the edges of the cauls and the base of the groove. The tape prevents the laminations from sticking to the form during glue-up.

7. Screw the concave caul back to the base.

A router trammel jig, whether commercial or shopmade, cuts the shape of the bending forms cleanly and easily.

Bent Lamination Form

9"

6"

Form is made from two layers of ¾" plywood, but only the top layer is routed.

34"

Location of screw connecting form layers

Radius 22½"

Radius 17½"

Radius 23½"

4"

1"

1"

Block, 1½" thick, raises trammel to the same height as form.

6"

Router trammel pivot point

the tablesaw can lead to severe kickback. The safest way to do this is to start with a 1-in.-thick board at least 6 in. wide, rip oversize strips from the offcut edge, and then plane them to ⅛ in. thick.

3. Lay out seven of the eight pieces and roll yellow glue on one face of each piece. In this application I used polyvinyl acetate (PVA). It's fast and easy, and is appropriate for this project because the piece isn't bent to a very tight radius, there are no voids, and it won't undergo much stress in use.

4. Stack the seven pieces, glue side up, then put the eighth on top.

5. Place the lamination on the form between the convex and concave side. Squeeze the laminate between the sides of the form, flat against the base.

6. Clamp across the center of the form to draw the sides and laminate tight together. Add clamps across the rest of the form (see **photo F**). Make sure that the lamination and convex side of the form lie flat against the base.

7. When the glue has dried (at least overnight), remove the lamination from the form and joint one edge, flattening it and cleaning off the glue squeeze-out.

8. Rip the lamination in half on the tablesaw. Do this carefully, keeping the jointed side against the rip fence and the convex side of the curve flat against the table next to the blade. This takes a continuous and curving motion, using a push stick to push the end of the lamination past the blade. If you're not comfortable doing this procedure on the tablesaw, either use a bandsaw or laminate two supports.

9. Plane the two pieces to ⅜ in. thick.

10. Finish-sand the arms to 150 grit.

Assembly and Finishing

1. Drill pilot holes through the back frame for the screws (locations shown in the drawings on p. 93).

2. Screw the lower shelf to the back frame flush with the bottom and sides.

Hanging Detail

Screws are located for easy access from front of rack.

Top screws are decorative brass. Install them straight into the wall.

Bottom screws are plain, installed at an angle between slats, and are hidden.

PHOTO G: After laying out the ends of the support arms, trim them to length and screw them in place.

3. Screw the upper shelf to the back frame 8 in. from the top.

4. Mark the locations for the support arms on the edges of the frames and hold the arms in place. Then mark where you need to trim the ends of the arms to fit.

5. Cut the ends of the arms (see **photo G**).

6. Drill and countersink the arms and screw them to the back and to the upper and lower frames.

7. Apply the finish of your choice to the rack. I used an oil finish, which is easy to apply to all the many, little parts.

8. When the finish is dry, attach four ⅛-in.-thick rubber bumpers to the back of the frame. This pushes the frame out from the wall a little and keeps very large plates from hitting the wall.

9. Drill pilot holes for the hanging screws (locations shown in the drawings on p. 93).

10. The specific length of the screws you use to hang the rack depends on the wall you're screwing into (see "Hanging Detail"). Try to choose attractive screws because they will show in the finished rack.

KITCHEN ISLAND AND STOOL

Niall Barrett

I N A LARGE KITCHEN, ESPECIALLY ONE with a U-shaped layout, an island can be a real time- and stepsaver. An island can anchor the room and organize the work flow, while providing accessible counter space from all directions.

There are no set guidelines for sizing an island, but there are a few rules for the spaces around it: For work aisles that face appliances, 42 in. is the suggested minimum, and there should be 36 in. between an island and wall. These standards help keep cooks from colliding and prevent appliance or cabinet doors on an island from banging into the ones opposite them when open.

This island is designed to separate the kitchen from another room. It has a storage side, which faces the kitchen, and on the opposite side is an overhang for stools. It could also work well as a traditional

island by removing the overhang. Build in one end and it will work as a peninsula.

This island is not presented as the best or most perfect island but something that is perhaps more difficult: an "average" island that is still appealing. It is an average size with average style. You can easily adapt the design to your kitchen. The details in this island, however, will show you what you need to know to construct your perfect island.

Also included are some easy-to-make handles and knobs. Sometimes these small details are just the thing to give your project that special zing.

Last, there's a sturdy, straightforward stool for those times when you want to sit and chat with the cook. A lot of people are hesitant to build seating, but as you can see by this example, a stool is really just an odd-looking table.

CENTER ISLAND

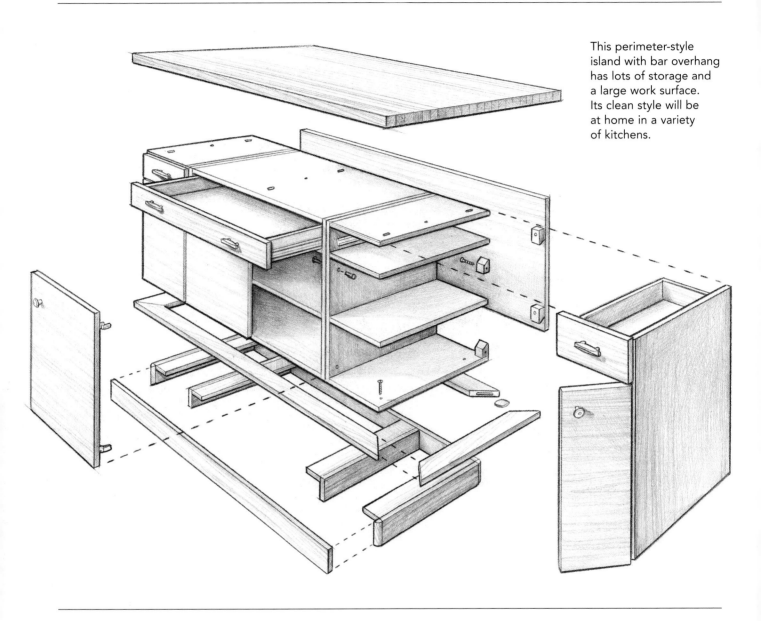

This perimeter-style island with bar overhang has lots of storage and a large work surface. Its clean style will be at home in a variety of kitchens.

Construction and Assembly

THE ISLAND IS CONSTRUCTED in sections or modules, which makes it manageable to build and easy to install. When I decided to make the doors plain (in an effort to allow the style to fit into as many existing kitchens as possible), I decided on flat doors, which might seem easy to make. The problem with flat doors is that unless they are perfectly flat they look terrible. No matter how much you adjust them, there are always one or two corners that stick out and interrupt the lines of the piece.

There are ways to make very flat doors, such as veneering over medium-density fiberboard (MDF) or honeycomb panels, but I wanted to use plywood, which almost

Views of Kitchen Island

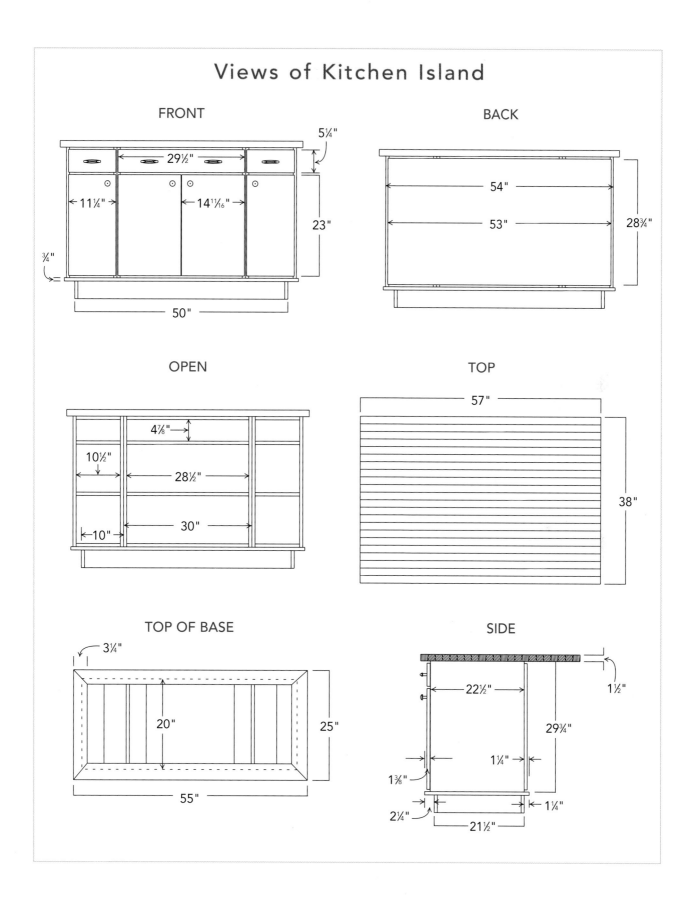

FRONT

BACK

OPEN

TOP

TOP OF BASE

SIDE

Base

2	Pieces	4" x 48½" x ¾"	cherry plywood
8	Pieces	4" x 20" x ¾"	cherry plywood
4	Pieces	4" x 19⅞" x ¾"	cherry plywood
4	Pieces	4" x ¾" x ¾"	solid cherry

Base Frame

2	Pieces	55" x 3¼" x ¹¹⁄₁₆"	solid cherry
2	Pieces	25" x 3¼" x ¹¹⁄₁₆"	solid cherry

Cabinet Boxes

6	Sides	29¾" x 22½" x ¾"	cherry plywood
6	Tops, bottoms, dividers (outside boxes)	10½" x 22½" x ¾"	cherry plywood
3	Tops, bottoms, dividers (center box)	28½" x 22½" x ¾"	cherry plywood
2	Shelves (outside boxes)	10⁷⁄₁₆" x 22⅜" x ¾"	cherry plywood
1	Shelf (center box)	28⁷⁄₁₆" x 22⅜" x ¾"	cherry plywood

Back

1	Piece	53" x 28¾" x ¾"	cherry plywood

Fronts

2	Drawer fronts (outside drawers)	11¼" x 5¼" x ¾"	cherry plywood
1	Drawer front (center drawer)	29½" x 5¼" x ¾"	cherry plywood
2	Doors (outside)	11¼" x 23" x ¾"	cherry plywood
2	Doors (center)	14¹¹⁄₁₆" x 23" x ¾"	cherry plywood

Drawers

6	Sides	22" x 4" x ½" [12mm]	Baltic birch plywood
2	Fronts (outside drawers)	8½" x 4" x ½" [12mm]	Baltic birch plywood
1	Front (center drawer)	26½" x 4" x ½" [12mm]	Baltic birch plywood
2	Backs (outside drawers)	8½" x 4" x ½" [12mm]	Baltic birch plywood
1	Back (center drawer)	26½" x 4" x ½" [12mm]	Baltic birch plywood
2	Bottoms (outside drawers)	9" x 21¾" x ¼" [6mm]	Baltic birch plywood
1	Bottom (center drawer)	27" x 21¾" x ¼" [6mm]	Baltic birch plywood

Top

22	Pieces	1¾" x 1½" x 57"	solid maple

CUT LIST FOR CENTER ISLAND

Other materials

100 ft.	Edge tape	maple
4	Hinges	110° full overlay, European concealed
4	Hinges	110° half overlay, European concealed
3 pr.	Drawer glides	¾-extension, epoxy-coated, bottom-mount
12	Shelf-support pins	
8	Hex-drive connector bolts and threaded sleeves	
8	Confirmat screws	
	Mineral oil	
	Lacquer	

never stays perfectly flat. My solution was to create a design element that would disguise any twists that might occur: a ½-in. space between the doors and drawer fronts. To emphasize this detail, I used a contrasting wood for the edges of the doors and drawer fronts as well as for the cabinet.

Making the Base

Start by building the base. It is important that the base be solid. Clearly it has to support the weight of the entire island. More important, since an island needs to be fastened to the floor (so it doesn't move around), it has to be able to resist lifting forces applied when people push against the island and lean down on the overhang.

1. Rip two 4-in. by 48½-in. and eight 4-in. by 20-in. strips of cherry plywood.

2. Biscuit the 20-in.-long pieces into four units with an L-shaped profile. They should be biscuited along their 20-in. sides, so that the units are 4 in. high by 4¾ in. wide by 20 in. long when assembled.

3. Put these aside for now and cut four ¾-in. by ¾-in. by 4-in. pieces of solid cherry, and biscuit, glue, and clamp these onto the ends of the 48½-in. plywood pieces. These become the corners of the base and will pro-

tect the fragile plywood corners from being damaged by feet or vacuum cleaners.

4. Once the glue is dry, sand off any excess glue. Now you're ready to biscuit the frame together.

5. Align the long sides parallel and 20 in. apart.

6. Position the four L-shaped units between the sides (see **photo A** on p. 106). One L-shaped unit forms each end, and the remaining two are positioned with the 4-in. leg directly underneath where the individual boxes join together. Make sure the 4¾-in. legs face toward the center of the base. These four L-shaped units will not only support the cabinets but also provide a means of attaching them to the base.

7. Biscuit, glue, and clamp these parts together.

8. When the glue is dry, sand all surfaces flush and rout a ⅛-in. quarter-round on each solid corner. Then finish-sand the outside of the base to 150 grit.

Making and assembling the decorative base frame

The next step is the decorative mitered frame that separates the base from the cabinets.

PHOTO A: The
decorative base
frame sits loosely
on top of the
base, around the
spacers screwed
to the tops of the
L-shaped units.

1. Mill up four pieces of solid cherry, two 3¼ in. by ¹¹⁄₁₆ in. by (a little over) 55 in. and two 3¼ in. by ¹¹⁄₁₆ in. by (a little over) 25 in. The extra length is to give you some room creep-up on the cut when cutting the miters.

2. Carefully miter the corners so that you end up with a frame 55 in. by 25 in.

I used my miter gauge on my tablesaw to cut these miters, but a radial-arm saw or chopsaw would also work. The important thing is accuracy. There is no such thing as a miter joint that's "good enough." Either it's just right or it's a bad joint. A bad joint may open up down the road, even when using biscuits. When the frame moves seasonally, there could be a fair amount of stress on these joints from time to time.

3. Cut a slot for a #20 biscuit in each joint.

4. Biscuit, glue, and clamp the frame together.

5. When the frame is dry, sand all joints flush.

6. Rout a ⅛-in. quarter-round, top and bottom, around the outside perimeter of the frame.

7. Cut four pieces of 3/4-in. plywood to 19⅞ in. long by 4¾ in. wide for spacers.

8. Screw the spacers on top of the L-shaped assemblies, centered, so they're ¹⁄₁₆ in. shy of the long base sides.

9. Position the base frame on top of the base, around the spacers (see **photo A**).

You are probably wondering why the frame is ¹¹⁄₁₆ in. thick and not ¾ in. Well, the frame basically sits loose on the base, held in position by the four pieces of ¾-in. plywood screwed to the top of the supports on the base. The ¾-in.-thick plywood, which is actually a little shy of ¾ in. thick, will be slightly higher than the frame and will take most of the weight of the cabinets.

Cabinet Boxes

1. Cut to size all the cherry plywood for the cabinet boxes. Use the dimensions in the cut list.

2. Cut biscuit slots for all the corner joints and the joints for the divider that separates the drawer section. These should be arranged so that the top, bottom, and divider (when joined) are between the sides.

3. This is also the time to cut the shelves. The shelves should be ¹⁄₁₆ in. smaller than the

DESIGN OPTION: TRAY STORAGE

The storage space in this island is pretty generic—just open drawers and cabinet space—but it doesn't have to remain that way. With a little extra thought and effort, you can customize the spaces for what you may need to store. There are many accessories you can buy, like pull-out storage baskets and drawer dividers, or you can make your own.

To get you started thinking along these lines, I have included an option my clients often ask me to include in their custom work.

Large trays or platters pose a difficult storage problem, but with just a couple of extra steps you can include storage for these items in your island. You could also build this storage afterward or add it to an existing cabinet by making it a separate box that slides into an existing space.

Before assembling one of the side cabinets, create some grooves in the top of the bottom of the cabinet and in the underside of the divider wide enough to fit some ¼-in. plywood panels. The spacing will depend on what exactly you wish to store, but you can always cut more grooves than you think you need and just use as many dividers as you want. The quickest way to cut these grooves is on your tablesaw using a dado blade.

Tray-Storage Option

This storage unit can be built as part of the cabinet (example B) or as a separate unit (example A) that can be built and inserted later. Spacing of the dividers is determined by the items that need to be stored.

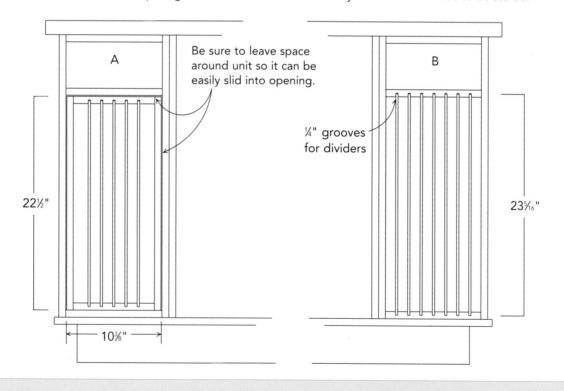

A

Be sure to leave space around unit so it can be easily slid into opening.

B

¼" grooves for dividers

22½"

23⁵⁄₁₆"

10⅜"

PHOTO B: Drill shelf pinholes for the adjustable shelves in the sides of the cabinets, using a commercial or shopmade jig.

width of the cabinet they fit into and ⅛ in. shorter front to back.

Shelf pinholes

The next step is to drill two rows of holes, front and back, in each side within the middle 12 in. of the lower section of the cabinet for shelf pins to support the shelves (see **photo B**). The most common shelf pins fit into either 5mm or ¼-in. holes, so choose which you will use before you drill these holes.

A good formula for locating these holes is one-sixth the total width in from the front and back edges. I use a commercial jig made by Festool®, but there are many jigs available; you can easily make your own by drilling a series of holes in a piece of plywood that fits the space. Even if the holes are not perfectly spaced, as long as each row is the same your shelves will lay flat. So make sure you always register the jig from the same edge.

Edgebanding

Before assembling the cabinet boxes, apply iron-on maple edgebanding to cover the exposed plywood edges. This includes all the front and back edges of the cabinets and the front edges of the shelves. The reason for banding the back edges of the cabinets is that since the back is exposed and the back panel is recessed ½ in. all around, these edges will show. Iron-on edgebanding is available from many woodworking suppliers and is easy to apply.

1. Break off a piece a little longer than you need.

2. Apply the edging with an ordinary household iron, set on high temperature and no steam. Start at one end and move along the edge bit by bit, softening the glue as you go until the edging sticks.

3. Trim off the excess length by scoring it lightly on the glue side and snapping it off. The edging is slightly wider that the plywood, so sand it flush.

4. Continue to finish-sand all the insides of the cabinets, including both sides of the dividers and the shelves, to 150 grit.

5. Biscuit, glue, and clamp the boxes together and set them aside.

The back

1. Cut a piece of ¾-in. cherry plywood for the back panel and cover the edges with maple edgebanding.

Remember to account for the thickness of the edgebanding when you cut the back. The edgebanding adds approximately ³⁄₃₂ in. to the length and width of the panel, so you must cut the back that much smaller before banding or you will have less than the ½-in. reveal that the design calls for. This is not all that critical for the back, but when you get to the doors and drawer fronts it is very important.

2. Finish-sand the back.

3. While you are waiting for the glue on the cabinets to dry, you can make the angled blocks that attach the back panel to the cabinet boxes (see "Back-Panel Attachment Blocks").

BACK-PANEL ATTACHMENT BLOCKS

There are many ways to attach backs to cabinets, but few of them completely hide their joinery. Rabbets work well in solid wood, but in plywood cabinets the edges would show. So I devised a very simple and easy knockdown method for this cabinet. This makes things simpler while building (giving access to the rear of cabinets for drawer-fitting and installation, for example) and is also more in line with its modular construction. In spite of being knockdown, it adds a lot of rigidity to the cabinet.

The back panel is attached using eight pairs of opposing-angled blocks. In the cabinets, one block is placed in each of the outside corners of the lower sections of the smaller boxes and in each of the four corners of the lower section of the center box. This arrangement allows the back to be lifted on and off easily. And the more you push down on it the tighter it wedges the back on. The location of the blocks in the corners keeps the cabinet boxes from racking.

The placement of the blocks is critical if the back is to be positioned correctly and be firmly attached. The blocks on the back panel itself must be as close as they can to where the sides of the cabinets will be without interfering with installing the back. All the blocks must be at exactly the right height, so that when the back is in place it is the correct height. So measure carefully. To make sure the back pulls tight to the cabinets before it bottoms out, position the blocks on the cabinets a little bit back from the edge (the thickness of the edge tape is a perfect distance).

The blocks are all identical: 2 in. long to the long point of the 45-degree bevel, 1½ in. wide, and ¾ in. thick. Screw the cabinet blocks to the sides of the cabinets through their sides, and screw the back-panel blocks to the panel through their faces. After the cabinets are assembled with the back installed—and you are sure everything is right—remove the blocks, apply a little glue, and screw them back on.

Back-Panel Attachment Blocks

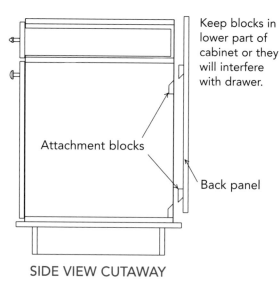

Keep blocks in lower part of cabinet or they will interfere with drawer.

Attachment blocks

Back panel

SIDE VIEW CUTAWAY

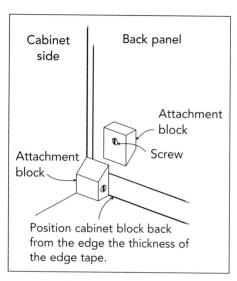

Cabinet side

Back panel

Attachment block

Screw

Attachment block

Position cabinet block back from the edge the thickness of the edge tape.

PHOTO C:
Assemble the
boxes separately,
then attach them
to the base and
to each other.

PHOTO D: Use hex-drive connector bolts and threaded
sleeves to connect the boxes to each other. Use Confirmat
screws to attach the boxes to the base.

Cabinet Assembly

Connecting the boxes

At this point, you are ready to assemble
everything you have made so far.

1. Remove the clamps from the cabinet
boxes and finish-sand the outsides.

2. Position the boxes on the base and temporarily clamp them together with all their
edges flush with their adjacent cabinets (see
photo C).

3. Mark out the holes for the connecting bolts.

I used two hex-drive connector bolts and
threaded sleeves along each of the front and
back edges, 1¼ in. up and down from the
inside corners of the cabinets, all located
1¼ in. in from the outside edges. There are
several versions of this type of connector
available through woodworking suppliers,
and the one you choose will determine the
size of the hole you need to drill.

Connecting the
boxes to the base

1. Assuming the cabinets are still positioned
correctly on the base layout, drill holes

through the bottom of the cabinets and into the crosspieces of the base (see **photo D**).

2. Screw the boxes down onto the base.

I used four Confirmat screws (also known as Euro screws) in the large center cabinet—one in each corner—and two each in the outside corners of the smaller cabinets. Again, the fasteners you choose will determine the size of the holes you drill. Make sure you position these holes far enough in that they clear the cherry frame on the top of the base.

Hanging the back

1. Make and attach the back-panel attachment blocks as described (see p. 109).

2. Hang the back in place and push down firmly (see **photo E**).

Drawer Construction and Installation

The drawers are constructed of ½-in. (12mm) Baltic birch plywood, biscuited together. You can certainly use solid wood if you prefer that look, but either way the construction is the same. The plywood boxes are slightly stronger because the orientation of the plies allows for more side-grain-to-side-grain gluing, in addition to the biscuits. The solid wood's end-grain-to-side-grain joint would rely primarily on the biscuits for strength. I have built both kinds of drawers, and I find either one works just fine in normal use.

1. Rip enough plywood 4 in. wide for the drawer boxes—sides, fronts, and backs.

2. Crosscut the pieces to length.

3. Pick out the back pieces of each drawer and rip them to 3⅜ in. wide. Making the backs of the drawers shallower will allow you to slide the drawer bottoms into the completed drawer boxes (see **photo F** on p. 112).

4. Leave the tablesaw set to 3⅜ in., and lower the blade to ¼ in. high.

5. Run a groove on the bottom inside edge of all the remaining parts.

PHOTO E: The back panel fits to the case with an attachment-block system.

6. Move the saw fence away from the blade by approximately half the width of the blade and run the same parts through again. One more time, and you should have a groove wide enough for your ¼-in. drawer bottoms.

You could use a ¼-in.-wide dado blade, but by the time you got it set up you could have the grooves cut with this method. You should have a piece of scrap handy as a test piece as well as a piece of the drawer-bottom material to test-fit the groove.

7. Size the groove so that the bottom fits snugly. If you have to reach for a hammer, the joint is too tight.

8. Sanding the drawer bottoms will remove enough material to allow you to slide them into the grooves easily.

9. Cut a slot for a #10 biscuit in each corner, making sure that the front and back of the drawer fits between the sides.

PHOTO F: The drawers are made entirely from Baltic birch plywood and use biscuit joints at each corner.

10. Finish-sand the insides of all the parts, then biscuit, glue, and clamp the drawer boxes together.

11. When the glue is dry, finish-sand the outsides of the drawers.

12. Cut the bottoms to fit, finish-sand them, and slide them into their grooves. Fasten them in place with a couple of small screws along the back edge.

13. Mount the drawer glides and install the drawers in their openings (see "Size, Location, and Fit of Drawers").

I used standard European-style, ¾-extension undermount glides. As their name suggests, they mount to the bottom of the drawer box. I have installed enough of these kind of glides that I have a special jig for installing the cabinet side of the glides. There are, however, many different kinds and styles of drawer glides available, and your choice will determine the exact installation positioning and technique. This process is a lot easier with the back off.

Size, Location, and Fit of Drawers

Middle drawer front is centered on drawer, but side drawer fronts are off-center, with less of a reveal on the outside edge to allow a consistent ½" space around drawers.

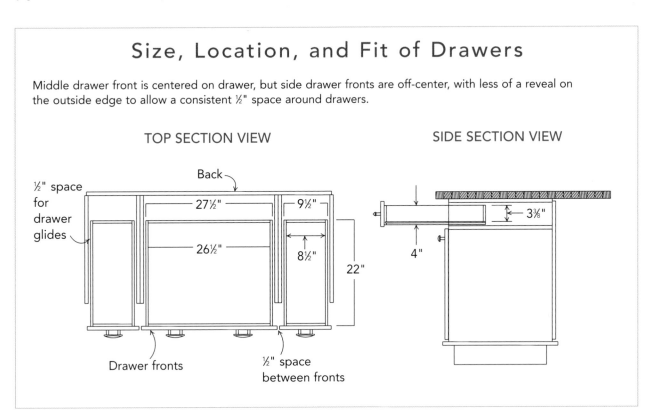

TOP SECTION VIEW

SIDE SECTION VIEW

½" space for drawer glides

Back

27½"

9½"

26½"

8½"

22"

3⅜"

4"

Drawer fronts

½" space between fronts

Hanging doors

Cut the cherry plywood for the doors and drawer fronts and edge-band them as you did the cabinet parts. Remember to account for the thickness of the edgebanding, as you did with the back panel (see **photo G**).

1. Once you have these parts edged, finish-sand them to 150 grit and install the hinges.

I used 110-degree European concealed hinges. The specifics of installing these type of hinges is somewhat dependent on the brand of hinge you buy, so follow the manufacturer's instructions (see "Choosing Hinges").

2. Once you have this sorted out, hang the doors and adjust the hinges until you have

PHOTO G: Apply edgebanding to all the doors and drawer fronts. Sand the corners flush when the glue sets.

CHOOSING HINGES

Be aware that you will have to use two different types of European hinges to hang the cabinet doors because of the ½-in. spacing between the doors and the ½-in. reveal around the edges.

The outside left and right doors overlay the cabinet side by ¼ in. (¾ in. less ½ in.) so you will need what is referred to as a half-overlay hinge. These hinges are designed to be used when two doors overlay a single ¾-in. cabinet side. They would normally position the door ⁵⁄₁₆ in. over the edge of the cabinet side, but ¼ in. is still within their adjustment range.

The center cabinet doors overlay their cabinet sides by ½ in. because there are two sides fastened together here, which adds up to 1½ in. Subtract the ½-in. space between the doors and you have 1 in. or ½-in. overlay per door. For these doors you will need what is referred to as a full-overlay hinge. These are normally used when one door covers a ¾-in. cabinet side. They normally position a door a little over ⅝ in. over the edge of the cabinet side, but ½ in. is within their adjustment range.

½ in. at the outside edges and ½ in. between and under the doors (see **photo H**).

Attaching drawer fronts

The drawer fronts are easier than the doors, but you will need a helper.

1. Cut some ½-in. spacer blocks from scrap wood and place them on top of the doors.

2. Position the drawer fronts one at a time on the spacers and align them side to side with the door or doors under them.

3. Place the palm of one hand on the back of the drawer box (the back panel is still off, right?) and the palm of your other hand on the drawer front and squeeze tightly as you open the drawer. This holds the drawer front in place while your helper places a couple of spring clamps on the drawer to hold the front in place.

4. From the inside of the drawer, drill four holes for the screws that attach the drawer front to the drawer box. Locate these holes 1¼ in. from the sides and 1¼ in. from the top and bottom of the drawer (see **photo I**). A small block 1¼ in. square will help you locate where to drill these holes.

If you find that you still need some adjustment, remove the front and enlarge the hole in the drawer box. This will give you a little room to move the drawer front around. There are special screws available for this application with extra large heads, but a screw and a washer works just as well.

PHOTO H: Hang the doors using 110° concealed hinges. They should hang flush with the fronts of the cabinet boxes.

PHOTO I: Attach the drawer fronts to the drawer boxes, using spring clamps to hold them in place as you drill and then screw them together.

Making the Butcher-Block Top

Making your own butcher-block top, while not difficult, is a lot of work and takes a lot of time. There is something to be said for buying a commercially made top. If this was a normal-width counter top (24 in.) I would probably have done just that, since they are relatively inexpensive. Unfortunately, this top is 38 in. wide; if you could find one this wide, it would be much more expensive.

The first thing to consider in a solid-wood top is stability. You want the top to be flat, straight, square, and rigid and to remain that way. The best way to accomplish this is to use quartersawn wood, but since slabs of quartersawn wood large enough to produce this top are rare, a butcher-block top is a better option.

The top of this island is 1½ in. thick, which is a little thicker than an average countertop. Any thinner, though, and it just doesn't look substantial enough. You could make it thicker, but then you would have to build the base lower, since your island would be higher than the standard 36 in.

1. Rip 8/4 flatsawn stock into 22 strips approximately 1⅝ in. wide and a little longer than the top.

2. Joint and thickness-plane the strips to 1¾ in. by 1½ in.

3. Glue the strips together in groups of five and six, then glue the groups together (see **photo J**). This will produce a quartersawn top 38½ in. wide, 1½ in. thick, and a little longer than 57 in. The extra width and length is for trimming the top straight and square later.

PHOTO J: Glue up the butcher-block top, first in groups of five and six pieces. After the glue sets, glue the assemblies together.

PHOTO K: Trim the ends of the top square with the edges. I used a circular saw and guide for this work.

If these strips are really straight and square you should have no trouble gluing up the top without biscuits, dowels, or splines. But if your stock is a little wild, don't hesitate to use them. Don't try to glue this top together all at once. It is difficult to spread glue quickly over so many surfaces and then get them aligned and evenly clamped. You will almost certainly lose control over some of them at some point and end up with a less-than-perfect top.

4. Sand the top flat when completely glued up and dry.

I used a stationary drum sander. If you don't have such a machine, you can thickness the smaller groups with a planer as you glue them up and then flatten the completed top with a handplane. Alternatively, you can have the finished top thickness-sanded at a commercial shop.

5. Rip the top to width and trim the ends. I used a straightedge/saw combination designed for this kind of operation, but a router and a straightedge would work fine (see **photo K**).

Finishing

I finished the island with satin spray lacquer and used a polymerized tung oil for the top. You can also use mineral oil for the top, but it won't wear as well and, once cured, the tung oil is safe for food surfaces, which is the main reason for using mineral oil. It really depends on what you plan to use your island for.

Attaching the Island to the Floor and the Top to the Island

Once you have the island completed, you will want to put it into use. There is more to this, however, than just setting it into place and laying on the top. Once in position, your island should be leveled, then firmly attached to the floor. This is more easily accomplished if you first remove the cabinet boxes from the base. Then you can shim and/or scribe the base level and attach it to the floor with some angle irons from the inside of the base. (This hardware is available from any hardware store or building center.) With the base secured to the floor, you can reassemble the cabinet boxes on the base and attach the top.

To attach the top, create eight elongated holes or slots in the tops of the cabinets: one in each corner of the center cabinet and two in the outside corners of each side cabinet. These slots should run front to back and will allow for seasonal wood movement without damaging either the cabinets or the top. Then attach the top through these holes with screws and washers.

Handles and Knobs

Decorative hardware is easily made and will set your project apart.

HANDLE

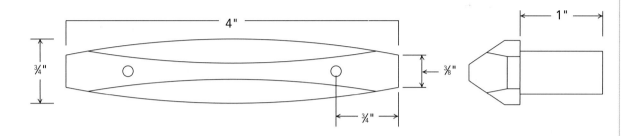

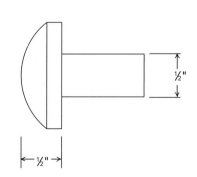

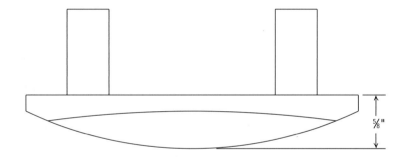

KNOB

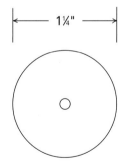

Steps for Shaping Handles

FRONT VIEW

END VIEW

Step 1: Chamfer the edges.

Step 2: Sand a gentle curve along the edges.

Step 3: Sand a gentle curve along the chamfers.

TOP VIEW

CUT LIST FOR HANDLES AND KNOBS			
4	Handles	¾" x ⅝" x 4"	bird's-eye maple
4	Knobs	1½" x 1½" x ½"	bird's-eye maple
Other materials			
1	Dowel	½" dia.	maple
10	Trim-head screws (black)	1⅝"	

Making the Handles

These handles have graceful curves but need no special jigs or techniques to create. They're so small, they can simply be sanded into shape (see "Steps for Shaping Handles").

1. Mill a piece of bird's-eye maple ¾ in. by ⅝ in. and long enough to make the handles you need plus a couple extra (just in case).

2. Rip a 30-degree angle along both ⅝-in.-wide edges, leaving a ³⁄₁₆-in. flat on each edge (see **photo L**).

3. Crosscut the piece into 4-in. lengths.

4. Belt-sand curves on each of the edges you just beveled. Create a curve that goes from nothing in the center flowing down to ³⁄₁₆ in. on each end (see **photo M**).

5. Sand a curve on the face of each piece that goes from nothing in the center curving down to ⁷⁄₁₆ in. on each end (see **photo N**). Make sure that you use a belt with the finest grit you have. You don't want to have to do a lot of finish-sanding that might soften the angles and planes you have created—you want them to remain crisp.

PHOTO L: Carefully rip a 30° angle on the edges of the blanks for the handles.

PHOTO M: Sand the top and bottom curves on the handle blanks. A stationary sander, or a belt sander in a vise, works well for this.

PHOTO N: Sand the curve on the face of the handles in the same way.

PHOTO O: Turn the faces of the knobs on a lathe, using whatever turning tool you're most comfortable with.

PHOTO P: Attach the handles and knobs to the doors and drawer fronts with mounting studs and screws.

Making the Knobs

The knobs are turned on a lathe.

1. Screw a piece of scrap plywood to a small faceplate. Attach a square of bird's-eye maple approximately 1½ in. square and ½ in. thick to the plywood, using some double-sided tape.

2. Mount this assembly on the lathe. Using a parting tool, create a 1¼-in.-dia. circle.

3. Using a small gouge or a skew chisel, whichever you find more comfortable, shape the face into a dome, leaving ³⁄₁₆ in. of flat around the outside edge (see **photo O**).

4. While it's still on the lathe, sand the knob to 150 grit.

5. Make the other three knobs.

6. On your drill press, drill holes for the trim-head screws in the center of each knob. Also, drill holes for the handles ¾ in. in from each end of the handles, centered top to bottom.

7. Cut a ½-in.-dia. maple dowel into ⁵⁄₈-in. lengths for the mounting studs and drill a pilot hole through the center of each. This hole will accept the screws that attach the handles and knobs to the drawers and doors. A good way to hold these small parts for drilling is to clamp them in a handscrew.

8. Attach the handles and knobs to the doors and drawers with trim-head screws through these mounting studs (see **photo P**).

Finishing

I finished these parts with the same oil I used on the top of the island, but any furniture oil will do. Oil brings out the figure a little better than a lot of spray finishes and will allow the handles and knobs to acquire a nice patina over time from handling.

STURDY, STRAIGHTFORWARD STOOL

This ash stool uses a combination of biscuit joinery and dowels for solid, effective construction.

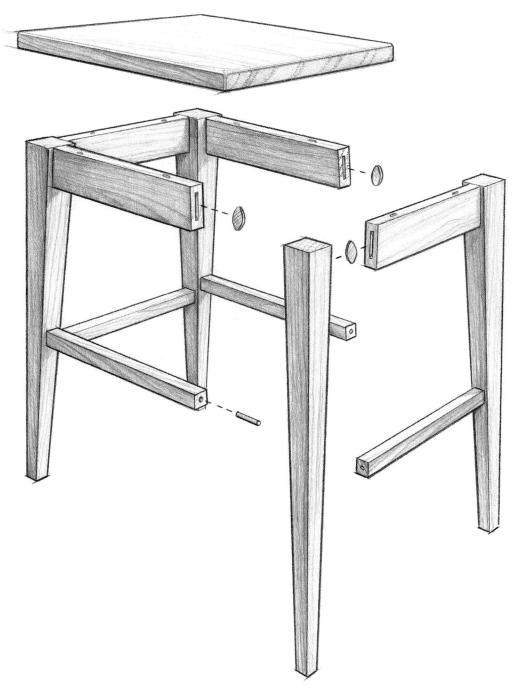

Views of Stool

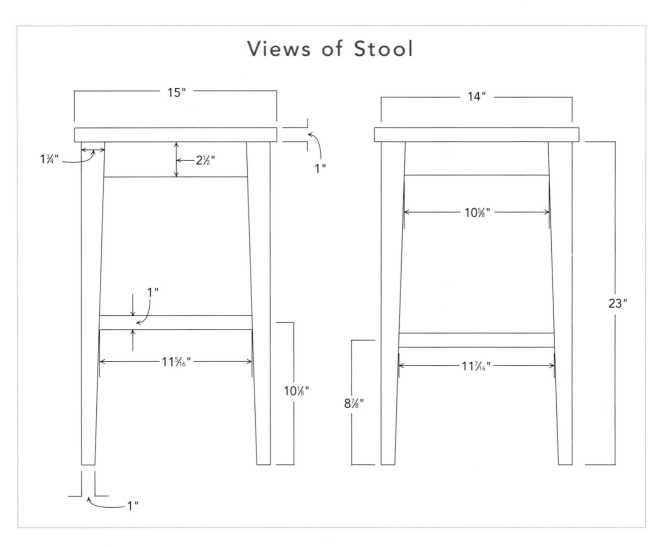

CUT LIST FOR STOOL			
1	Seat	15" x 15" x 1"	ash
4	Legs	1¾" x 1¾" x 23"	ash
4	Aprons	2½" x 10⅝" x 1"	ash
4	Stretchers	1" x 1" x 12⁷⁄₁₆"	ash

Milling the Parts

This piece is constructed entirely of solid wood, so since you have a fair amount of milling to do, it's a good idea to do it all at once.

1. Mill all the parts for the legs, aprons, and stretchers to the dimensions in the cut list.

Leave all but the legs a little longer than finished size.

2. Mill at least three pieces to glue up for the seat. I prefer to use an odd number of boards when I do solid-wood glue-ups and to alternate the growth rings in adjacent boards. This way any cupping should average out rather than having the entire piece cup in one direction.

Tapering the Legs

The legs taper on the two inside faces from 1¾ in. at the top (the full thickness of the leg) to 1 in. at the bottom.

1. Make a simple jig made of plywood with two stops angled to register the leg in the cut (see "Leg Tapering Jig").

PHOTO Q: Taper the legs for the stool using a tablesaw jig.

2. Place the leg in the jig with your tablesaw fence set to the width of the jig's plywood base. Run it through your saw (see **photo Q**).

3. Rotate the leg 90 degrees and run it through again.

4. Repeat the process for all the legs.

Sizing and Joinery for the Aprons and Stretchers

The apron and stretcher pieces meet the legs on the tapered sides, so they will have to be crosscut at the same angle.

1. Lay one apron piece and one stretcher under two legs, with the top of the apron piece flush with the tops of the legs and the stretcher placed the correct distance up from the bottom of the legs. Make sure the legs are parallel to each other and square to the apron and stretcher.

2. Mark where the legs cross the apron and stretcher. Remember that there are two different stretcher locations, so you will have to do this twice (see **photo R** on p. 124).

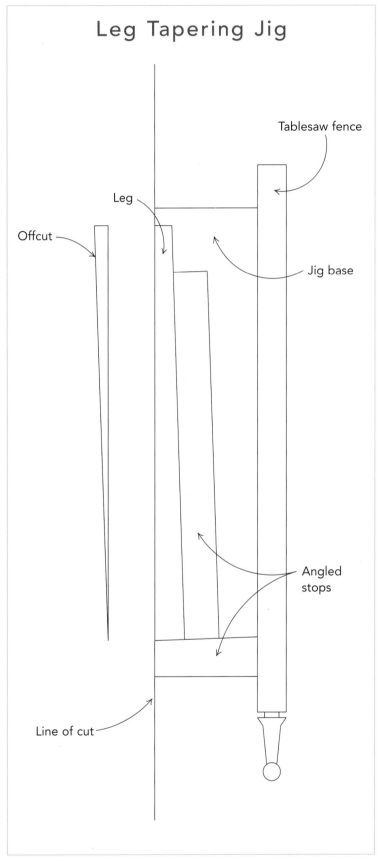

Leg Tapering Jig

Tablesaw fence

Leg

Offcut

Jig base

Angled stops

Line of cut

PHOTO S: Single biscuits join the tops of the legs to the aprons.

3. Crosscut these parts to length at the marked angle on your tablesaw using your miter gauge.

4. Drill countersunk holes in the underside of the apron pieces large enough to easily accept the heads of the screws and deep enough to allow the screws to enter the seat approximately ¾ in. The seat will be attached to the base with two screws through each of the apron pieces.

5. Drill oversized holes the rest of the way through the pieces. The oversized holes will allow the seat to expand and contract seasonally without damaging either the seat or the base.

6. Cut the biscuit slots that connect the apron pieces to the legs (see **photo S**). The apron pieces are recessed ½ in. from the outside faces of the legs, so you will have to set your biscuit-joiner fence deeper when you cut the slots in the legs; otherwise, these are

normal #20 biscuit joints. Making the recess exactly ½ in. is not critical—a little more or less is fine.

7. Drill ⅜-in.-dia. holes in the center of the ends of the stretchers and centered on the legs at the correct heights (remember there are two different heights). I used a horizontal-mortising machine, but a drill press with a little care, ingenuity, and a jig will work fine—just mind how the tapers pull the drill bit to one side (see **photo T**).

Assembly

Assembly is pretty straightforward: The biscuit joints and the dowel joints get glued and clamped together. To make your life easier, however, I suggest that you assemble the stool in stages.

1. Before starting assembly, finish-sand all the parts to 150 grit. This is also a good time

PHOTO U: Assemble the stool frame in stages: First glue up two sets of legs, aprons, and stretchers; then attach the two assemblies with the remaining aprons and stretchers.

to size and finish-sand the seat (I'm sure it's dry by now).

2. Glue and clamp two sets of legs, an apron, and a stretcher, and set them aside to dry.

3. When dry, you can easily connect these two assemblies with the remaining apron pieces and stretchers (see **photo U** on p. 125).

Finishing

I finished the stool with a satin spray lacquer, but a nice oil finish would also look nice and feel better to the touch. When you are done with the finishing, attach the seat (see **photo V**).

PHOTO V: Screw the stool frame to the seat through the aprons.

DESIGN OPTION: UPHOLSTERED SEAT

I think this is a nice-looking stool as is. But if you want to dress it up a little and make it more comfortable, it is a simple matter to replace the seat with an upholstered version.

In one way this is actually easier to make, since you don't have to construct the solid-wood seat. A piece of plywood makes an excellent base for the upholstery and has the benefit of being dimensionally stable so you don't have to take seasonal movement into account.

An upholstered seat is more comfortable and not that difficult to make.

You will need to purchase an 18-in. square of fabric and a 16-in. square of 2-in. high-density foam for each seat. Most fabric stores will carry both items.

1. Cut a piece of ¾-in. plywood 14 in. by 14 in. When centered on the base, this will leave ½ in. all around that will be taken up with foam.

2. Take the square of foam and bevel the outside edge so that the square is 14 in. by 14 in. on the bottom and 16 in. by 16 in. on the top. A bandsaw works surprisingly well for this, but a sharp handsaw or bread knife will also work (the result doesn't have to be pretty).

3. Using some spray contact cement, glue this foam to the plywood.

4. Place this assembly upside-down on the fabric.

5. Fold and stretch one side of the fabric up and across the plywood until the foam folds up and covers the edge of the plywood. Staple it in place.

6. Repeat this on all four sides. At this point, you will have a fabric pocket at each corner. Pull and stretch these pockets diagonally across the plywood, and staple in place.

That's it! If this was your first time doing this, there is a good chance it doesn't look all that great. Don't despair—just remove the staples and try again. It's a matter of getting the stretching right and sometimes it takes a few tries.

Cross Section of Upholstered Seat

A sandwich of plywood, foam, and fabric makes an attractive and comfortable seat.

Fabric

2" foam

14" square of ¾" plywood

Finished seat

Fabric is folded under plywood, compressing foam to 1" and pulling beveled edge down to fill ½" space around the edge of the plywood, for a finished 15"-square seat.

Staple fabric to plywood.

MEDICINE CABINET

Paul Anthony

MOST MEDICINE CABINETS are not designed to safely and discreetly store medicines. The drugs typically sit on shelves within the grasp of youngsters and within plain view of anyone who decides to take an interest in them. Kids are notoriously fascinated by anything that looks like candy, and childproof bottles won't necessarily keep kids out. In another vein, some surveys report that as many as half the visitors to a home snoop in the medicine cabinet.

With this in mind (not that I *personally* have anything to hide), I designed this snoop-proof medicine cabinet with a lockable compartment. For easy access, the compartment can stay unlocked most of the time—its door held shut with a ball catch. But for security, a half-mortise lock can easily be activated with a key. For protection against key scratches, I installed an inset escutcheon. The drop-down compartment door is installed with knife hinges, which are low-profile and perfect for this particular application.

I used spalted sycamore for my cabinet, but any wood will do. You may want to use something that matches your existing cabinetry. The door stiles are a bit proud of the rails, lending visual interest to the door joints. The pulls are made of wenge, but another contrasting wood could work nicely too.

MEDICINE CABINET

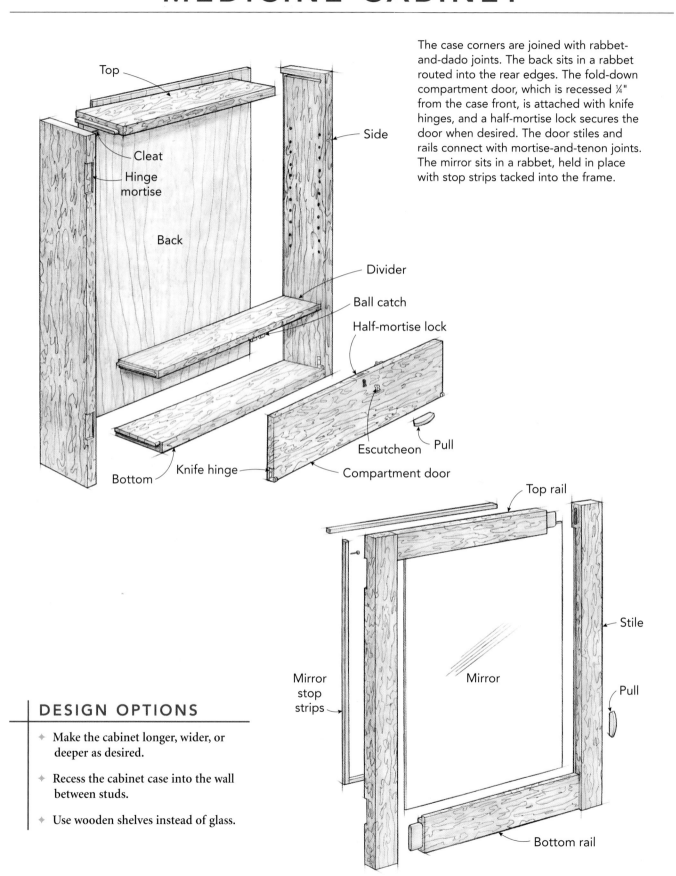

The case corners are joined with rabbet-and-dado joints. The back sits in a rabbet routed into the rear edges. The fold-down compartment door, which is recessed ¼" from the case front, is attached with knife hinges, and a half-mortise lock secures the door when desired. The door stiles and rails connect with mortise-and-tenon joints. The mirror sits in a rabbet, held in place with stop strips tacked into the frame.

Top

Cleat

Hinge mortise

Back

Side

Divider

Ball catch

Half-mortise lock

Escutcheon

Pull

Knife hinge

Bottom

Compartment door

Top rail

Stile

Mirror stop strips

Mirror

Pull

Bottom rail

DESIGN OPTIONS

✦ Make the cabinet longer, wider, or deeper as desired.

✦ Recess the cabinet case into the wall between studs.

✦ Use wooden shelves instead of glass.

Front, Side, and Top Views

FRONT VIEW

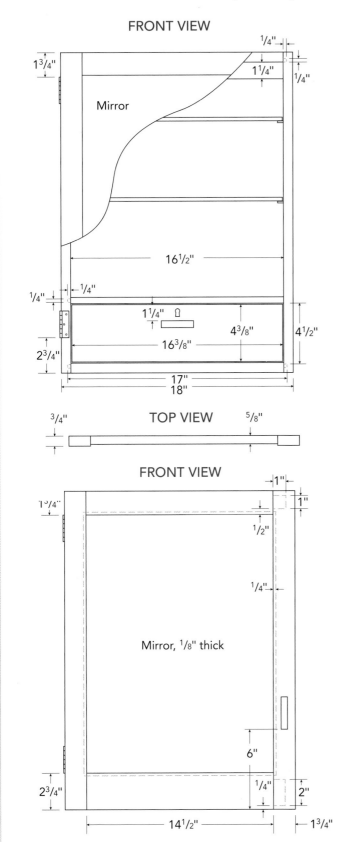

Mirror

1³/₄"

¹/₄"

1¹/₄"

¹/₄"

16¹/₂"

¹/₄"

¹/₄"

1¹/₄"

4³/₈"

4¹/₂"

16³/₈"

2³/₄"

17"

18"

TOP VIEW

³/₄"

⁵/₈"

FRONT VIEW

1³/₄"

1"

1"

¹/₂"

¹/₄"

Mirror, ¹/₈" thick

6"

¹/₄"

2³/₄"

2"

14¹/₂"

1³/₄"

SIDE VIEW (side removed)

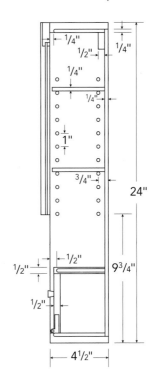

¹/₄"

¹/₂"

¹/₄"

¹/₄"

¹/₄"

1"

³/₄"

24"

¹/₂"

9³/₄"

¹/₂"

¹/₂"

4¹/₂"

SIDE VIEW (stile removed)

¹/₄"

¹/₄"

¹/₄"

¹/₈"

Mirror

24"

¹/₂"

¹/₄"

Case

2	Sides	¾" x 4½" x 24"	solid wood
2	Top and bottom	¾" x 4½" x 17"	solid wood
1	Divider	½" x 4" x 17"	solid wood
1	Compartment door	½" x 4⅜" x 16⅜"	solid wood
1	Cleat	½" x 1¼" x 16½"	solid wood
1	Back	¼" x 17" x 23"	hardwood plywood

Door

1	Top rail	⅝" x 1¾" x 16½"	solid wood
1	Bottom rail	⅝" x 2¾" x 16½"	solid wood
2	Stiles	¾" x 1¾" x 24"	solid wood
2	Stop strips	¼" x ¼" x 14½"	solid wood
2	Stop strips	¼" x ¼" x 20"	solid wood
2	Pulls	½" x ½" x ½"	solid wood

Other materials

2	Extruded hinges	2½" x 1½"	from Woodcraft®; item #16Q51
2	Knife hinge	⅝" (offset 1⅜")	from Lee Valley™; item #01B1415
1	Extruded escutcheon	½" (inside height)	from Lee Valley; item #00A03.01
1	Cupboard lock	2" (standard cut)	from Lee Valley; item #00P2920
2	Ball catch	1¾" x ⁵⁄₁₆"	from Rockler℠; item #28613
1	Mirror	distance between rabbets minus ¹⁄₁₆"	
2	Shelves (glass)	¼" x 4" x 16⅜"	
8	Shelf support pins	¼" (flat spoon style)	from Woodcraft; item #27I11

TIP

If you don't have a screwdriver short enough to fit in a tight space, you can use a power driver tip, turning it with a small wrench.

BUILD THE CASE FIRST; then I fit the compartment door and install the half-mortise lock. After that, I make the cabinet door, fit the hinges, apply finish, install the mirror, and hang the door.

Constructing the Case

Mill the pieces and cut the joints

1. Lay out the case pieces. Next, joint, plane, and saw them to size.

2. Lay out the ¼-in.-wide stopped dadoes on the sides. Note that the top and bottom dadoes stop ¼ in. from the case front and the divider dado stops ½ in. from the case front.

3. Rout the dadoes. I guide the router with a shopmade fence.

4. Cut the rabbets in the top and bottom pieces to create the ¼-in. by ¼-in. tongues to fit in the case dadoes. I fit my saw with a dado blade and auxiliary fence and then cut the rabbets with the stock lying flat on the saw table. Back the pieces up with a miter gauge for safe feeding.

5. Leaving the rip fence set where it is, drop the blade to saw the opposing ⅛-in.-deep rabbets that create the tongue on each end of the divider. Begin with the blade set lower than you need and cut both rabbets. Test the fit; then raise the blade a bit and try again. Creep up on the final cuts for a snug fit in the divider dadoes.

6. Raise the blade to ⅜ in. high and saw off the front section of each tongue on all of the pieces.

7. Rout the ¼-in. by ¼-in. rabbets in the rear edges of the top, bottom, and sides. I did this on the router table using a ⁵⁄₁₆-in.-diameter straight bit and laying the workpieces flat on the table. Make sure to stop the case side rabbets ½ in. from the ends of the sides.

Cut the knife hinge mortises

The knife hinge mortises need to be cut in the case sides before assembly, because it would be difficult to do afterward.

1. Dry-assemble the top and bottom to the sides, leaving the divider out.

PHOTO A: Bore a hole to accept the knife hinge knuckle. Make the hole as deep as the hinge leaf is thick.

2. One leaf of each hinge has a pin and one doesn't. Using the pinless leaf, lay out the hinge mortises. Place the knuckle ¹⁄₁₆ in. back from the case front and pressed against the case bottom (see "Medicine Compartment"). Trace around the hinge and inside the pin hole with a sharp pencil. Mark the center of the pin hole with a small awl.

3. Using a ⁵⁄₁₆-in.-diameter brad-point drill bit in the drill press, bore a ¹⁄₈-in.-deep hole for the knuckle recess (see **photo A**).

4. Using a ¼-in.-diameter straight bit, rout the majority of the waste from the rest of the mortise (see **photo B** on p. 134). Stay clear of the layout lines.

5. Using a razor-sharp chisel, pare back to the layout lines, testing the fit of the leaf as you go (see **photo C** on p. 134).

6. Drill the pilot holes for the screws now, as it will be difficult to maneuver a drill in the case corner after assembly.

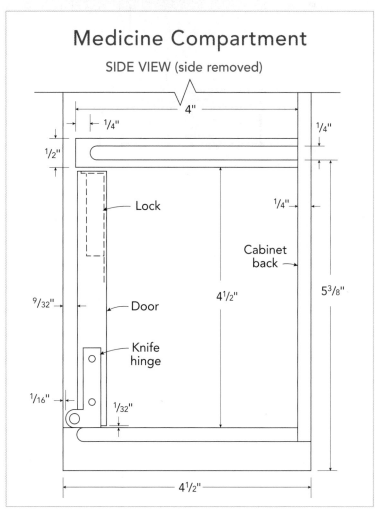

Medicine Compartment

SIDE VIEW (side removed)

4"

¼"

¼"

½"

¼"

Lock

¼"

Cabinet back

4½"

5³⁄₈"

⁹⁄₃₂"

Door

Knife hinge

¹⁄₁₆"

¹⁄₃₂"

4½"

PHOTO B: Rout away most of the waste to the depth of the hole while staying clear of the layout lines.

PHOTO C: Using a sharp chisel, gradually pare to the layout lines until the hinge leaf fits very snugly.

Assemble the case and install the cleat

1. Dry-clamp the case together to check the joint fit and to rehearse your assembly procedures. Lay the case flat on the bench and use cauls to distribute pressure evenly across the joints. Make the back and place it into its rabbets to square up the case before applying the last clamp to the divider (see **photo D**).

2. Glue the case together, then immediately wipe away any glue squeeze-out with a clean, wet rag.

3. After the glue dries, make and fit the cleat and glue it to the case top.

4. Drill the shelf-pin holes using a thick, prebored plywood template. If you prefer, you could lay out the holes on the case sides and drill them on the drill press before assembling the case, but I find template drilling more accurate.

5. Plane the front and rear edges of the case flush to each other.

Constructing the Compartment Door

Make and fit the parts

1. Make the flip-down door for the compartment, measuring the compartment opening and subtracting 1/16 in. from the height and width to determine the size of the door. Use quartersawn stock, if possible, to minimize potential warpage (see "Stability Is in the Cut" on p. 8).

2. Lay out the knife hinge mortise in each end of the door. The lower end of each hinge should project 1/32 in. beyond the door's bottom edge, as shown in the drawing on p. 133.

3. After adjusting your router bit depth to the thickness of the hinge leaf, rout away most of the waste (see **photo E** on p. 136). Then pare to the layout lines (see **photo F** on p. 136).

4. Drill the pilot holes and prethread them using a steel screw that matches the size of the hinge's brass screws.

5. Test-fit the doors after attaching the case half of each hinge to the case. Screw one door leaf to the door and hang the other door leaf on its mating leaf. Slip the installed leaves together; then slide the uninstalled door leaf into its mortise and screw it in place.

6. With the door installed, check the gaps around it. Mark cut lines to correct any inconsistencies in the gap, remove the door, and plane to the cut lines. Afterward, reinstall the door, recheck its fit, and make any final corrections in the same manner.

Install the escutcheon, lock, and catch

1. Install the inset escutcheon (see "Installing an Inset Escutcheon" on p. 137). Alternatively, you could tack on a surface-mount escutcheon after installing the lock.

2. Install the half-mortise lock (see "Installing a Half-Mortise Lock" on p. 139). When routing the lock body mortise, use a carbide bit because you'll be cutting partially into the brass escutcheon.

3. Rout the mortise for the lock bolt using a slot-cutting bit (see **photo G** on p. 138). To determine the distance of the mortise from the front edge of the divider, measure from the front of the door to the front of the bolt and add ½ in.

4. Install the ball catch after replacing the stock springs with springs from a ball-point pen. I attach the pronged half of the catch to the door, lock the door, press the case half of the catch onto the prong, and then mark the screw holes (see **photo H** on p. 138). Drill the pilot holes using a right-angle drill attachment.

5. Prethread the pilot holes using a ⅜-in.-long steel screw, then attach the case half of the catch in place with brass screws. The brass screws that came with my catch were too long, so I ground them down to ⅜ in. long on my bench grinder.

PHOTO D: Before gluing up the case, do a dry-fit to check your joints and rehearse your clamping procedures. The back, cut to fit tightly in its rabbets, helps hold the case square while the glue cures.

TIP

Don't fret if you rout a hinge mortise a bit too deep. You can simply shim the hinge during installation. Masking tape, business cards, and playing cards all make great shims.

PHOTO E: Clamp the end of the compartment door flush to the benchtop for routing the majority of the waste from the knife hinge mortise.

Constructing the Cabinet Door

The rails are thinner than the stiles on this door, which creates "stepped" joints—adding visual interest to the frame. Keep the different thicknesses in mind as you mill the stock and lay out the joints.

Prepare the pieces

1. Mill the pieces and cut them to length. Make the stiles $\frac{1}{32}$ in. oversize in width and length. That way, you'll later be able to trim the slightly oversize door to fit the case exactly. Mill a bit of extra rail stock for saw setups when cutting the tenons.

2. Lay the pieces out for pleasing grain orientation (see "Grain Layout" on p. 17).

3. Lay out the mortise lengths on the stiles. Then lay out the width of one mortise to use as a reference for setting your router edge guide. The $\frac{1}{4}$-in.-wide mortises are inset $\frac{3}{16}$ in. from the back side of the stiles.

4. Using a router edge guide, rout the 1-in.-deep mortises in the stiles.

PHOTO F:
Complete the mortise by paring to the layout lines. Notice that the knuckle will project beyond the face of the door.

INSTALLING AN INSET ESCUTCHEON

Although many styles of surface-mount keyhole escutcheons are available, I prefer the subtle elegance of an inset escutcheon. This keyhole-shaped piece of extruded brass fits into a mortise rather than being tacked onto the workpiece like typical surface-mount escutcheons. Fit an inset escutcheon before installing the lock.

1. Locate the position of the lock pin on the door, then drill a hole that matches the outside diameter of the round escutcheon head. Use a brad-point bit to prevent tearout and drill to a depth about ½2 in. less than the depth of the escutcheon.

2. Clamp the escutcheon in place over the hole, with its tapered side down. Trace around the skirted area using a very sharp knife.

3. Remove the waste in the skirted area using a razor-sharp chisel. Cut only to the depth of the drilled hole (see photo below). Work carefully, test-fitting the escutcheon occasionally without pressing it in completely.

4. Line the walls of the mortise with a mixture of sanding dust and epoxy or cyanoacrylate glue, then clamp the escutcheon in place with waxed paper on top of it.

5. After the adhesive has cured, sand the surface flush.

6. Using a bit that matches the inside diameter of the escutcheon head, bore a hole completely through the door.

7. After installing the lock, saw away the waste in the skirted area using a coping saw.

5. Saw the tenons. I do this with a dado blade on the tablesaw, first cutting the ³⁄₁₆-in. by 1-in. rabbet on the back side of each rail. Next, I adjust the height of the dado blade and cut the rabbets on the face side (see **photo I** on p. 140). Adjust the blade height again to cut the ¼-in. and ½-in. shoulders.

6. File and pare the edges of the tenons to approximately match the radius of the mortise.

7. Sand the faces and inside edges of the rails and stiles through 220 grit, rounding the edges gently. Then apply one coat of finish to the faces and interior edges of the rails and to the area adjacent to the mortises. This will make removal of excess glue at the stepped joints much easier later.

Assemble the door

1. Dry-fit the door to make sure the joints fit well and that they clamp up squarely and lie flat on the bench. If not, make any necessary adjustments.

2. Glue and clamp the door, making sure it's flat on the bench and that the clamp screws are centered across the thickness of the stock

to prevent the pieces from cocking out of alignment.

3. After the glue cures, plane or belt-sand the back of the door flat.

4. Rout the ¼-in.-wide by ⅜-in.-deep rabbet in the back side to accept the mirror and stop strips. Chisel the rabbet corners square after routing.

5. Rip the ¼-in. by ¼-in. stop strips to fit.

6. Measure for the mirror by subtracting 1/16 in. from the distance between the rabbet walls. When ordering the mirror, specify that you want it cut accurately. At the same time, order the glass shelves. I had the shelf edges "polished" (or "eased") to round them slightly.

Hang the door

Because this is an overlay door, it's easy to install. You'll cut the hinge mortises, temporarily attach the hinges, and then trim the door flush to the case.

PHOTO G: Use a slot-cutting bit to rout the mortise for the lock bolt. Clamp square scrap to the divider to steady the router. (The masking tape here simply provides a better view of the bit.)

TIP

I love the elegant little brass ball catches used in this cabinet, but their springs can be too strong for a small door like this. No problem. Simply unscrew the spring caps, remove the two springs, and replace them with ball-point pen springs cut to the same length as the stock springs.

PHOTO H: After attaching the pronged half of the ball catch to the door, snap the other half in place from behind the cabinet and mark the screw holes.

INSTALLING A HALF-MORTISE LOCK

Half-mortise locks provide a strong, discreet way to secure doors, drawers, and box lids. Although lock bolt configurations differ depending on the application, the mounting procedure is the same for all lock bodies. Installation simply requires cutting three different mortises: a large one to accommodate the lock box and two shallow ones to recess the thin backplate and selvage.

1. First, lay out the lock pin location. Measure the backset of the lock—the distance between the outer face of the selvage and the center of the pin. Transfer that distance in from the outer edge of your door and mark the pin location with an awl.

2. Using a brad-point bit that matches the diameter of the keyhole, drill all the way through the door at the pin location. (When using an inset escutcheon, as here, install the escutcheon before this step.)

3. Using a ruler and square, lay out the mortise for the box, positioning it so the lock pin lines up with your drilled hole. Then rout it

about 1/32 in. deeper than the combined thickness of the box and backplate. Cut the mortise a bit wider and longer than the box; the backplate will cover any gaps.

4. Lay out the mortise for the backplate. First place the box in its mortise, centering the pin side to side in your drilled hole. Score the outline of the backplate onto the door using a sharp knife. Rout out the majority of the waste to a depth that matches the thickness of the backplate. Then pare to your knife lines using a razor-sharp chisel.

5. Lay out the selvage mortise on the edge of the door. Press the lock into its mortises and trace around the selvage with a sharp knife. Rout and chisel the mortise as before.

6. Widen the backplate mortise just enough for the selvage to seat in its mortise. With the selvage pressed into its mortise and the backplate resting on the back of the door, trace the bottom edge of the backplate with a knife, then pare to the lines (see photo above).

7. Using the lock's keyhole opening as a guide for size, lay out the skirted section of the keyhole, flaring the edges out a few degrees. Then cut the shape with a coping saw and screw the lock in place.

A HALF-MORTISE LOCK

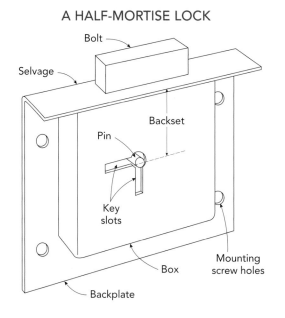

Bolt

Selvage

Pin

Backset

Key slots

Box

Mounting screw holes

Backplate

PHOTO I: To saw tenons with a dado blade, use the rip fence as a stop block and back up narrow workpieces with the miter gauge for safe feeding. For long tenons that require more than one pass over the blade, cut the waste at the end first, moving toward the tenon shoulder in subsequent passes.

Pulls

FRONT VIEW

1/2"

2 1/2"

SIDE VIEW

3/16"

3/16"

1/16"

END VIEW

10°

1/2" cabinet door pull

7/16" compartment door pull

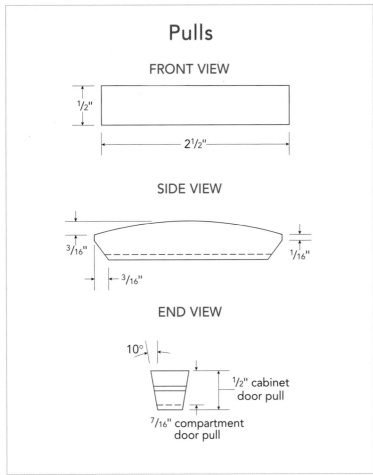

1. Clamp the hinges to the case and trace around each leaf with a sharp knife.

2. Outfit your router with a ¼-in.-diameter straight bit and edge guide. Adjust the edge guide for a cut that reaches the far wall of the mortise. If you're using good-quality extruded hinges, as I suggest, adjust the bit depth to the exact thickness of the hinge leaf. If you're using typical stamped hardware store hinges, adjust the bit so it projects about ⅟₃₂ in. below the center of the hinge pin, with the hinge lying on the upside down router base.

3. Rout the case mortises, staying clear of the knife lines on the shorter edges of the mortise (see **photo J**). Afterward, pare to the remaining knife lines with a sharp chisel.

TIP

When tacking in stop strips for mirror or glass, use as small a hammer as possible and lay a piece of corrugated cardboard over the glass in the area that you're working.

4. Install a hinge in each mortise using a single screw. Drill a pilot hole first, offsetting it very slightly so the screw will pull the hinge toward the rear mortise wall.

5. Fold the hinges over and place the door on the case, aligning the hinged side of the door and the case. Split any overlap between the top and bottom evenly. Slide a sharp knife against each edge of a leaf and into the edge of the door to transfer the hinge placement. Then use a square to extend knife lines across the back face of the stile to mark the hinge outlines.

6. Rout and chisel the hinge mortises in the stile as you did in the case, then attach the door to the hinges with one screw only.

7. With the door attached, plane or sand the door edges flush to the case edges.

Make the pulls

1. Lay out the profile of the pulls on ½-in.-thick stock (see "Pulls"). This is a great opportunity to use a bit of that special accent wood you've been hoarding. Note that the compartment pull is ¹⁄₁₆ in. shallower than the door pull.

2. Shape the side profile. I used a disk sander, but you could use a belt sander or scrollsaw.

3. Handplane the 10-degree bevel on each side of the pull, then sand the pulls through 220 grit.

Finishing Up

Sand and apply the finish

1. Remove all of the hardware and sand everything through 220-grit. Then glue the pulls in place.

2. Apply a good water-resistant finish. I rubbed on four coats of wiping varnish (see the section "A Favorite Finish" on p. 19). I used a small artist's brush to work finish into the shelf-pin holes.

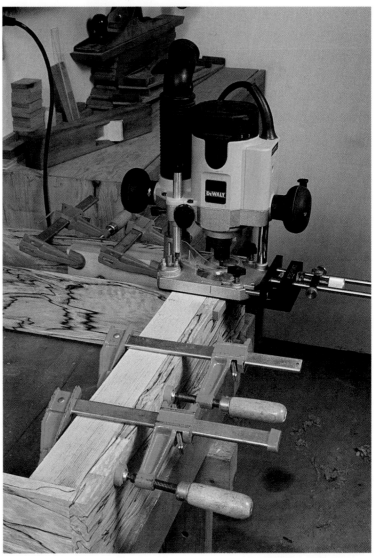

PHOTO J: By using the same router edge guide setting when routing the hinge mortises on both the case and the door, you're assured of good door–case alignment.

Assemble the cabinet

1. Reinstall the compartment door hinges, lock, and catch.

2. Place the mirror into its rabbets and tack the stop strips in place. I predrill the nail holes to prevent splitting the stops.

3. Hang the door and install a ball catch behind the pull.

4. Nail or staple the back on. Then hang the cabinet, screwing through the cleat into a wall stud. Install the shelf pins and shelves.

PART TWO

Around The House

WINE RACK

Niall Barrett

WINE CELLARS ARE ROMANTIC places. Dusty bottles sleep in orderly rows in a dark, moist, cool climate, waiting to be dusted off, brought upstairs, and enjoyed.

But you don't really need a fancy, expensive cellar to store and age your wines. In fact, not all wines are meant to be aged. If you're like most wine consumers, you'll enjoy your wines soon after you bring them home. A relatively small wine rack, located in an appropriate place, will be fine for housing your wines.

Wine cellars are ideal places to store wine. But it's possible to store wine upstairs quite well by keeping a few things in mind. Temperature fluctuations, sunlight, and movement are the biggest enemies of wine.

People commonly make the mistake of storing wine in a rack in a brightly lit room where it gets both hot and cold. It may look nice, but the wine will turn quickly. Ultraviolet light will penetrate even dark-colored glass, so avoid direct sunlight.

Ideal storage temperature is between 55°F and 65°F. More important, the temperature should be constant. A slow change of 10 or so degrees between seasons is not a big problem. But this kind of fluctuation on a regular basis will damage your wines.

Last, vibration disturbs a red wine's sediment and can be harmful to all wines, so the top of your refrigerator is not the best location.

This rack will hold about 17 bottles of wine and, like all good wine-rack designs, stores the wine horizontally so that the wine stays in contact with the cork. This prevents the cork from drying and shrinking, which would allow air to enter the bottle and negatively affect the wine's flavor. The solid sides keep the wine in relative shade.

WINE RACK

This mahogany wine rack will store
at least 17 bottles of wine horizontally.
The solid sides keep most light out.

Front and Side Views

FRONT

SIDE

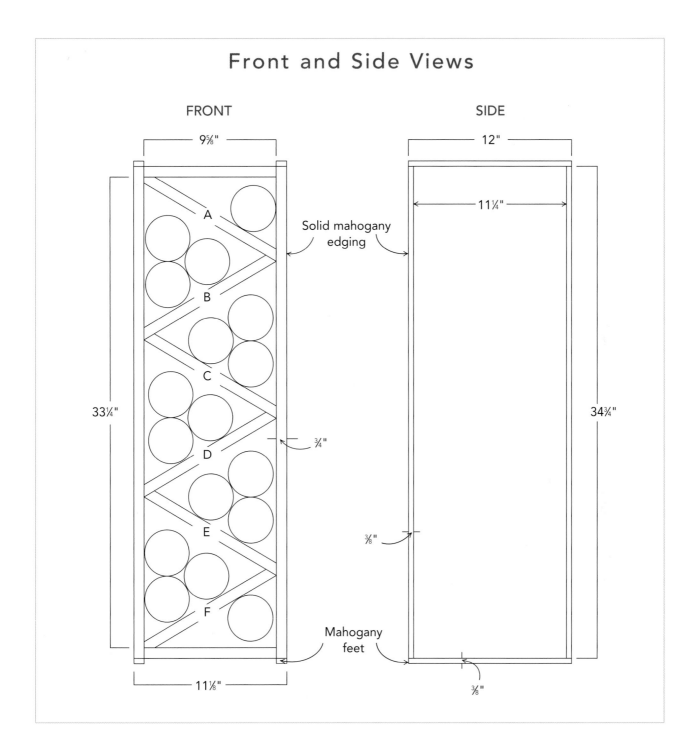

9⅝"

12"

11¼"

Solid mahogany edging

33¼"

¾"

A

B

C

D

E

F

34¾"

⅜"

Mahogany feet

11⅛"

⅜"

Construction and Assembly

WHILE THIS DESIGN LOOKS simple, it's a little tricky to build. If you follow my directions precisely, though, I guarantee it will all work out. It's a matter of accuracy: The interior dimensions of the box have to be exactly as given in the drawing. The space thus created is precisely the right size to hold the partitions, provided they are cut to the right size and their angles are exact (see "Exact Partition Sizes" on p. 148). If the box size changes slightly, the length of and angles on the ends of the partitions must also slightly

CUT LIST FOR WINE RACK			
2	Top and bottom	9 5/8" x 11 1/4" x 3/4"	mahogany plywood
2	Sides	34 3/4" x 11 1/4" x 3/4"	mahogany plywood
5	Partitions	11 1/8" x 10 1/2" x 3/4"	mahogany plywood
1	Top partition	11 1/8" x 10 1/2" x 3/4"	mahogany plywood
4	Feet	12" x 3/8" x 13/16"	solid mahogany
20 linear ft.	Edging	3/8" x 3/4"	solid mahogany
Other materials			
12	Brass screws	#10 x 3/4"	

Exact Partition Sizes

All partitions are cut on the ends at 60°. The last cuts on partitions A and F are at 90° to the 60° cut.

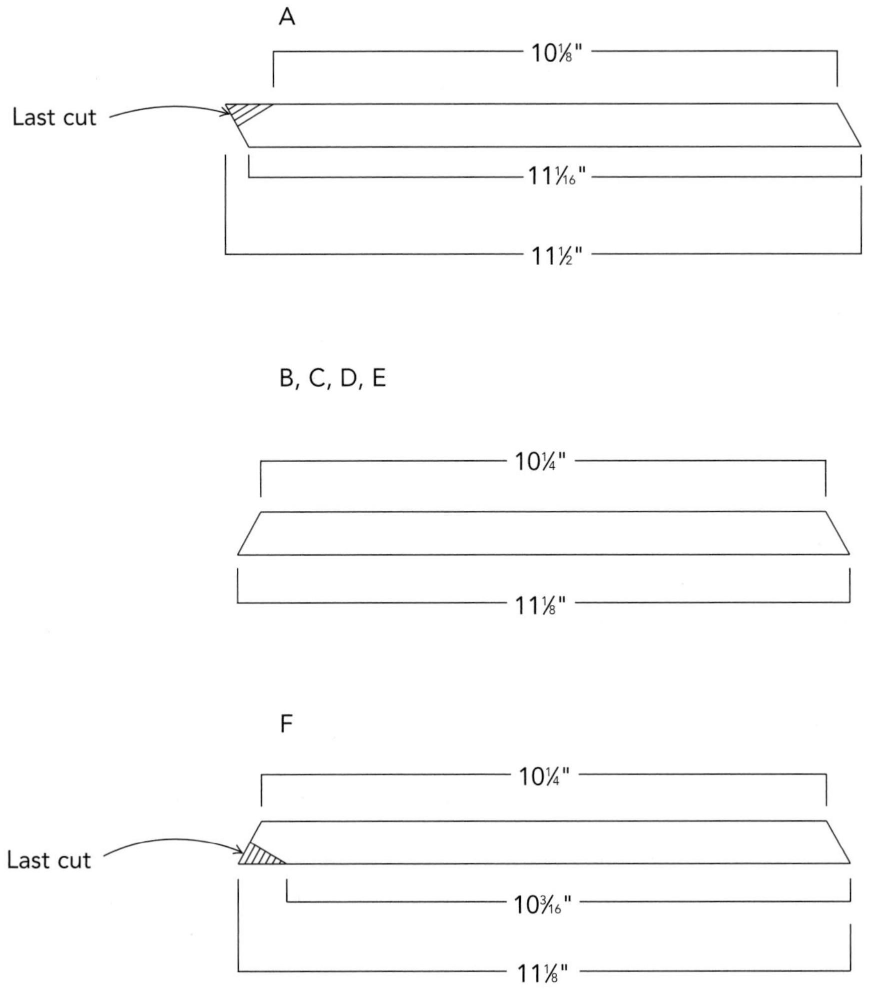
A
10 1/8"
Last cut
11 1/16"
11 1/2"
B, C, D, E
10 1/4"
11 1/8"
F
10 1/4"
Last cut
10 3/16"
11 1/8"

change. You can see the potential nightmare of adding $\frac{5}{32}$ in. to each partition and trying to cut something like a 58¼-degree angle.

Cutting the Sides and Partitions to Size

The first step is to cut all the plywood parts.

1. Cut all the parts to the widths given in the cut list, leaving all the parts about 2 in. too long. The sides for the box are ¾ in. wider than the partitions because the partitions are inset front and back by as much.

2. Mill enough solid-mahogany edging stock to cover the front and back edges of all the parts.

3. Glue and clamp this edging to all these edges and set them aside to dry. It's easiest to leave this edging a little wide and long, so you can trim it flush after the glue has dried. This kind of edging is difficult to align perfectly, so if you leave some extra and it slides a little while being clamped, it will still cover the edges. When these parts are dry, trim all the edging flush with the faces of the plywood.

4. First trim the excess off the ends. This can be done very quickly by crosscutting ¼ in. or so off each end, which should still leave about 1½ in. of extra length.

5. Trim the excess from the sides. The quickest way to accomplish this is with a flush-trimming bit in your router. As long as you haven't left too much extra, you shouldn't have any splintering problems. You could also use a sharp block plane or even a sanding block. Regardless of the method you use, make sure that the edging ends up completely flush and level with the sides. If there is any rounding, it will show where all the parts come together.

Building the Box

It's hard to get out of the rut of measuring outside dimensions, but the most important thing to remember for this project is that the inside measurements are what count. I have also given you outside measurements for this wine rack, but these assume that the plywood you are using is exactly ¾ in. thick. As you may or may not know, ¾-in. plywood is rarely exactly ¾ in. and can be as much as $\frac{1}{16}$ in. under. If you multiply this by two (the number of sides), you can make a box with interior dimensions as much as ⅛ in. off, more than enough to throw off the fit of the partitions. Other than that, it's just a box put together with biscuits.

1. Size the sides, top, and bottom for a box with inside dimensions of 33¼ in. by 9⅝ in., factoring in any stock-thickness variations.

2. Cut the biscuit slots so that the top and bottom are between the sides when assembled.

3. Finish-sand the inside faces of the box parts to 150 grit.

4. Glue, biscuit, and clamp the parts together. Make sure the box is still a true rectangle when clamped up.

5. When the glue is dry, finish-sand the outside.

Making the Feet

The box has four feet, attached with some brass screws over the plywood edges that show on the top and bottom of the box. Not only will these cover the raw plywood edges, but they also lift the bottom of the box slightly.

1. Mill four pieces of mahogany 12 in. by ⅜ in. by $\frac{13}{16}$ in. for the feet.

2. Drill three countersunk holes, sized to brass screws at even intervals in each foot.

Making the Partitions

This part is not difficult, nor will it take very long, but you must be accurate (see "Summary of Cutting Sequence for Partitions" on p. 150).

1. Set the blade on your tablesaw to 60 degrees.

Summary of Cutting Sequence for Partitions

All cuts are made on the tablesaw.

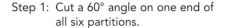

Step 1: Cut a 60° angle on one end of all six partitions.

Step 2: Take five partitions, and cut matching angles on the opposite ends.

Step 3: Take the remaining partition, and cut a complementary 60° angle on its opposite end.

Step 4: Take the piece from Step 3. Using an angle-block carrier, hold the piece at 60° to the blade and cut the end off.

Step 5: Take one of the pieces from Step 2. Using an angle-block carrier, hold the piece at 60° to the blade and cut the end off.

PHOTO A: Cut 60° angles on the ends of every partition.

2. Set the fence so that each cut will take off about ⅛ in. to ¼ in. more than you need. This will ensure a splinter-free cut.

3. Rip a 60-degree angle on one end of all six of the partitions (see **photo A**).

4. Reset the fence to 11⅛ in. and rip a matching 60-degree angle on the opposite end of five of the six partitions. The same face of the partition should ride on the table during the cut.

5. Attach an auxiliary fence that sits perfectly flush with the table and set the fence to cut at 11½ in. This auxiliary fence must lay tight to the table surface. The next cut requires that the long point of the last partition rides on the table and against the fence. You don't want any space under the rip fence under which the point could slip.

6. Cut a complementary 60-degree angle without a bevel on the end of the last partition (see **photo B**). (This partition is shown as "A" in "Exact Partition Sizes" on p. 148.)

7. Make an angle-block carrier to hold the top and bottom partitions ("A" and "F" on p. 148) at 60 degrees to the sawblade. This allows you to cut the secondary angles that are at 90 degrees to the 60-degree angles. A simple block of wood about 18 in. long by 1¾ in. high by 2½ in. wide will work fine (see "Positioning Angle-Block Carrier").

8. Attach one of the two partitions to this block with some double-sided tape. (Both of these partitions will be cut the same way, with the same exact setup.)

PHOTO B: Cut a complementary 60° angle on the ends of the top partition ("A" on p. 148).

Positioning Angle-Block Carrier

Partition

Rip fence

Angle-block carrier, 1¾" high x 2½" wide x 18" long

Sawblade

Offcut

Distance from fence to sawblade is 1¹⁵⁄₁₆".

PHOTO C: An auxiliary block angles the top and bottom partitions to cut the corners of one edge at 90° to the 60° bevel.

9. With the blade at 90 degrees to the table, set the rip fence 1¹⁵⁄₁₆ in. away from the blade. Then run the partition through (see **photo C**). Repeat the procedure for the other partition. (Use "Exact Partition Sizes" on p. 148 to check that you've got your angles oriented properly.)

Assembly

Before you glue the partitions in place, do a dry assembly to check the fit.
1. Stand the box on end.
2. Starting at the bottom, place the partitions in the box one on top of the other (see **photo D**).

The accumulating weight of the partitions will spread the sides of the box a little, which is good since it will allow room for the last partition to be inserted. However, it will make it look as though nothing fits right, since the partitions are settling toward the bottom of the box. Don't worry.
3. Take some clamps and, working from the bottom up, position them front and back across the box at the joint of each partition.

PHOTO D: As you stack the partitions in the box, the sides will bow a little bit, making it easy to insert the top partition.

4. Lightly tighten the clamps as you go until the partitions fill up the space. If all the partitions have been cut correctly, they will lie nicely one on top of the other with all the intersecting joints tight.
5. Just to be sure, check that the box is the same width in the center as it is at the top and at the bottom; also, check the diagonals to be sure it is square.
6. Once you are satisfied with the fit, remove the partitions and finish-sand them to 150 grit.

7. Starting at the bottom again, carefully apply a light bead of glue down the center of each end of the first partition and place it in the box. Remember that the partitions are set in ⅜ in. front and back from the edges of the box. Make sure to keep glue away from the last inch or so of the edge at the front and back. This will be plenty of glue to hold things together, and this way it shouldn't make a mess (which otherwise would be very difficult to clean up).

8. Continue gluing and installing partitions until they are all in. The box should spread a little like before, and you should have no problem getting the top partition in without smearing glue on the inside of the box. If it's tight, just spread the sides a little with your hands and it should be fine.

9. Clamp it up just as you did during the dry assembly and check for square (see **photo E**). That's it!

Finishing

This is a very difficult piece to spray finish (or oil for that matter). The compartments created by the partitions make it difficult to get the finish inside. But like an old cabinet-maker I used to know once said, it's also difficult for anyone to see if it's finished in there! So I ended up spraying it the best I could with some satin lacquer. It looks fine—but don't you dare pull out a bottle just to see how well it's finished inside.

PHOTO E: Clamp the case sides together at each partition joint, both front and back. The clamping will make the top partition joint snug.

CONVERTIBLE WINE CABINET

Paul Anthony

UNLESS YOU'RE AN AVOWED WINE collector, you don't need a wine cellar or huge cabinet dedicated to your prized fermentations. However, even the most modest of wine connoisseurs needs a way to store bottles on their sides to keep the corks swelled.

Many wine cabinets consist of X-shaped grids that support bottles lying on their sides. The problem with a grid design is that if your collection dwindles, you've got a lot of wasted space. Plus, a grid cabinet is very difficult to clean if wine is spilled or glass is broken inside.

This cherry wine cabinet, designed and built by professional cabinetmaker Adolph Schneider, solves both problems neatly. Wine bottles are cradled in racks that can be easily removed for cleaning or for temporary replacement with regular shelves when your wine supplies are low. The cabinet also includes racks for hanging wineglasses. This particular cabinet will accommodate nine bottles of wine without glasses, or six bottles with glasses. The cabinet shown in the drawings is a couple of inches taller than the one shown in the photo, to allow a bit more room for taller glasses.

Of course, you can make the cabinet any size you like—longer, wider, taller, whatever. Just follow the basic bottle spacing shown. Although most people like to display their wines, you could also make racks to fit inside your existing kitchen base cabinets.

CONVERTIBLE WINE CABINET

The hardwood plywood case is joined with splined miters, then the plywood edges are covered with veneer tape. The solid-wood bottle racks are joined with screwed and glued rabbets. The wineglass rails are attached with screws after finishing.

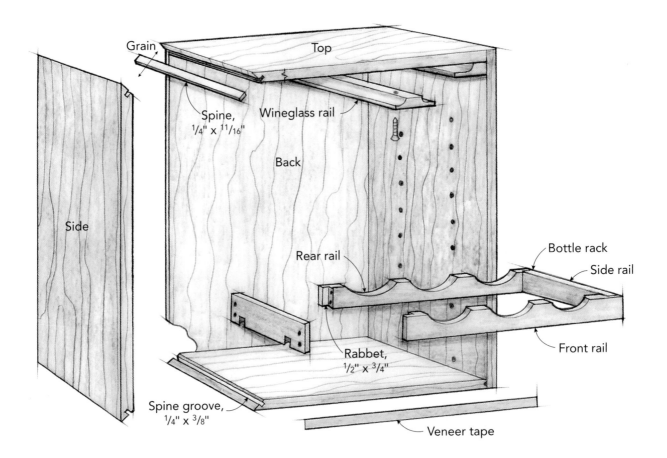

Grain

Top

Spine,
$1/4$" x $^{11}/_{16}$"

Wineglass rail

Back

Side

Rear rail

Bottle rack

Side rail

Rabbet,
$1/2$" x $^3/4$"

Front rail

Spine groove,
$1/4$" x $^3/8$"

Veneer tape

DESIGN OPTIONS

✦ Make the wine cabinet case to match existing kitchen cabinetry, then modify the wall cabinets to accommodate the wine cabinet.

✦ Make a dedicated base cabinet with wine racks and standard shelves.

Side and Front Views

SECTION THROUGH SIDE

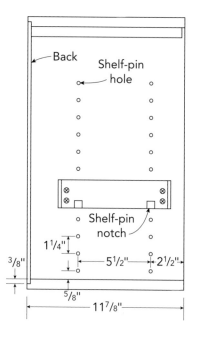

FRONT VIEW

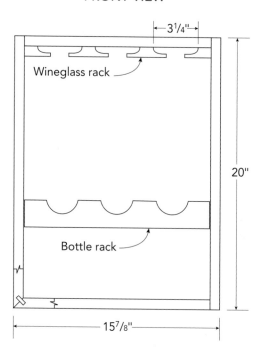

THIS CASE IS MADE from hardwood plywood that's mitered at the corners and reinforced with splines. The raw plywood edge is covered by veneer tape that's applied after the case is assembled. The interior bottle racks and wineglass rails are fitted after the case is assembled. The wineglass rails are simply screwed in place and the adjustable racks fit over shelf supports.

Constructing the Case

Layout and joinery

If you're customizing the size of the case, first determine the case width based on the bottle layout of the racks. Allow 4¼ in. between bottle centers and 3 in. between the center of an end bottle and the end of the rack.

1. Lay out the case sides, top, and bottom end to end so that the grain will flow continuously around the top.

CUT LIST FOR WINE CABINET

Case			
2	Sides	¾" x 11⅞" x 20"	hardwood plywood
2	Top and bottom	¾" x 11⅞" x 15⅞"	hardwood plywood
1	Back	¼" x 11⅛" x 15⅛"	hardwood plywood
	Veneer tape as needed		
Bottle rack			
2	Side rails	¾" x 2" x 14⅚"	solid wood
2	Front/rear rails	¾" x 2" x 8"	solid wood
Wineglass rack			
2	Outer rails	¾" x 2⁵⁄₁₆" x 11⅜"	solid wood
2	Inner rails	¾" x 3" x 11⅜"	solid wood
Other materials			
12	Shelf supports	*from* Woodworker's Hardware℠; item #WT8010	

Parts for a single bottle rack.

Rack Layout

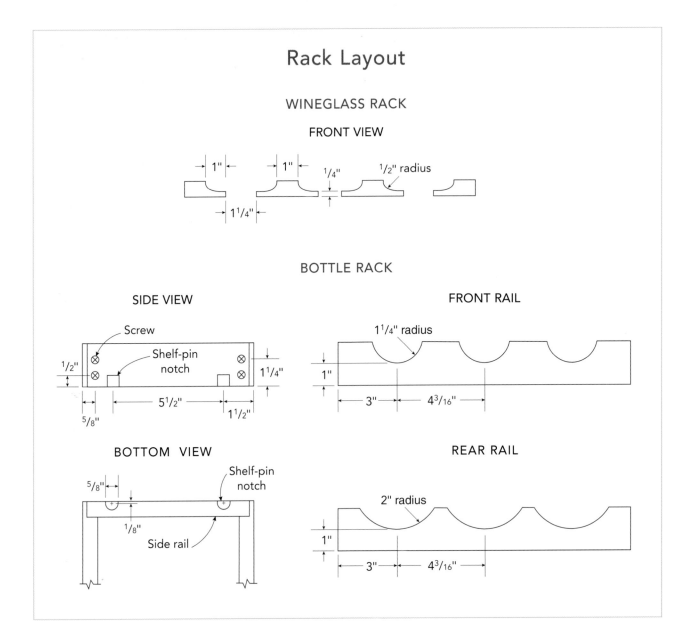

WINEGLASS RACK

FRONT VIEW

1"   1"   1/4"   1/2" radius

1 1/4"

BOTTLE RACK

SIDE VIEW

Screw

Shelf-pin notch

1/2"   1 1/4"

5 1/2"

1 1/2"

5/8"

FRONT RAIL

1 1/4" radius

1"

3"   4 3/16"

BOTTOM VIEW

5/8"

Shelf-pin notch

1/8"

Side rail

REAR RAIL

2" radius

1"

3"   4 3/16"

2. Saw the pieces to size using a good-quality blade to prevent grain tearout.
3. Miter both ends of the case sides, top, and bottom.
4. Rout a ¼-in.-wide by ⅜-in.-deep spline groove in each miter, favoring the inside edge of the miter. An easy way to do this is to clamp the pieces together and then use an edge guide to steer the router.
5. Saw a ¼-in. by ⅜-in. rabbet in the rear edge of each piece to accept the case back.
6. Make the ¼-in. by ¹¹⁄₁₆-in. splines. Good joint alignment depends on splines that fit snugly into their grooves. It's easiest to crosscut the splines from ¼-in.-thick construction plywood, sanding them if necessary for a good fit. Avoid hardwood plywood, which is typically thinner than its nominal size.
7. Dry-clamp the pieces together to check for good joint fit. You could use band clamps, but miter clamping cauls pull the joints together more neatly.
8. With the case still clamped up, cut the back to fit snugly within its rabbets.

TIP

Before laying out pieces on a large plywood panel, inspect it using a strong, glancing sidelight. This will clearly emphasize any scratches or other damage to avoid.

Shelf-support holes and assembly

1. Disassemble the case and lay out the spacing for the shelf-support holes in the sides.

2. Drill the 5mm-dia. holes on the drill press, then sand the inside face of each piece through 220 grit.

3. Assemble the case, gluing only the corner joints for now. Place the back into its grooves unglued to hold the case square while the glue cures. Make sure the tips of the miters meet neatly.

4. Apply veneer tape to the front edges of the case, then sand it flush to the case sides.

5. Glue and nail the back into its rabbets. Wipe off any excess glue immediately.

6. Sand the outsides of the case through 220 grit. Be careful not to sand through the veneer, especially at the corners.

Constructing the Racks

Make the bottle racks

1. Plane and saw the rail pieces to size.

2. Lay out the arcs in the front and rear rails.

3. Saw the ½-in. by ¾-in. rabbets in the front and back rails that will accept the side rails.

4. Drill the arcs on the front rails using a 2½-in.-dia. hole saw on the drill press (see **photo A**).

5. Cut the arcs in the rear rails using a jigsaw or bandsaw.

6. Sand the arcs smooth. A large drum sander mounted on the drill press works well for this.

7. Slightly round over the inside edges of the front and back rails. Schneider uses a

PHOTO A: Use a hole saw to drill the arcs in the front rail of the bottle rack. Place the workpiece against a fence that sits ½ in. forward of the hole saw pilot bit.

⅛-in.-radius roundover bit set a bit shy of a complete quarter-round.

8. Drill and countersink the angled clearance holes for the screws that will hold the side rails in their rabbets (see **photo B** on p. 160).

9. Glue and screw the side rails into their rabbets using 1¼-in.-long screws in the upper holes to prevent the screws from projecting into the rear arcs. Use 1⅜-in.-long screws in the lower holes. If you need to drill a pilot first, make it small to prevent the screws from stripping out the end grain.

10. Lay out the shelf-support notches on the bottom edges of the side rails (see "Rack Layout").

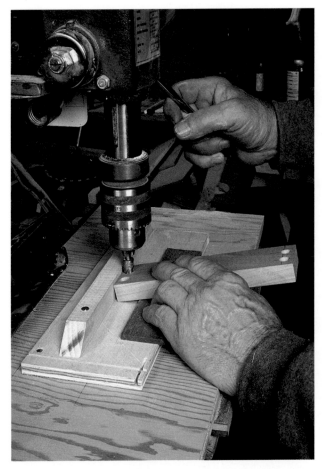

PHOTO B: Drill and countersink clearance holes in the end rails of the bottle racks for attachment to the front rails. To angle the holes, rest the workpiece on a ³⁄₁₆-in.-thick shim set back 1¼ in. from the drill-press fence.

PHOTO C: Schneider uses a ⅝-in.-dia. Forstner bit to drill the shelf-support notches in the undersides of the bottle rack side holes.

TIP

When drilling shelf-support holes, use a brad-point drill bit to minimize grain tearout.

11. Drill the shelf-support notches using a flat-bottom bit, such as a Forstner bit (see **photo C**).
12. Slightly round over all the remaining edges on the racks and sand the racks through 220 grit.

Make the wineglass racks

1. Plane and saw the rails to size.
2. Cut the cove profiles in the edges. Schneider used a molding head on the tablesaw, but you could rout the profile after wasting most of the cove on the tablesaw (see "Cutting the Wineglass Rack Rail Profile").

3. Drill and countersink two screw clearance holes in each rail for attachment to the case top.
4. Sand the rails through 220 grit.

Finishing Up

1. Touch-up sand the case and racks as necessary.
2. Apply an alcohol-resistant finish. This cabinet was finished with several coats of wiping varnish (see the section "A Favorite Finish" on p. 19).
3. Attach the wineglass rails with #6 by 1¼-in. screws (see **photo D**).
4. Fill cabinet with wine, and celebrate with a glass of Merlot.

Cutting the Wineglass Rack Rail Profile

Step 2.
Rout remainder
of cove.

Router table
fence

Step 1.
Waste bulk of
cove on table saw.

Wineglass rail
(end view)

Router table

$\frac{1}{2}$"-diameter corebox bit

PHOTO D: Screw the wineglass racks to the underside of the case top through predrilled countersunk clearance holes.

TOY CHEST

Jeff Miller

A TOY CHEST IS SOMETHING different for a grown-up than it is for a child. For the child it's simply a place to stash everything when told to put stuff away. It needs to be big. Once in a while, it's also a place to play; either on or in. It should be fun. For a grown-up it represents all that, plus a preserve for orderliness or at least a place to hide the mess. But first and foremost it has to be safe. The lid must be well supported so it can't slam on fingers, and it must not close airtight, in case someone does decide to play inside of it.

This toy chest fills the requirements for both. It's also fairly easy to build, being relatively free of complicated woodworking joints. It can be made of a hardwood or edge-banded plywood, nicely finished, or poplar or soft maple that is painted and decorated. There's an optional inner tray to help organize some of the junk inside. For safety, there is a lid stay (support)—not at all optional—to prevent the lid from slamming. The front edge of the box is lowered to protect fingers further and to provide ventilation in case a child closes himself or herself inside.

TOY CHEST

The five panels that make up the box of the toy chest are screwed together, making for simple joinery. The ball feet are purchased but are modified using a special jig. The molding that runs around the box adds character to it all and is easy to make with a drill press.

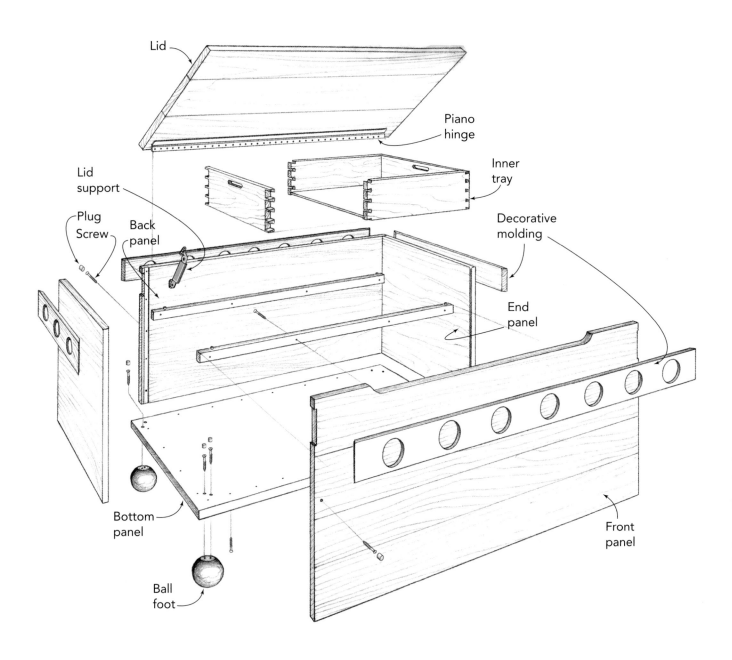

Lid

Piano hinge

Inner tray

Lid support

Plug Screw

Back panel

Decorative molding

End panel

Bottom panel

Ball foot

Front panel

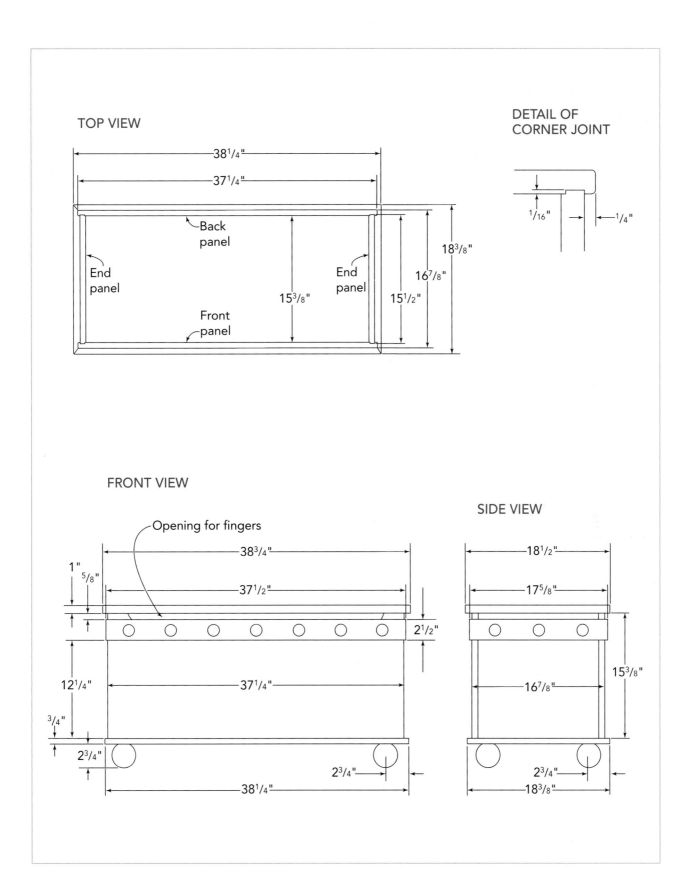

TOP VIEW

38¹/₄"

37¹/₄"

Back panel

End panel

End panel

Front panel

18³/₈"

16⁷/₈"

15¹/₂"

15³/₈"

DETAIL OF
CORNER JOINT

¹/₁₆"

¹/₄"

FRONT VIEW

Opening for fingers

38³/₄"

37¹/₂"

1"

⁵/₈"

2¹/₂"

12¹/₄"

37¹/₄"

³/₄"

2³/₄"

2³/₄"

38¹/₄"

SIDE VIEW

18¹/₂"

17⁵/₈"

15³/₈"

16⁷/₈"

2³/₄"

18³/₈"

CUT LIST FOR TOY CHEST		
2	Panels (1 front and 1 back)	¾" x 15⅜" x 37¼"
2	End panels	¾" x 15⅜" x 15½"
1	Bottom panel	¾" x 15½" x 35½"*
2	Edge pieces	¾" x 1⅜" x 38¼" (cut to fit)
2	Edge pieces	¾" x 1⅜" x 18¼" (cut to fit)
4	Wooden balls	3" dia.
1	Top	1" x 18½" x 38¾"
2	Decorative molding pieces	⅜" x 2½" x 17½"
2	Decorative molding pieces	⅜" x 2½" x 37½"
Hardware		
	Screws	#6 x 1⅝"
	Screws	#6 x 2"
	Wooden plugs	
1	Piano hinge	1½" x 36" (cut down to 34")
1	Lid stay	
Optional Inner Tray		
2	Sides	½" x 4½" x 15"
2	Ends	½" x 4½" x 15¼"
1	Bottom	¼" plywood, 14½" x 14¾"
2	Cleats	¾" x 1" x 35¼"
4	Screw-on rubber bumpers	⅝" dia.

*Hardwood plywood

Three-Quarter View

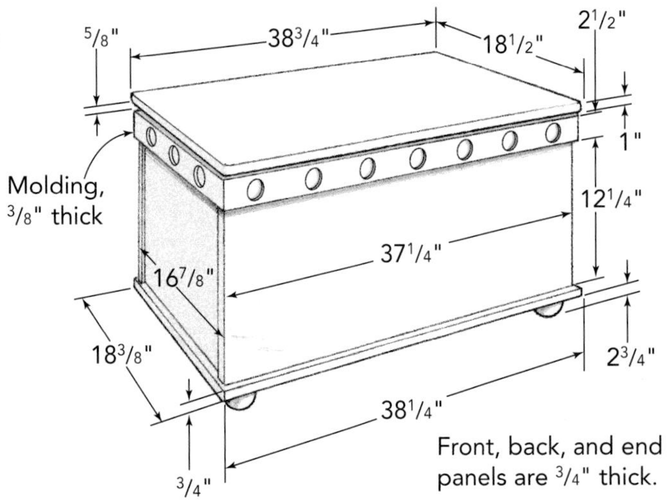
5/8"
38 3/4"
18 1/2"
2 1/2"
1"
Molding,
3/8" thick
12 1/4"
37 1/4"
16 7/8"
18 3/8"
2 3/4"
38 1/4"
3/4"
Front, back, and end
panels are 3/4" thick.

THERE ARE LOTS OF WAYS to put together the four sides of a box like this. I opted for the relative simplicity of dadoes and screws, because I didn't really want to see a lot of joinery at the corners.

Making the Box

Preparing the panels

Start by preparing all of the panels that will make up the box.

1. Mill all of the wood for the chest front, back, and sides to ¾ in. thick. If you're making a chest of a nice hardwood, you might rip all of this stock to the same width or along lines that yield the best of the wood's figure.

2. Mill the wood for the top to 1 in. thick.

3. Joint all edges straight and smooth.

4. Arrange the boards the way you want them and mark them with a layout triangle so you can put them back together in order.

5. Check the edges to be sure they are all straight. If not, rejoint and check again.

6. Get everything you'll need for a glue-up, then glue the boards together. Leave the boards in clamps for at least 1 hour or 2 hours if you're using yellow glue. Don't move on to smoothing out the panels for at least 24 hours.

7. Plane, scrape, and/or sand the panels flat and smooth.

8. Cut the panels to size.

9. Round over the ends of the front and back panels slightly. I used a 1/8-in. round-over bit in the router.

Cutting the box joinery

It doesn't really matter how you put the boards together, as long as the basic box is secure. I dadoed the front and back panels, rabbeted the sides to fit, and then screwed the box together (see "Joinery Details").

1. Cut a 1/16-in.-deep by 5/8-in.-wide dado on the inside face of both ends of the front and back panels, 1/4 in. away from the edges (see **Photo A**).

2. Cut a shallow rabbet on the inside of each end of the end panels, then fit the end panels into the dadoes in the front and rear panels.

3. Drill four countersunk pilot holes for #6 by 1⅝-in. screws in the front and rear panels so the screws will be centered on the end panels; these should be ¹¹/₁₆ in. from the ends of the front and back panels.

4. Lay out and cut the notches for the decorative molding ⅝ in. down from the top edge of both the front and the back panels (see "Joinery Details"). These notches should be 2½ in. wide (exactly the same as the molding) and at least deep enough to reach the dado for the end panels. Because it is not critical that the bottoms of the notches be

Joinery Details

Because of variations in thickness, solid panels are often easier to fit in a groove if cut to a shallow rabbet.

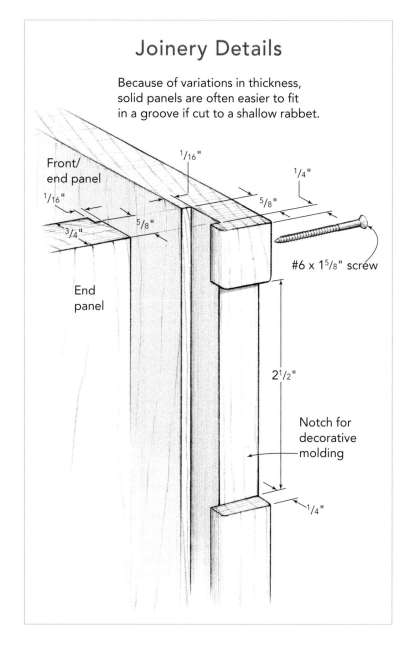

Front/end panel

1/16"

1/16"

3/4"

5/8"

5/8"

1/4"

End panel

#6 x 1⅝" screw

2½"

Notch for decorative molding

1/4"

PHOTO A: Cut the dadoes on the front and rear panels on the tablesaw. A crosscut sled makes the job safer and easier.

PHOTO B: I cut the notches for the decorative molding on the bandsaw. After cutting both ends of the notch, I nibbled away enough wood to leave room for the blade and then I cut along the bottom of the notch.

PHOTO C: You can use the hinge itself as an accurate positioning jig for drilling the pilot holes for the screws. A self-centering drill bit makes the job much easier.

perfectly smooth, I just cut out the notches on the bandsaw, which required no special setup (see **Photo B**).

Assembling the box

1. Spread a small amount of glue into each of the dadoes.
2. Fit the panels into position, aligning the top and bottom edges and holding them together with clamps. Then drive the screws into the pilot holes.
3. Plug the holes.

Sanding the outside and leveling the edges

1. When the glue is dry, cut off the plugs and sand them flush with the panel surface.
2. Go over the rest of the box and sand where necessary. Be sure to sand the end grain on the front and rear panels.
3. Level off the top and bottom edges by planing or sanding carefully with a sanding block. On the bottom, the goal is a flat edge that will mate well with the bottom of the toy chest. The top back and side edges should be eased enough so they will not cause any scrapes or scratches. Don't worry about the front edge for now.

Locating the lid hinge

Because the decorative molding will get in the way of setting up the piano hinge on the back of the box, this is a good time to drill the pilot holes for all of the screws.
1. Cut the piano hinge to 34 in. long or close to that length while cutting at a seam. File the cut edges smooth.
2. Open the piano hinge as far as it will go (this should be roughly 270 degrees), and place it on the back edge of the chest with the knuckle up and to the outside and with the unfolded leaf extending down outside of the back. This unfolded leaf will work as a stop to hold the hinge in the right position (see **Photo C**).
3. Drill the pilot holes for the screws. This is easy to do with a self-centering drill bit.
4. Set aside the hinge and the screws for later.

Making the decorative molding

The molding has no function, but it is one of the things that makes the overall design work.
1. Mill the stock for the molding to ⅜ in. thick and rip to width. It's a good idea to sand the outside face now as well, before you start drilling the holes in it.
2. Cut the strips roughly to length (a couple inches long is fine for now). Miter one end of each strip.
3. Fit each piece to the case and mark out the opposite end. It may help to have a

mitered piece of scrap to hold around the corner, so you're sure that the end is in exactly the right place before marking the end you need to cut. Cut each of the strips to length.

4. Lay out the locations for the holes (see "Decorative Molding").

5. Drill the holes, then ease all of the outside edges.

6. Attach the molding to the box by gluing and clamping in place. Be careful with the glue so you don't have to clean up a lot of squeeze-out inside the holes.

Making the Base of the Chest

Begin work on the bottom of the toy chest by cutting a piece of hardwood plywood to about ⅛ in. less than the outer dimensions of your box. This way, the seam for the solid-wood edge-banding will remain covered.

Edging the bottom of the chest

1. Mill the wood for the edge pieces to ¾ in. thick (about ½₂ in. thicker than the plywood) and rip to 1⅜ in. wide. Cut into pieces long enough for each edge (including the miters on the ends).

2. Miter one end of each of the edge pieces.

3. Scribe the location of the opposite corner onto the inside of the edge pieces (see **Photo D**).

4. Cut the miter on this corner so it just touches your scribed line. Note that the two pieces may be slightly different if your plywood is not exactly square. Mark carefully so you know which piece goes on which side.

5. Glue the two longer pieces of edging to the plywood bottom.

6. When the glue is dry, remove the clamps and work on getting the short edge pieces to fit. Mark carefully, then cut to size. I like to start long and work slowly toward a perfect fit. Repeat for the other end.

7. Glue the end pieces on. Spread some glue on the miters as well as on the edges, and clamp in place.

8. Plane and sand the edging flush with the panels. It's best not to plane through

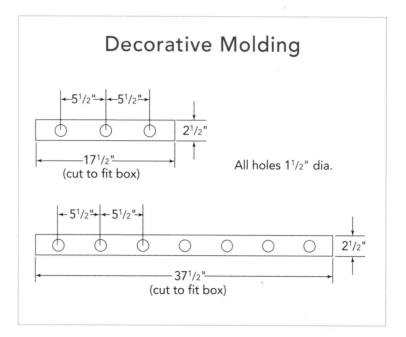

Decorative Molding

All holes 1½" dia.

PHOTO D: Accuracy when cutting the mitered edge pieces comes from working methodically and checking each piece in its place.

the veneer on the panel, but don't worry about it too much, since the seam is hidden from view.

9. Sand the edges smooth. Then round over both the top and bottom edges on all four sides with a ¼-in. roundover bit in a router.

Making the ball feet

The feet are 3-in.-dia. round balls that are commercially available in maple. You can turn your own ball feet, if you'd like.

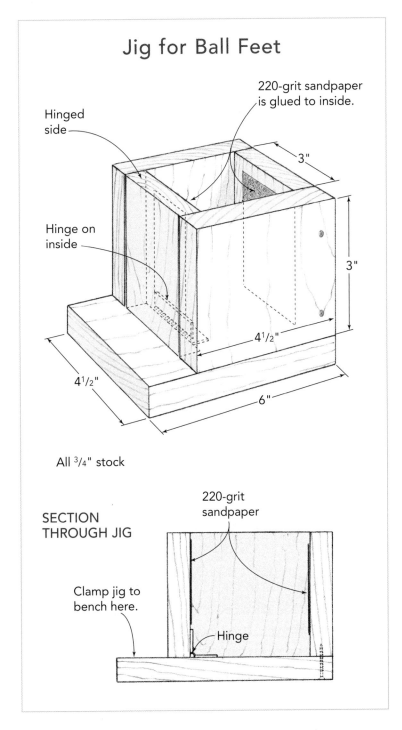

Jig for Ball Feet

Hinged side

220-grit sandpaper is glued to inside.

Hinge on inside

3"

3"

4½"

4½"

6"

All ¾" stock

SECTION THROUGH JIG

220-grit sandpaper

Clamp jig to bench here.

Hinge

PHOTO E: Clamp the ball tightly in the jig and the jig securely to the bench. Then rout the flat on the top with a straight bit.

1. You need to cut a flat on the top of each of the balls. Removing about ¼ in. will leave a flat that is roughly 1½ in. in diameter. For this, you need to make a jig to hold the ball securely during the work (see **Photo E** and "Jig for Ball Feet").

2. While the ball is still in the jig, mark out a spot roughly in the center of the flat, then drill a ³⁄₃₂-in. pilot hole about 1½ in. deep for the screw that will attach the ball to the bottom of the chest.

Attaching the feet to the bottom

Attach the feet to the bottom of the chest with screws and glue.

1. Mark out the location for each of the feet on the top of the bottom panel at a point 2¾ in. from each of the edges. Mark the upper face of the bottom panel.

2. Drill countersunk pilot holes down from the top of the bottom panel on your marks.

3. Put a daub of glue on the flat on the top of the foot, then insert a #6 by 2-in. screw in the pilot hole closest to the corner in the bottom panel until it just sticks out the underside. Place a foot in place and screw down tight (see **Photo F**). Add the second screw. Repeat for each of the other feet.

4. Plug the countersunk holes, then cut off the plugs and sand them flush with the surface of the bottom panel.

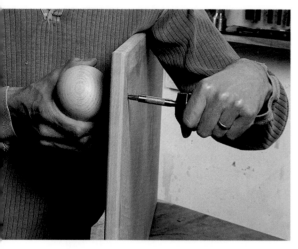

PHOTO F: Hold the ball foot to keep it from turning when you tighten the screw.

Attaching the bottom to the chest

1. Mark out and drill countersunk pilot holes for the screws to attach the bottom to the box. There should be three evenly spaced holes on each end and five evenly spaced holes on each side. Be sure to drill and countersink from the underside of the bottom panel.

2. Place the box upside down on a pair of sawhorses or a workbench and position the bottom panel carefully. When the panel is centered on the box, clamp in place and secure with #6 by 1⅝-in. screws.

3. Plug all of the holes, then trim off with a chisel or saw and sand the plugs flush with the bottom.

Making the Lid

The lid is 2 in. longer but only 1⅝ in. wider than the box (the back can't overhang as much as the sides or front).

1. Cut the lid to size (see "Lid Details").

2. Smooth all of the edges and use a ⅜-in.-rad. router bit to round over all but the back underside edge where the hinge will go.

3. A solid-wood top on an enclosed box like this would usually be subject to some warping, since the moisture content of the air outside a closed box can be different from that on the inside. The ventilation slot and the fact that the lid does not sit completely tight to the box help equalize things here. If

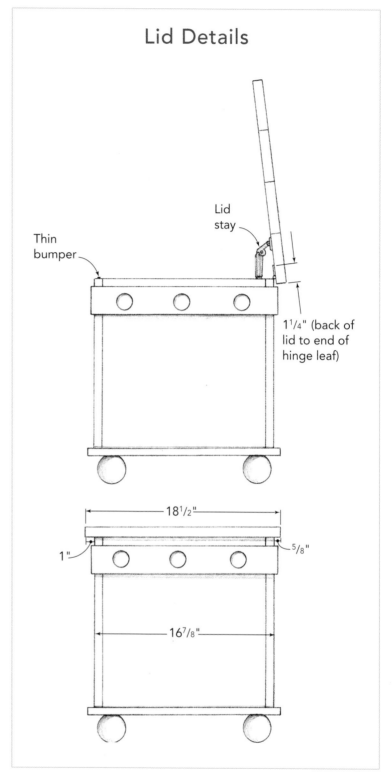

Lid Details

Thin bumper

Lid stay

1¼" (back of lid to end of hinge leaf)

18½"

1"

⅝"

16⅞"

you have problems with warping, you can add battens to the underside of the lid. The outer holes for screwing the battens to the lid must be elongated to allow for wood movement; the center holes do not need this.

PHOTO G: The bearing of the flush-trimming bit references off the edge of the decorative molding. The cut is stopped when the router base contacts the box.

PHOTO H: Mark the hinge location on the underside of the lid after centering the lid on the chest.

Routing the front top edge of the box

The top edge of the front of the box is recessed to keep fingers from getting smashed there when the lid is closed and to provide ventilation in case someone decides to play inside the box.

1. Tip the box forward onto the front face.

2. Using a router with a flush-trimming bit, rout the top of the front panel flush with the decorative molding. You may want to clamp

a piece of scrap into place on the right side of the box to prevent the router from chipping out some of the edge as it exits the cut (see **Photo G**).

3. Sand the routed edge smooth and ease the corners.

Hinging the lid

The lid can overhang the back of the box by only ⅜ in.; any longer and it will bang into the molding on the back. The lid will not be able to open more than 90 degrees because of the lid stay, so the overhang, which would otherwise keep it from opening more than that, won't be a problem.

1. Place the hinge on the back edge of the box and drive in a few screws to hold it in position. Close the hinge. Place the top on the box, positioning it so that it's centered from side to side and the back edge is flush with the outside of the box. Mark out the ends of the hinge on the underside of the top (see **Photo H**). Remove the lid, and unscrew and remove the hinge.

2. Transfer your end marks forward 1 in.; then scribe a line 1¼ in. from the back edge of the lid.

3. Clamp the hinge in position with the edge of the leaf on the scribed line and the ends lined up with the end marks.

4. Drill pilot holes for the screws.

5. Screw the hinge to the box. Then hold the lid in place and screw the other leaf of the hinge to the lid.

Adding the lid stay

It is critical that you add a lid stay to support the lid in any position so it can't drop down on fingers. Lid stays generally come with specific mounting instructions. The lid stay I used has a strong spring and a cam. It is very effective.

Finishing

However you decide to finish the outside of the toy chest, don't use an oil finish on the inside. This will smell rancid after just a short time. I used an oil-and-wax finish on the outside and shellac on the inside.

THE OPTIONAL INNER TRAY

Make the optional inner tray about 15 in. long and ⅛ in. less in length than the inside distance between the front and the back. I made the tray 4½ in. high, which left room to rout handles on the ends. The tray sides should be ½ in. thick. Join the tray together however you please, as long as it will be sturdy enough to stand up to some abuse.

Installing the Cleats

Screw the cleats that will support the inner tray into place 5½ in. down from the top. Attach screw-on rubber bumpers to the cleats on both sides. These will keep the tray from banging into the sides of the box and will leave room for the lid stay to fold down. If the lid stay needs more room, move the bumper on that side farther away from the end panel.

This peek inside the toy chest shows the optional inner tray, the cleats it rests on, the rubber bumpers, and the lid support.

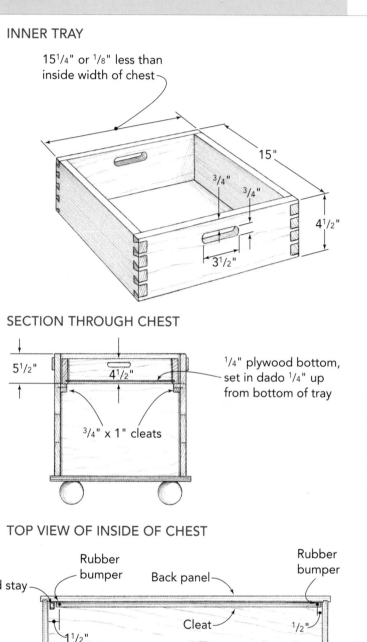

INNER TRAY

15¼" or ⅛" less than inside width of chest

15"

¾"

¾"

4½"

3½"

SECTION THROUGH CHEST

5½"

4½"

¼" plywood bottom, set in dado ¼" up from bottom of tray

¾" x 1" cleats

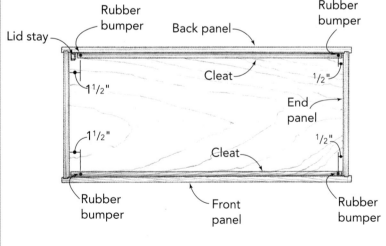

TOP VIEW OF INSIDE OF CHEST

Rubber bumper

Lid stay

Back panel

Rubber bumper

Cleat

½"

1½"

End panel

1½"

Cleat

½"

Rubber bumper

Front panel

Rubber bumper

MOBILE CLOSET

Paul Anthony

I

T'S NOT UNUSUAL FOR AN APARTMENT or house to lack closet space. And it's often simply not feasible to construct a built-in closet, especially if you're renting. Well, here's an unusual solution, a closet that's both easy to make and extremely portable.

Furniture maker Denis Kissane designed this portable closet as an entry for a national design competition, where it won an award in the "contract furniture" division. Kissane intended it for use in hostels and hotels, but has found it to also be very popular for guest bedrooms. The open case makes the unit lightweight and allows clothes to air out. Kissane used a commercially made chrome clothes bar, but you could use dowel rod instead.

Because it was designed for production, the closet is fairly easy to make. The tops, shelves, and divider are all the same width, and the tops and shelves are all the same length. Kissane built the case from cherry plywood, complimenting it with solid maple drawer fronts, posts, and rails. For aesthetic reasons, he made the case top, bottom, and divider 1 in. thick, gluing together ¾-in.-thick plywood and ¼-in.-thick plywood. But if you like, you can simply make those pieces from ¾-in.-thick plywood to save on time and materials.

MOBILE CLOSET

All the panels are edged with ¼"-thick solid wood and then joined together with #10 biscuits. The posts and rails are also joined to the case with biscuits. The drawers ride on center-mounted wooden slides.

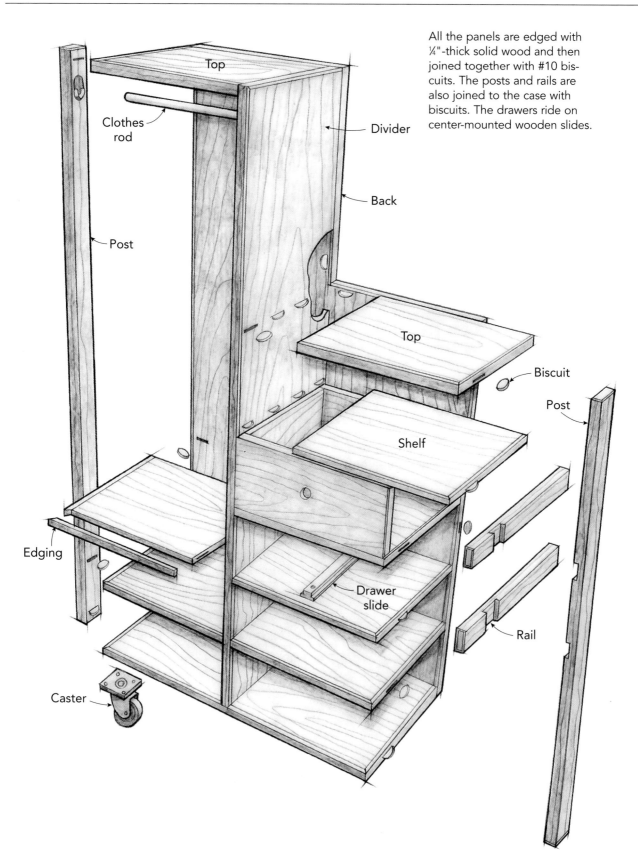

Top

Clothes rod

Divider

Back

Post

Top

Biscuit

Post

Shelf

Edging

Drawer slide

Rail

Caster

Side and Front Views

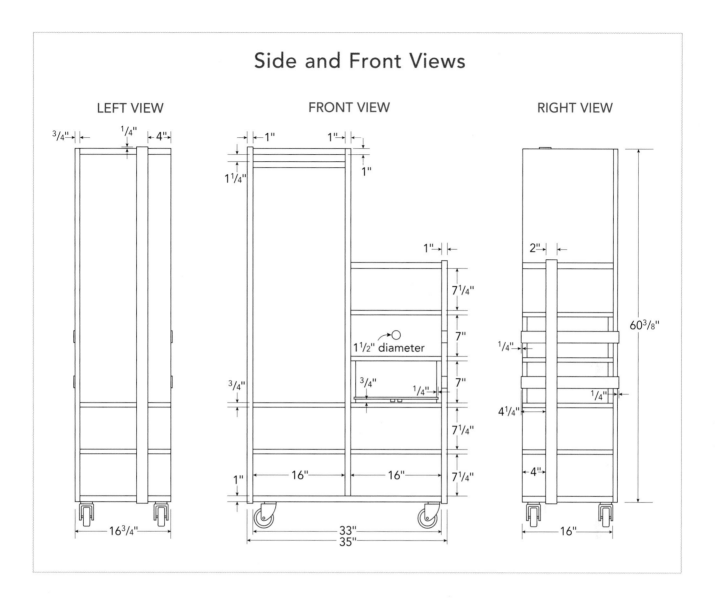

LEFT VIEW

FRONT VIEW

RIGHT VIEW

DESIGN OPTIONS

✦ Use ¾-in.-thick plywood for the divider, top, and bottom.

✦ Totally enclose the cabinet with sides and overlay doors.

✦ Install more drawers in the compartments and use commercial pulls, if desired.

✦ Install an overlay door over the clothes rod compartment.

BEGIN BY MAKING THE CASE and then the drawers. You'll saw all of the plywood pieces to size and then apply edging to them. After milling the posts and rails, you'll cut the joints and assemble the case. All that remains at that point is to make the drawers and apply a finish.

Building the Case

Make the pieces

1. Inspect your plywood sheets in preparation for laying out the parts. I shut off my overhead shop lights, draw the window blinds, and use a strong sidelight to inspect for scratches, dings, and imperfections (see **photos A** and **B** on p. 179).

CUT LIST FOR MOBILE CLOSET

Case

1	Divider	¾" x 15¾" x 59⅛" (59⅜")	hardwood plywood
1	Divider	¼" x 15¾" x 59⅛" (omit)	hardwood plywood
2	Tops	¾" x 15¾" x 15¾"	hardwood plywood
2	Tops	¼" x 15¾" x 15¾" (omit)	hardwood plywood
1	Bottom	¾" x 15¾" x 32½" (32¼")	hardwood plywood
1	Bottom	¼" x 15¾" x 32½" (omit)	hardwood plywood
6	Shelves	¾" x 15¾" x 15¾"	hardwood plywood
1	Back	¾" x 32½" (32¼") x 60⅛"	hardwood plywood
1	Post	1" x 2" x 60⅞"	solid wood
1	Post	1" x 2" x 41¼"	solid wood
2	Rails	1" x 2" x 17¼"	solid wood
	Edging	¼" x appropriate width and length	solid wood

Drawers

4	Front/backs	¾" x 6⅞" x 15⅞"	solid wood
4	Sides	¾" x 6⅞" x 14⁷⁄₁₆"	solid wood
2	Bottoms	¼" x 14¹⁵⁄₁₆" x 14⅞"	hardwood plywood

Other materials

2	Drawer slides (wood; center-mount)		from Rockler; item # 24877
4	Casters (total-lock)	3"	from Rockler; item # 31870
1	Oval clothes rod (chrome)		from Woodworker's Hardware; item #KV0880 CHR96

If using ¾"-thick tops, dividers, and bottom, cut to dimensions in parentheses.

2. Lay out the parts for the tops, shelves, bottom, and divider. If the plywood has imperfections, try to hide them on the undersides of shelves or within the drawer compartments.

3. Cut the pieces. If you're going to make the tops, divider, and bottom 1 in. thick, as Kissane did, cut all those pieces slightly oversize in length and width. You'll trim them to final size afterward. If you're going to simply use ¾-in.-thick material for those parts, go ahead and cut them to final size now.

4. Glue together the ¼-in.-thick and ¾-in.-thick plywood to make the 1-in. thickness for the tops, divider, and bottom. As these are fairly large panels and you may not have the panel-pressing equipment, this may be a time to improvise. You can weigh down the panels with a sheet of ¾-in.-thick particleboard loaded down with cinderblocks or other heavy objects.

5. Saw the laminated panels to final size.

6. Lay out the back panel. When marking for the L-shaped cutout, remember to account for the ¼-in.-thick solid-wood edging all around the panel edges.

7. Saw the back panel. After cutting it to length and width, saw the L-shaped cutout. You can make the longer cut on the tablesaw, stopping short at the end and finishing the cut with a jigsaw. The shorter cut can be made by guiding a portable circular saw against a straightedge. Make the cut a bit wide, then rout to the cut line with a straight bit to smooth the edge.

8. Plane, joint, rip, and crosscut the rails and posts to size. At the same time, mill a couple extra short pieces of stock to use for test material when setting up the saw to cut the post-and-rail half-lap joint.

TIP

Although contact cement is a very convenient way of laminating panels, many woodworkers have found that the bond can be unreliable in the long run. If you don't want to risk future delamination, use white or yellow glue instead.

9. Make the edging, ripping the strips from a board that you've planed to ¹⁄₁₆ in. thicker than the edge to be covered. Also, crosscut the strips to about ¼ in. oversize in length. The edging will be trimmed flush to the plywood after attaching it.

Apply and trim the edging

There's quite a bit of mitered edging to apply to these pieces. If you work systematically and carefully, the work should go fairly quickly—and the result will be beautiful.

1. In preparation for the next steps, lay out the pieces for orientation, marking the rear edges of the pieces with triangles (see "Triangle Marking System" on p. 18).

2. Miter one end of each edging piece for the tops and shelves. Glue one of each pair to its plywood, carefully lining up the inside of the miter with the corner of the plywood. The ends opposite the miters should run a bit long, but you'll trim them later (see **photo C**).

3. After the glue cures, rout and plane the first piece of edging flush to the plywood (see **photo D** on p. 180). Then attach the remaining piece, also routing and planing it flush after the glue cures.

4. Fit the edging pieces to the case bottom. Carefully miter both ends of the front piece first, glue it in place, and trim it flush. Then fit and attach the side edging pieces, leaving them a bit long at the rear.

5. Fit and attach the edging to the divider and back. Try to fit the long pieces closely to length. You'll be paring the excess later, as it will be difficult to trim off on the tablesaw. Use cauls as necessary to distribute clamping pressure evenly on the edging.

6. Trim the square end of each edging piece flush to the plywood using a shim on the tablesaw (see **photo E** on p. 180). Because the divider and back can be awkward to feed on the tablesaw, flush up their ends using a very sharp chisel.

7. Finish-sand the faces of all the plywood panels now, because sanding into the corners

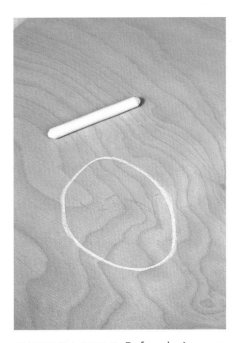

PHOTOS A AND B: Before laying out your plywood, inspect it for flaws using a strong, glancing sidelight in a darkened shop. The scar circled in chalk in the left photo is barely visible in normal light, but under a sidelight (right photo), it's immediately apparent.

PHOTO C: When fitting mitered edging pieces to length, rest the panels on thin shims and carefully align the inner edge of each miter to its panel corner. Test the fit by holding the adjacent pieces of mitered edging in place against the first miters.

will be difficult after assembly. Don't sand the edges yet. You'll do that after assembly.

Make the post-and-rail assembly

1. Lay out the half-lap joints that connect the rails to the right-hand post, as shown in the drawing on p. 176. The post is set back 4¼ in. from the front ends of the rails.

2. Mount a dado blade on your tablesaw and adjust its height to about ⁷⁄₁₆ in.

3. Using the extra pieces of stock you milled, fine-tune the height of the blade to cut exactly halfway through each piece. The easiest approach is to take a cut at each end of a piece and then fit them together for a look. Re-adjust the height of the blade a bit, take another pass on each piece, and check again. Repeat until the pieces are flush.

4. Glue and clamp the rails to the posts.

5. Using a sharp block plane, cut a small chamfer completely around the end of each post and rail.

PHOTO D: A laminate trimmer with a flush-trimming bit quickly routs the edging flush to the plywood panel. Afterward, smooth the joint with a block plane set for a very fine cut.

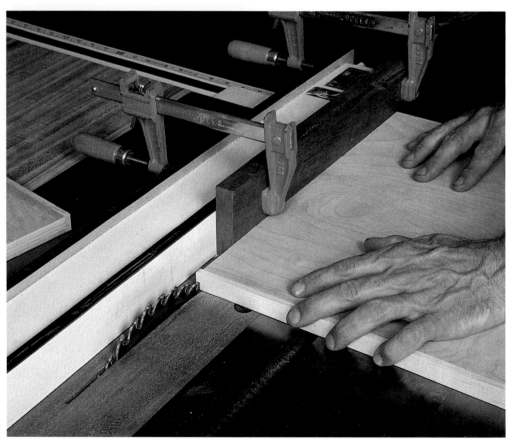

PHOTO E: To trim the ends of the edging, clamp a shim to your rip fence, aligning it with the outside edges of the sawteeth.

PHOTO F: After laying out the location of the top face of each shelf on the divider, clamp the shelf upside down with its edge aligned to the layout line. Mark the biscuit slot locations on the underside of the shelf.

Cut the biscuit joints

Now that all the parts are prepared, you're ready to cut the biscuit joints. If you don't have a biscuit joiner, you could dowel all of the parts together, working very carefully to align the dowel holes.

1. Lay out the shelf and right-hand top locations on the divider. Also lay out the divider location on the bottom. You need only gauge a short line where the top edge of each shelf meets the divider and where one side of the divider meets the bottom.

2. Lay out and cut the biscuit slots for the shelves and for the divider-to-bottom joint (see **photos F** and **G** and **photo H** on p. 182).

3. Lay out and cut the biscuit slots for joining the left-hand top to the divider. Right-angle joints like this involve registering the drop-down fence on the biscuit joiner against the end of the divider and the top edge of the shelf.

4. Lay out and cut the biscuit slots for joining the tops, bottom, shelves, and divider to the back.

5. Lay out and cut the biscuit slots for joining the posts and rails to the case. Note that the ends of the posts and rails all extend ¼ in. past the case edges.

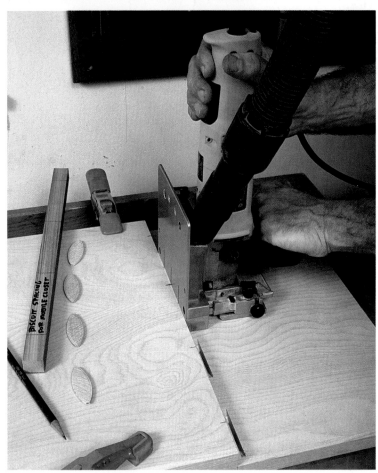

PHOTO G: Set the biscuit joiner for a #10 slot, align the center index line on the bottom of the joiner with the biscuit location mark, and plunge into the divider.

PHOTO H: Register the base of the biscuit jointer on the divider, align the biscuit joiner center index line with the biscuit location mark, and plunge into the edge of the shelf. The parts should now align perfectly.

Assemble the case

Gluing up the case needs to be done in stages. Because of the lack of case sides to help hold the pieces in place, assembly can be a bit awkward. Get a helper if you can and definitely rehearse every clamp-up procedure before getting out the glue bottle. After gluing each joint, immediately clean up excess glue with a clean rag and clean water.

1. Assemble the right-hand top and right-hand shelves to the divider. Use thick hardwood cauls to span the divider and pull the joint together tightly. Make sure everything is square under clamp pressure. Temporarily screwing a brace to the opposite ends of the shelves will help stabilize them. Attach the screws at the post location.

2. Glue and clamp the left-hand top and shelves to the divider.

3. Glue the divider to the bottom. You can use screws instead of clamps to pull this joint home.

4. Glue and clamp the left-hand post in place. If you don't have a deep-throat clamp large enough to reach from the edge of the shelf to the post, you can use band clamps.

5. Glue and clamp the back in place. Use thick, long, crowned cauls to distribute clamp pressure across the joints (see "Clamping Cauls" on p. 19).

6. Glue and clamp the post-and-rail assembly to the right-hand side of the case, again spanning the post with cauls if you don't have deep-throat clamps. Alternatively, you could attach the assembly with screws though counterbored holes, which you could plug later.

7. After the glue cures, plane or scrape all adjacent joints flush to each other.

Building the Drawers

The drawers are easy to make. They are simply boxes biscuited together at the corners. The bottoms sit in grooves routed in the front, sides, and back. The drawers ride on center-mounted wooden drawer slides.

Make the drawers

1. Cut the fronts, backs, and sides to size.
2. Rout the ¼-in. by ¼-in. grooves in all of the pieces to accept the drawer bottoms. The grooves sit ¾ in. up from the bottom edge of the pieces. The grooves in the front and back stop ½ in. from the ends.
3. Lay out and cut the slots at the corners for the #10 biscuits. Cut the lowest slots as close as possible to the drawer bottom groove without intruding into it.
4. On the drill press, bore the 1½-in.-dia. finger hole through the center of each drawer front.
5. Saw the drawer bottoms to size.
6. Dry-assemble the drawers to check the joint fit.
7. Glue and clamp the drawers. Make sure they are sitting on a flat surface and that they're square while under clamp pressure. Spot glue the bottoms into their grooves. Let the glue cure thoroughly.

Fit the drawers

Kissane used commercially available wooden slides, but you could make your own.

1. Fit the drawer half of the slide to the drawer, notching out the bottom edges of the drawer front and back and then gluing the slide in place (see "Wooden Drawer Slide"). Make certain that the slide is mounted perpendicular to the drawer front.

2. Cut the case half of each slide to length. The front end of the slide should stop ¾ in. short of the front edge of the shelf.

3. Center the case half of each slide across the width of its shelf and tack it in place with a small finish nail at each end. Insert the drawer and check to make sure it's centered. If necessary, tap the case half of the slide to better position it. When the drawer is centered, attach the slide using flat-head screws, countersinking them into the slide.

4. Check the gap all around the drawer to make sure it's consistent. If necessary, plane or sand the edges for a neat ¹⁄₁₆-in. reveal all around the front. To create the reveal at the bottom of the drawer front, plane it to create a bevel that rises slightly upward from the rear edge of the front.

5. Sand the drawers through 220 grit. Take care not to round over the exposed edges and corners too much. You want a crisp but friendly look here.

Finishing Up

1. Touch-up sand the panel faces where the grain was raised by the glue cleanup. Using 220-grit sandpaper, gently round over all edges and corners without over-sanding them.

2. Apply a finish. Kissane sprayed the closet with several coats of lacquer, but you could use any finish you like. Although the unit isn't likely to suffer much water or alcohol damage, the finish should be tough enough to resist some abrasion.

3. Attach the casters. Kissane used heavy-duty locking swivel casters, which ensure safety and allow great maneuverability.

4. Install the clothes rod brackets and cut the rod to size. Kissane used a commercial, oval-shaped, chrome rod, but you could use a wooden rod from a home-supply store.

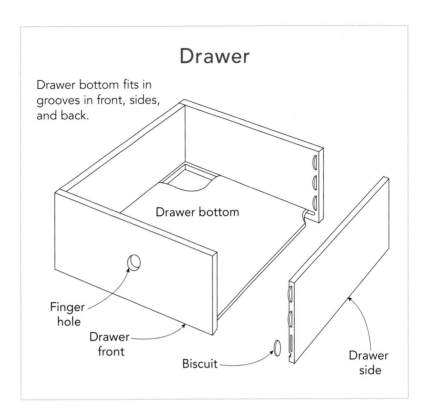

Drawer

Drawer bottom fits in grooves in front, sides, and back.

Drawer bottom

Finger hole

Drawer front

Biscuit

Drawer side

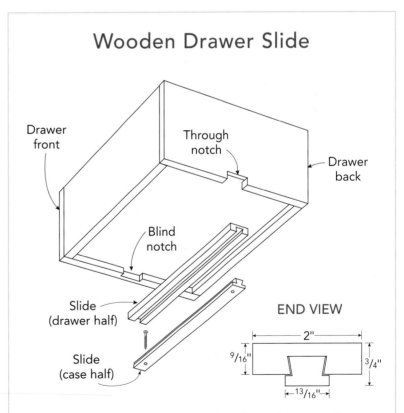

Wooden Drawer Slide

Drawer front

Through notch

Drawer back

Blind notch

Slide (drawer half)

Slide (case half)

END VIEW

2"

⁹⁄₁₆"

³⁄₄"

¹³⁄₁₆"

The drawer half of the slide is glued at the ends into notches cut into the drawer front and back. The case half is screwed to the shelf with countersunk flat-head screws.

STORAGE BED

Paul Anthony

ALMOST EVERYONE stashes things under the bed, particularly large items. But if you were to peek under the typical bed, you would find a jumble of stuff, usually shoved together in a dusty pile. Some solutions for underbed storage include using cardboard boxes or roll-out trays. But these are only partial fixes, as boxes need to be pulled entirely out to be opened, and most roll-out trays don't have lids to keep out dust.

Professional woodworker Ken Burton designed and built a bed platform that solves these problems. The platform consists of a pair of drawer cases that serve as a pedestal for his queen-size bed. The drawers provide clean storage with quick access,

and the space between the two cases creates a cavity for stashing long objects like skis, fishing poles, and bolts of fabric. Each case contains three large drawers joined at the corners with dovetails for great strength. A cavity at one end of the case allows access for bolting a headboard to the cases.

Burton used ¾-in.-thick fir AC-grade construction plywood for his cases because it's less expensive than hardwood plywood. The plywood shows only at the foot of an undraped bed. If you like, you can cover it there with veneer or more attractive panels. Burton's drawer fronts are walnut, but of course you can use any wood.

STORAGE BED

The twin cases are made from ¾"-thick plywood joined with glue and screws, using biscuits for easy alignment. The plywood edges around the drawer openings are covered with ¼"-thick solid-wood strips. The drawers are joined with through dovetails at the rear and half-blind dovetails at the front.

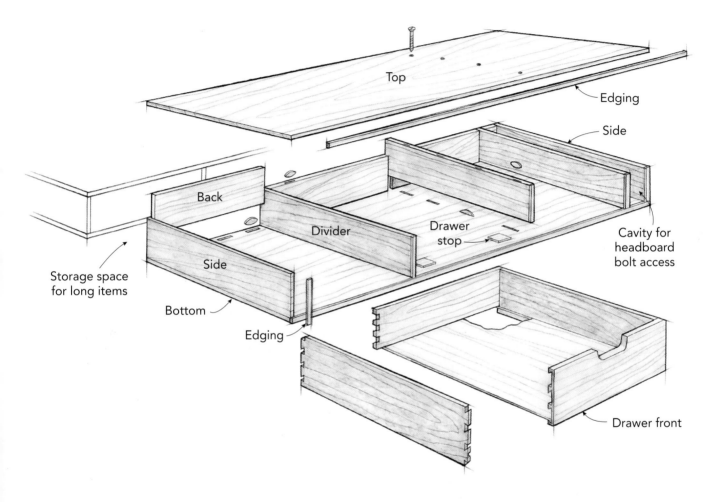

Top

Edging

Side

Back

Divider

Drawer stop

Cavity for headboard bolt access

Storage space for long items

Side

Bottom

Edging

Drawer front

DESIGN OPTIONS

✦ If the box springs are omitted, the drawers can be made deeper or stacked two high.

✦ A single case can be made to suit a twin bed mattress set.

✦ The drawers can be reduced in width by 1 in. and mounted on commercial slides.

✦ The headboard bolt cavity can be covered with a removable panel or omitted if no headboard is desired.

Top, Side, and Front Views

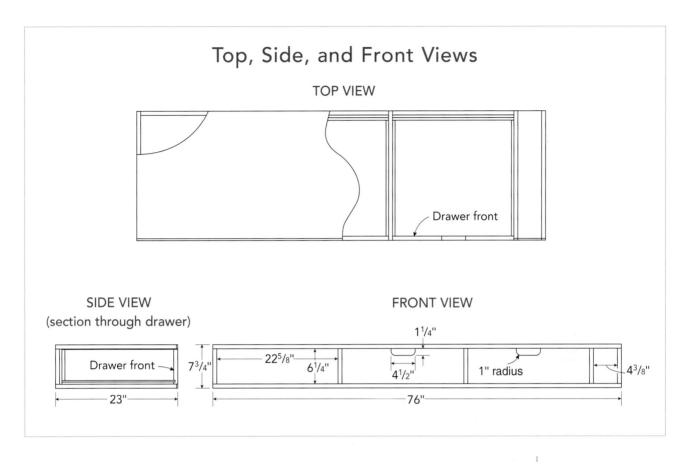

TOP VIEW

SIDE VIEW
(section through drawer)

Drawer front

23"

7³/₄"

FRONT VIEW

Drawer front

1¹/₄"

22⁵/₈"

6¹/₄"

4¹/₂"

1" radius

4³/₈"

76"

THE PEDESTAL CONSISTS simply of the cases and the drawers. The cases, which are easy to build, are made first. Then the drawers are constructed and fit to their openings.

Making the Case

Cut the pieces and apply the edging

1. Lay out the plywood pieces.
2. Cut the pieces to size. Rip the back pieces to width, but crosscut them about ⅛ in. oversize in length for now.
3. Mill the edging, ripping the strips from a ¹³/₁₆-in.-thick board. Crosscut each strip slightly longer than the edge to be covered.
4. Glue the edging to the pieces.
5. Scrape or sand the edging flush to the panels; then trim the ends flush.

Assemble the case

1. Lay out the biscuit joints on the inside faces of the top and bottom panels and on the top and bottom edges of the sides, dividers, and backs.
2. Cut the biscuit slots.
3. Dry-fit the sides and dividers between the top and bottom panels, then cut the backs to fit exactly into their openings. A good fit here will help keep the case square for a good drawer fit.
4. Test-fit the backs and double-check the entire case for good joint fits.
5. Glue and screw the case together, making sure that everything is as square as possible before driving the screws home. Wipe up any excess glue immediately with a clean, wet rag.

Making the Drawers

For the best fit, size the drawers to fit the height of their openings exactly, then hand-plane them for a snug but easy sliding fit after assembly. Dovetails are the best joint

TIP

When gluing edging strips to similarly sized panels, clamp up the panels in pairs with the strips in the center. The panels themselves will serve as clamping cauls to provide even pressure across the strips.

CUT LIST FOR BED PEDESTAL

Case			
2	Top and bottom	¾" x 22¾" x 76"	plywood
5	Dividers	¾" x 6¼" x 22½"	plywood
3	Backs	¾" x 6¼" x 22⅝"	plywood
	Edging stock	¼" x ¾" x 16'	solid wood
Drawers			
3	Fronts	¾" x 6¼" x 22⅝"	solid wood
3	Backs	9/16" x 5 9/16" x 22⅝"	solid wood
6	Sides	9/16" x 6¼" x 20¼"	solid wood
3	Bottoms	¼" x 20" x 21⅞"	hardwood plywood

Case parts are for one unit; drawer parts are for one case.

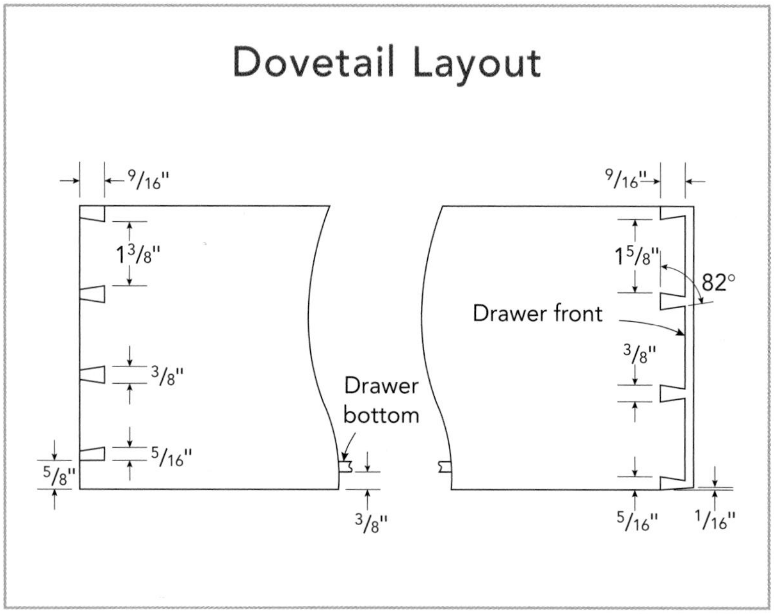

to use for large heavy drawers because they can withstand strong pulling forces. However, if you don't feel like tackling dovetails, you could use rabbet-and-dado joints with applied drawer fronts (see the instructions for the file cabinet on p. 270).

Prepare the stock

1. Mill stock for the drawer fronts. If possible, use one long board for each run of adjacent drawer fronts.

2. Lay out the drawer fronts, noting their sequence for continuous grain orientation in the case later.

3. Mill stock for the sides and backs.

4. Rip all of the pieces to width, taking measurements directly from the drawer openings. Rip the drawer fronts and sides to exactly the height of the openings. Rip the drawer backs ⅝ in. less than that.

5. Crosscut the pieces to length, making each drawer front and its matching back 3/32 in. less than the width of their drawer opening.

Cut the dovetails

These drawers use half-blind dovetails for the fronts and through dovetails for the drawer backs. Although we're using a hand dovetail technique here, you could also use one of the many popular router jigs for this operation.

1. Saw the ¼-in.-deep drawer bottom grooves in the front and sides. The grooves sit ⅜ in. up from the bottom edges.

2. Set a marking gauge to the thickness of the drawer side, then use it to scribe the dovetail-pin baseline across both faces of each pin board and tail board. Also scribe across the edges of the tail boards.

3. Using a bevel gauge set to about 82 degrees, lay out the angle of the pins with a sharp pencil (see **photo A**).

4. Saw the pins, staying to the waste side of the lines. A fine-tooth saw that cuts cleanly and tracks well makes all the difference when sawing dovetails. Lines extending from the workpiece edge to the scribed baseline help guide your cut (see **photo B**).

5. To remove the waste, begin by tapping just outside the baseline with a sharp chisel. With the bevel side of the chisel facing toward the end of the board, the force of the mallet will drive the chisel backward to the baseline.

6. Lean the chisel steeply and make a light V-cut back to the baseline to establish a shoulder for registering subsequent baseline cuts (see **photo C** on p. 190).

7. Deepen the baseline cut, angling the chisel just a bit to create a slight undercut

Dovetailed Drawer Construction

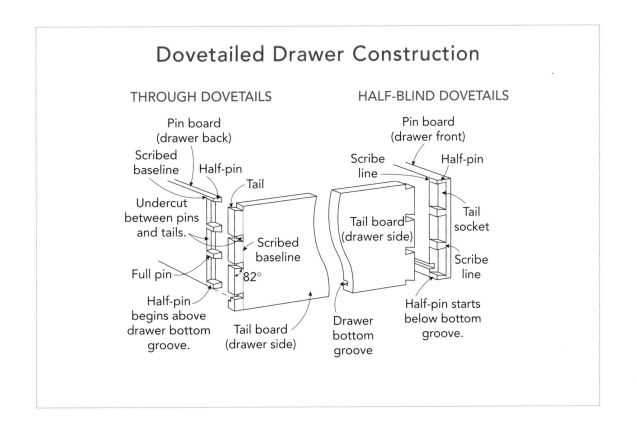

THROUGH DOVETAILS

Pin board (drawer back)

Scribed baseline

Half-pin

Tail

Undercut between pins and tails.

Scribed baseline

82°

Full pin

Half-pin begins above drawer bottom groove.

Tail board (drawer side)

HALF-BLIND DOVETAILS

Pin board (drawer front)

Scribe line

Half-pin

Tail board (drawer side)

Tail socket

Scribe line

Drawer bottom groove

Half-pin starts below bottom groove.

PHOTO A: Lay out the dovetail pins first, setting the bevel gauge to about 82°.

PHOTO B: Saw down carefully to the scribed baseline, keeping the saw vertical.

PHOTO C: Leaning the chisel helps establish a shoulder for the cuts.

PHOTO D: After chopping halfway through the pin board, flip it over and remove the remaining waste from the opposite side.

of the shoulder, which will help the joints close tightly.

8. Chisel backward at a steep angle to remove more waste. Make subsequent cuts in the same manner—first at the shoulder, then at a steep backward angle to remove the waste. Repeat until you're halfway through the workpiece.

9. Flip the workpiece over and chop away the remainder of the waste from the other side, working in the same way (see **photo D**).

10. Clean out any chips in the corners using a sharp knife.

11. Stand the pin board on the tail board and trace around the pins. Use a sharp pencil or knife, pulling it toward the wide face of the pins. Afterward, extend the lines across the end of the workpiece to help you cut squarely (see **photo E**).

12. To cut the tails, keep the sawblade to the waste side of a cut line, splitting it in half. Avoid cutting the tails so fat that you have to chisel them for a good fit—a very time-consuming practice.

13. Chisel away the waste between the tails as you did for the pins, again undercutting

PHOTO E: The tails are marked from the completed pins. Afterward, layout lines are extended squarely across the end of the tail board.

at the shoulder. Take care not to dig into the tails when leaning the chisel over (see **photo F**).

14. Saw away the waste at the edges, again splitting the line.

15. To lay out the half-blind pins, first set a marking gauge to the thickness of a drawer side; then scribe the inside face and edge of the drawer front (see **photo G.**)

16. After laying out the pins, saw as much of their cheeks as possible by angling the saw between the two scribed lines. Notice that the lower half-pin lies outside the drawer bottom groove (see **photo H** on p. 192).

17. Use a thin, unburnished scraper to deepen the cut, but be careful not to split the workpiece, especially if it's a hardwood. This technique works best with softer woods like poplar and pine (see **photo I** on p. 192).

18. After chiseling out the bulk of the waste, flatten the bottom of the tail socket down to the scribed line (see **photo J** on p. 193).

19. Stand the pin board on the tail board, aligning the bottom of the tail sockets with the end of the tail board, then trace the pins. Saw and chop the tails as before.

PHOTO F: Remove the waste between the tails, taking care not to dig into the crisp edges.

PHOTO G: With a marking gauge, scribe the inside faces and ends of the drawer fronts to begin layout of the half-blind dovetails.

PHOTO H: A saw starts the half-blind dovetail pins with an angled cut that joins the two layout lines.

Finish and assemble the drawers

1. Lay out the handholds. Then drill the ends of the cutouts on the drill press (see **photo K**).

2. Cut the straight bottom section of each handhold with a jigsaw or bandsaw, then sand the profile smooth with a drum sander. Rout both the inside and outside edges with a ¼-in.-dia. roundover bit to soften the feel.

3. Dry-assemble the drawers. Then cut the drawer bottoms to fit snugly between their grooves.

4. Glue up the drawers. If your joints were cut well, you shouldn't need to use clamps. However, if you need to clamp the joints, use cauls placed directly over the tails, with slots cut on the underside to span the pins (see "Dovetail Cauls"). Insert the drawer bottoms to keep the drawers square while the glue dries.

5. Screw each drawer bottom to the bottom edge of its drawer back.

Fit the drawers

1. Plane any saw marks off the top and bottom edge of each drawer, then lay the drawer on a flat surface to check for any

PHOTO I: Gently tap a scraper into the established kerf to finish the cut.

rocking. Plane the bottom if necessary to make the drawer rest flat.

2. Check the fit of each drawer in its opening. Plane the top edges until you've got an easy, sliding fit in the opening. If you're doing this during the humid summer season, leave the fit fairly tight. If you're working during the dry winter months, plane off a bit more to prevent the drawers from sticking when they swell during summertime.

3. Plane or sand the edges of the drawer front until you achieve an even gap of about ⅟₁₆ in. all around the drawer. Because of the drawer sides, the bottom edge of the drawer front would be difficult to plane squarely. Instead, plane it at an angle to create a gap at the front (see "Dovetail Layout" on p. 188).

4. Make the drawer stops from ¼-in.-thick wood and install two behind each drawer front to align it flush to the drawer case.

Finishing Up

1. Sand the case edging and the drawer fronts through 220 grit in preparation for finishing.

2. Apply a finish to the edging and drawer fronts. Burton wiped on four coats of a commercial oil and varnish blend, scrubbing between coats with 0000 steel wool.

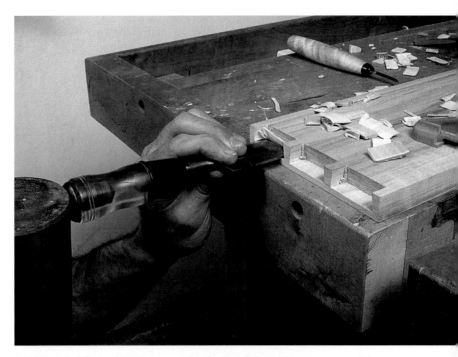

PHOTO J: After chiseling out the bulk of the waste, use a wide flat chisel to pare down to the layout lines.

Dovetail Cauls

Clamping caul

Pin　　Tail

If you need to clamp dovetail joints due to slightly loose fits or cupped boards, use notched cauls that span the pins.

PHOTO K: To create each drawer front hand hole, drill two holes with a 2-in.-dia. bit, then saw between the lower quadrants with a jigsaw or bandsaw to complete the cutout.

PART THREE
Media Areas

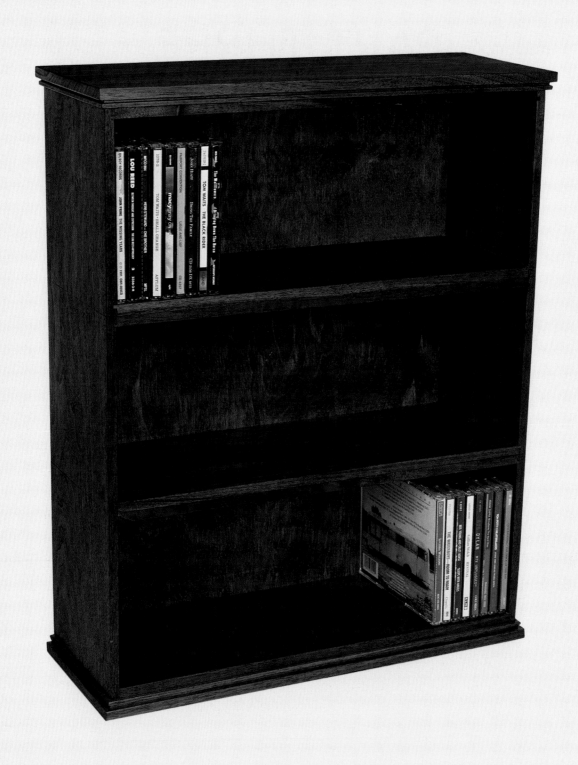

MODULAR COMPACT DISC CABINET

Paul Anthony

COMPACT DISCS have become almost as common as books these days. Music CDs have largely replaced vinyl records, and you'll usually find a stack of computer program CDs within reach of any computer. While CDs can be stored almost anywhere, there are few spaces ideally suited to them. Placed on a typical bookshelf, they waste a lot of space. Stored in a drawer, they'll scatter unless restrained within compartments. Commercial storage units for CDs are often unattractive, poorly made, and ill-suited to the size of your particular collection. A large unit may sit mostly empty for a long time, but a small unit can fill up more quickly than you'd think.

To solve those problems, I designed these cabinets as individual boxes, or modules, that are screwed together. A modular cabinet can be built to suit your current collection, but can be easily expanded to accommodate future discs when needed. The walnut cabinet shown here is composed of three modules stacked vertically, but you can configure the boxes any way you like. The modules are visually tied together by sandwiching them between top and bottom "caps," creating the look of a finished cabinet. As your CD collection grows, you can simply unscrew a cap, add a module, then reattach the cap. If you like, you can hang the cabinets on a wall by screwing through the plywood back into wall studs.

MODULAR COMPACT DISC CABINET

Like barrister bookcases, these CD modules are stacked together to create the look of a single cabinet. The modules are screwed together and sandwiched between top and bottom caps.

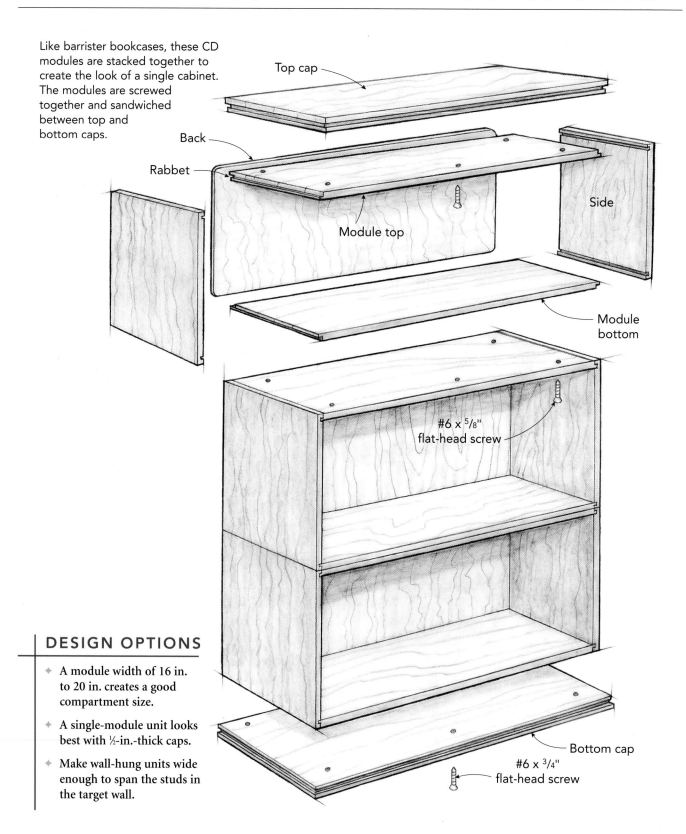

Top cap

Back

Rabbet

Module top

Side

Module bottom

#6 x $^5/_8$"
flat-head screw

DESIGN OPTIONS

✦ A module width of 16 in. to 20 in. creates a good compartment size.

✦ A single-module unit looks best with ½-in.-thick caps.

✦ Make wall-hung units wide enough to span the studs in the target wall.

Bottom cap

#6 x $^3/_4$"
flat-head screw

Cabinet Modules

To expand the cabinet vertically, remove a cap, add a module, and re-attach the cap. To expand the cabinet horizontally, make new top and bottom caps for the new modules.

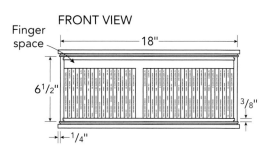

SINGLE-MODULE CABINET

FRONT VIEW

Finger space

18"

6½"

3/8"

1/4"

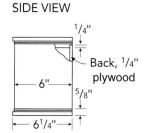

SIDE VIEW

1/4"

Back, 1/4" plywood

6"

5/8"

6¼"

FOUR-MODULE CABINET

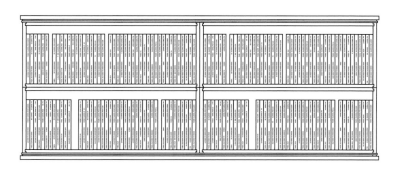

THREE-MODULE CABINET

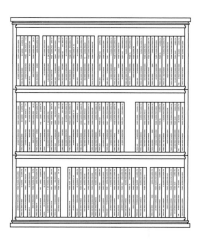

T HE CABINET MODULES use simple rabbet-and-dado joint construction with a plywood back. The top and bottom caps provide a lot of the appeal and are simply attached to the modules, tying them together visually.

Milling and Shaping the Stock

Lay out and prepare the stock

You could plane the ⅜-in.-thick stock down from store-bought ¾-in.-thick lumber, but it's much less wasteful to resaw the pieces from thick roughsawn stock. You'll get the best yield by using 6/4 or thicker stock, but

CUT LIST FOR COMPACT DISC CABINET

6	Sides	⅜" x 6" x 6½"	solid wood
6	Box tops and bottoms	⅜" x 6" x 17½"	solid wood
2	Caps	⅝" x 6¼" x 18½"	solid wood
3	Backs	¼" x 6¼" x 17¾"	hardwood plywood

Other materials

15	#6 x ⅝" flat-head wood screws
5	#6 x ¾" flat-head wood screws

Dimensions for an 18"-wide, three-module unit.

RESAWING ON THE BANDSAW

Resawing is a great way to economize on lumber when making thin pieces. But to do it successfully, your saw needs to be tuned properly and the fence needs to be set to accommodate "blade drift"—the blade's tendency to pull to one side.

Here are a few tips:

+ Use the widest blade your saw will accept and tension it so there is no more than ¼-in. flex with the blade guides set at maximum height. New blades cut and track the best.

+ Set the thrust bearings just a few thousandths of an inch behind the blade.

+ Set the guide blocks a few thousands of an inch (the thickness of a dollar bill) to the sides of the blade and just behind the tooth gullets.

+ Make a tall, flat, straight fence and set it to the angle of your blade drift. Make sure the blade and fence are parallel to each other.

+ Saw using a steady, even feed pressure, holding the workpiece firmly against the fence just in front of the blade, as shown at left. Pull the last inch or so through from the outfeed side of the saw.

+ Before making each subsequent slice from a workpiece, joint the face that will abut the fence.

if you're careful you can even saw two ⅜-in.-thick pieces from roughsawn 4/4 stock.

1. Lay out the pieces, allowing a couple of inches extra in length. Gang the side pieces together end to end to make for safer jointing and planing and to provide grain continuity on the cabinet sides, if desired. Lay out some extra stock for tool setup purposes and to allow for mistakes.

2. Cut the tops, bottoms, and caps to rough length, but keep the ganged sides together as a continuous piece for right now.

3. Joint one edge of each piece straight, rip it about ¼-in. oversize in width, then joint one face flat.

4. Resaw the pieces, then plane them to finished thickness (see "Resawing on the Bandsaw").

5. Joint one edge of each piece straight and square, rip the pieces to final width, and crosscut one end of each piece square.

6. Draw a line across the side pieces to register their relationships to each other, then crosscut all pieces to finished length. Use a stop block to ensure consistency of length.

Saw the joints and cap edging

1. Determine the inside face of each piece, then sand all the inside faces to 220-grit, being careful not to round over the edges.

2. Saw the ⅛-in. by ⅛-in. dadoes in the side pieces (see "Details"). Space the dadoes in from the ends so that the sides will overhang the top and bottom by about ¼₄ in. To create a relatively flat-bottom dado, use a sawblade that includes raker teeth (see **photo A**).

3. Using scrap, set up your saw to cut the ⅛-in. by ¼-in. rabbets in the tops and bottoms. Cut the tongue to thickness first, making the test cut a bit fat. Remove the rabbet waste using a different saw so that you can leave your tablesaw set up as is. Next, test-fit the tongue in a dado. Adjust the saw fence until the tongue fits snugly, but not too tightly, then cut the tongues on all of the pieces (see **photo B** on p. 202).

4. Saw the rabbet shoulders (see **photo C** on p. 202). Again, use scrap for the initial setup.

5. With the raker-tooth blade on your saw, rip the profile in the front and side edges of the caps.

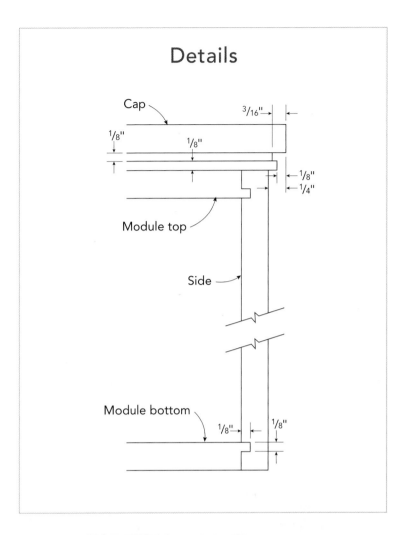

Details

Cap

3/16"

1/8"

1/8"

Module top

1/8"

1/4"

Side

Module bottom

1/8"

1/8"

PHOTO A: Press the stock firmly against the saw table to ensure dadoes of consistent depth.

PHOTO B: To make the rabbets on the box tops and bottoms, first cut each tongue to thickness, sliding it firmly against the table-saw rip fence.

PHOTO C: Cut the shoulder of the rabbet using a board clamped to the rip fence above the rabbet to prevent the cutoff from jamming between the blade and fence.

PHOTO D: Place thick hardwood cauls against the box sides to distribute clamping pressure along the joints.

Assembling the Case

Assemble and rout the modules

1. Mark all the pieces for their final position, remembering to pair up the sides to ensure continuous grain, if desired. I use the triangle marking system, shown on p. 18, to orient the pieces.

2. Glue up each module using thick cauls against the sides to distribute clamping pressure across the joints (see **photo D**). After clamping, check for square by comparing the diagonal measurements. If necessary, cock the clamps to bring the unit into square.

3. After the glue has cured, plane the edges of each module. Also plane the ends of the sides flush to the tops and bottoms.

4. Rout the ¼-in. by ¼-in. rabbet in the back edges of each module to accept a plywood back. Use a bit with a small bearing that can reach well into the corner. An auxiliary router base will stabilize the router on the thin workpiece edge (see **photo E**).

PHOTO E: To prevent tearout on the interior rabbet shoulder, first make a shallow "climb cut," carefully moving the router in a counterclockwise direction. Finish up by routing in a clockwise direction, as shown here.

SETTING THE DRIFT ANGLE

Any given bandsaw blade tends to cut in a particular direction, which isn't necessarily parallel to the edges of the saw table. To resaw successfully, your fence must be set to the angle the blade wants to cut.

1. Gauge a line parallel to the straight edge of a piece of scrap about 20 in. long (see top photo at left).

2. Carefully cut freehand to the line, stopping about halfway through the cut. Without changing the feed angle, hold the scrap firmly to the table and turn the saw off.

3. Trace the straight edge of the scrap onto the bandsaw table using a fine-tipped felt marker (see bottom photo at left).

4. Set the fence parallel to the line at a distance equal to the desired resaw thickness plus about 1/32 in. and clamp it in place (see photo below).

5. Test the setup using scrap. The blade should track nicely without pulling the workpiece into or away from the fence. Adjust the fence as necessary to fine-tune the drift angle.

Attach the modules and caps

1. Clamp the top two modules and the top cap together upside down to the bench. Drill pilot holes and countersink holes for #6 by ⅝-in. flat-head screws (see **photo F**). If you don't have a right-angle drill, you can use a right-angle adapter (see **photo G**).

2. Unclamp the modules and enlarge the pilot holes in the countersunk pieces to allow the screw to slip through and draw the two pieces tightly together.

3. Clamp the bottom module and bottom cap to the center module and repeat the above processes. (I clamp the modules in steps because it's awkward to align and clamp a lot of pieces at once.) Counterbore for #6 by ¾-in. flat-head screws to attach the bottom cap.

4. Screw the modules together, leaving the caps off for now.

5. Touch-up sand the insides of the modules and sand or plane the outsides flush to each other.

6. Sand the caps and screw them to the modules.

Make the backs

1. Cut the backs for a tight fit within their rabbets. Then sand or saw the corners to match the radius of the rabbet corner.

2. If you're going to stain the backs to match the color of the modules, do it now. To preserve a perimeter of raw wood for gluing, lightly trace around the inside of the module onto the back, mask just outside of the lines, and then stain.

3. Use glue and nails or staples to fasten the backs. Even if you're not planning to hang the cabinets, it's wise to glue the backs anyway, in case someone decides to hang them later.

Finishing Up

You can use just about any finish you like on a CD cabinet because it's not likely to be subjected to liquids or abrasion. I typically use several coats of a wiping varnish on the ones I build (see the section "A Favorite Finish" on p. 19).

PHOTO F: Drill for the screw holes using a combination pilot/countersink bit. Afterward, enlarge the hole in the countersunk piece to allow the screw to pull the modules tightly together.

PHOTO G: A right-angle drill adapter is an inexpensive alternative to a right-angle drill. This particular adapter accepts hex shanks. Other types incorporate adjustable chucks.

HOME OFFICE

Niall Barrett
Paul Anthony

LMOST ALL OF US have some kind of work space in our homes. Often it's nothing more than a corner of the kitchen where bills pile up and phone calls are answered, but just as often a small room or portion of a room is devoted to the normal paperwork generated from running a household. For the self-employed or telecommuters, this space does double duty as a location for home and business paperwork. For others, the home office is a place to enjoy surfing the Internet.

Since desktop computers became a household fixture, manufacturers have flooded the market with equipment such as printers, copiers, scanners, and telephones. Of course, putting all this electronic stuff on a small table will do in a pinch. Or you could make due with a desk from an office superstore. But if you have basic woodworking skills you can build your own home office furniture that will look better and most certainly last longer.

Part of the fun of working at home is deciding how you want your office to look, especially because there is no need to re-create the look of a commercial office. So take some time to plan how to arrange the elements of the office to best work for you. In this chapter we show how you can create integrated modules that can be rearranged in many ways. We also suggest some design options to change the style to suit your taste.

If you can put together a basic plywood box, you can build file cabinets, a desk, bookcases, and other accessories. At the end of the chapter are some stand alone accessories—a printer stand and a file cabinet—in case the idea of building a whole suite of office furniture is too daunting.

FILE DRAWER PEDESTAL

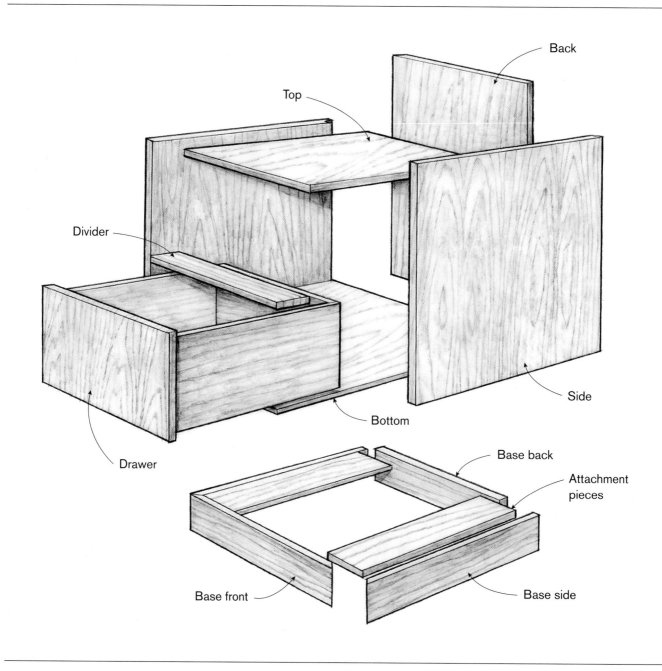

Back

Top

Divider

Side

Drawer

Bottom

Base back

Attachment pieces

Base front

Base side

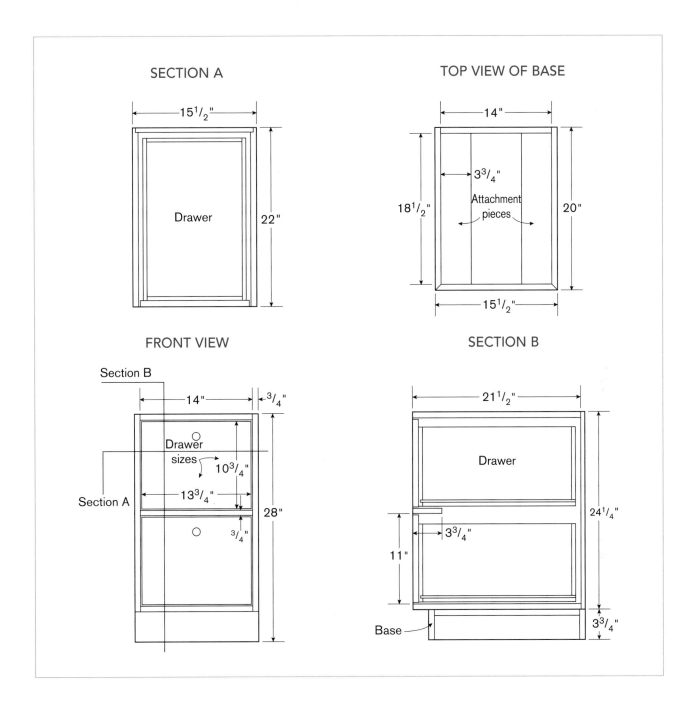

SECTION A

15¹/₂"

Drawer

22"

TOP VIEW OF BASE

14"

3³/₄"

Attachment pieces

18¹/₂"

20"

15¹/₂"

FRONT VIEW

Section B

14"

³/₄"

Drawer sizes

10³/₄"

13³/₄"

Section A

28"

³/₄"

SECTION B

21¹/₂"

Drawer

24¹/₄"

11"

3³/₄"

3³/₄"

Base

Construction and Assembly

THE MOST IMPORTANT ITEMS stored in offices are typically files. Two file sizes are in common use in the United States: letter size (8½ in. by 11 in.) and legal size (8½ in. by 14 in.). In a home office, most files will be letter size. With this in mind, I've designed the file drawers in this pedestal unit to be wide enough to fit letter-size files. However, you can fit legal-size files in the drawers if you store them side to side rather than front to back.

Layout

All of the projects in this book are constructed primarily of cherry veneer plywood, a relatively expensive material that is normally sold in 4x8 sheets. You don't want to waste material. On the other hand, you can't let material size drive all your decisions. I've tried to design most of the parts so they

CUT LIST FOR FILE DRAWER PEDESTAL

Base

1 Front	15½" x 3¾"	¾" cherry plywood
1 Back	14" x 3¾"	¾" cherry plywood
2 Sides	20" x 3¾"	¾" cherry plywood
2 Attachment pieces	18½" x 3¾"	¾" cherry plywood

Cabinet Box

1 Top	21½" x 14"	¾" cherry plywood
1 Bottom	21½" x 14"	¾" cherry plywood
1 Divider	14" x 3¾"	¾" cherry plywood
2 Sides	24¼" x 22"	¾" cherry plywood
1 Back	24¼" x 14¾"	½" cherry plywood

Drawers

4 Sides	20" x 9½"	½" Baltic birch plywood
2 Fronts	12" x 9½"	½" Baltic birch plywood
2 Backs	12" x 8⅞"	½" Baltic birch plywood
2 Bottoms	19¾" x 12½"	¼" Baltic birch plywood
2 Drawer fronts	13¾" x 10¾"	¾" cherry plywood

Other Materials

Approximately 20 linear ft. edge tape	cherry
2 Pair drawer glides	
2 Drawer pulls	
4 Confirmat screws	
#20 biscuits	
#10 biscuits	
Finish	

can be cut from sheets of this size without undue waste.

Sometimes I couldn't avoid having material left over. For example, the sides of the cabinets in this chapter are 24¼ in. high, so you can cut only three of them from an 8-ft. length of plywood. If I'd shortened the cabinet so you could cut all four pieces from a single length, it wouldn't have had room for two file drawers. Even in this case, you'll find you can use the leftover pieces of plywood in other parts of these cabinets or in other projects in this book.

Before you decide how to divide up the material, you should also consider wood grain. Just cutting up the sheets into usable sizes may not produce the most attractive grain pattern on all of the pieces. By this time you should already have planned out your space and decided how many cabinets you need and of what kind. Take the time to think about your office as a whole, and lay out your materials carefully so you can make the best and most attractive use of them.

One last thing to keep in mind when laying out your materials is that you need to cut the parts slightly larger than their finished dimensions. The saw is going to remove material, and you'll lose additional

PHOTO A: A careful layout will ensure efficient use of your material.

Example Layout and Cut Sequence for Plywood

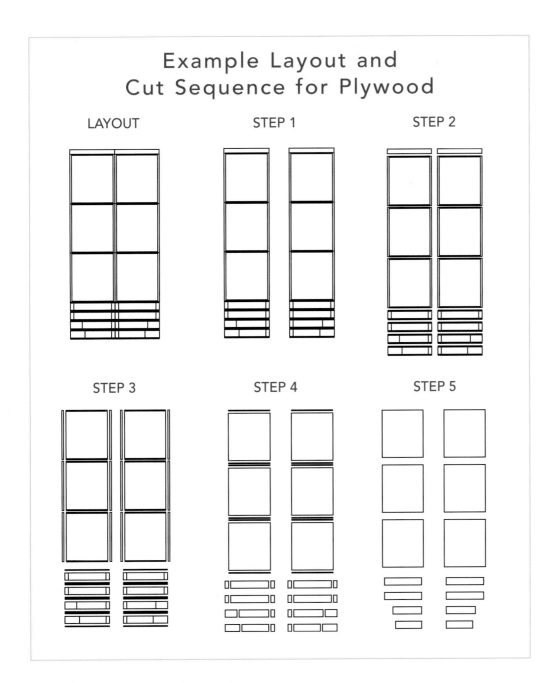

LAYOUT   STEP 1   STEP 2

STEP 3   STEP 4   STEP 5

material in truing and squaring the edges (see **photo A**).

Cabinet Boxes

Once your material is layed out, cut all of the cherry plywood for the cabinet boxes and drawer fronts to size. The dimensions of the drawer fronts include the edgebanding, so you will have to take into account the actual thickness of the tape you are planning to use and subtract twice that thickness from each dimension when you size the drawer fronts.

The dimensions in the cut list give you the finished sizes, but to assure clean, square parts when sizing plywood I suggest cutting the plywood in the following sequence:

1. Following the illustration above, lay out the parts on the sheet of plywood. Add at least ¾ in. to the length and width of each part, plus the waste from the thickness of your sawblade.

2. Make any rip cuts on a tablesaw (see **photo B** on p. 212). In this case the only rip cut is down the center of the sheet.

3. Make the crosscuts using a circular saw with an edge guide or using a radial-arm saw (see **photo C**).

4. Returning to the tablesaw, rip the parts to their finished dimensions in two passes. First remove half the waste from one edge to produce a straight, clean edge. Then with this edge against the fence, cut the parts to their finished dimensions. Be sure to cut all like-dimensioned parts one after the other, without resetting the fence, so that they will be identical.

5. Returning to the circular saw or the radial-arm saw, repeat this process to cut the parts to finished length.

PHOTO B: Ripping the plywood sheet in half first will make subsequent cuts more manageable.

PHOTO C: A radial-arm saw makes short work of cutting the cabinet parts, but you c6an also use a circular saw and edge guide as shown in the sidebar on the facing page.

Cutting the rabbets

Once all of the parts for this cabinet box are sized, it's time to cut the rabbets that the back will fit into. For this cabinet, you'll cut rabbets only in the inside back edges of the cabinet sides, since these are the only places that show. You don't need to hide the back in rabbets at the top and bottom of the cabinet, since these can't be seen in the finished office—the bottom of the cabinet sits on the base and the top will be covered by the desktop. To accommodate the back, the top and bottom of the cabinet are cut ½ in. shorter than the sides, front to back.

1. To cut the rabbets, install a sharp, piloted rabbeting bit in your router. I recommend using a ½-in. collet router with at least 1½ hp. Set the bit to cut a ½-in.-wide rabbet, ⅜ in. deep (half the thickness of the plywood).

2. Clamp the workpiece so its edge overhangs your workbench.

3. Rout the rabbet, taking care at the beginning and the end of the cut not to let the

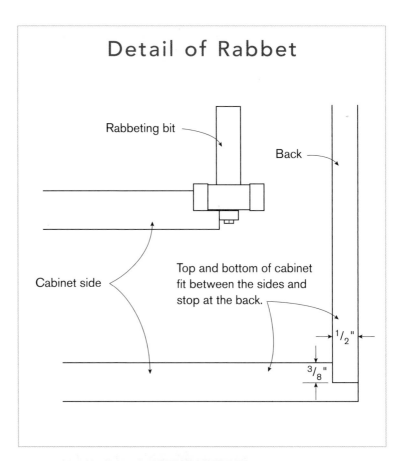

Detail of Rabbet

Rabbeting bit

Back

Cabinet side

Top and bottom of cabinet fit between the sides and stop at the back.

$\frac{1}{2}$"

$\frac{3}{8}$"

PHOTO D: A large router and a sharp bit are necessary for a cleanly cut rabbet.

bearing roll around either corner (see **photo D** on p. 213).

Cutting the biscuit slots

The corner joints and the joints for the drawer section divider are configured so as to put the sides of the cabinet on the outside and the top, bottom, and divider between the sides.

1. Lay out and cut three biscuit slots for each of the corner joints: one in the center and one 2 in. in from each of the front and back edges. Be sure to take into account that the top and bottom are ½ in. shorter front to back than the sides, with the shortfall at the back.

2. Lay out and cut one biscuit slot in the center of each end of the divider and a mating slot halfway down each side (see **photo E**).

Edgebanding

Before assembling the cabinet boxes, apply iron-on cherry edgebanding to cover the exposed plywood edges on the front of the sides, top, bottom, and divider. Iron-on edgebanding is available from many woodworking suppliers and is easy to apply. It comes in many different species of wood and has hot-melt glue on the back.

1. Break off a piece of edgebanding a little longer than you will need.

2. Set an ordinary household iron to high temperature and no steam. Using the iron to apply the edgebanding, move it along the edge bit by bit and soften the glue as you go until the edging sticks (see **photo F**).

3. Trim off the excess length by scoring the edgebanding lightly on the glue side and snapping it off.

4. Since the edgebanding is slightly wider than the plywood, sand it flush with the sides of the plywood.

5. Finish-sand all of the insides of the cabinets, including both sides of the divider, to 150 grit.

Assembly

1. After clearing a suitable space and gathering all the clamps, glue, and biscuits you'll need for the glue-up, lay the two sides down with their insides facing up. Glue biscuits into all of the slots in their faces.

2. Apply glue to the slots in the ends of the top, bottom, and divider.

3. Position the top, bottom, and divider onto their respective biscuits on one of the sides, making sure all of the front edges are flush, and press down firmly.

4. Next, turn over the other side piece and position it on the ends of the top, bottom,

PHOTO G: Placing a clamp at each biscuit location will ensure that the joints close up tight.

BASE CONSTRUCTION
AND ATTACHMENTS

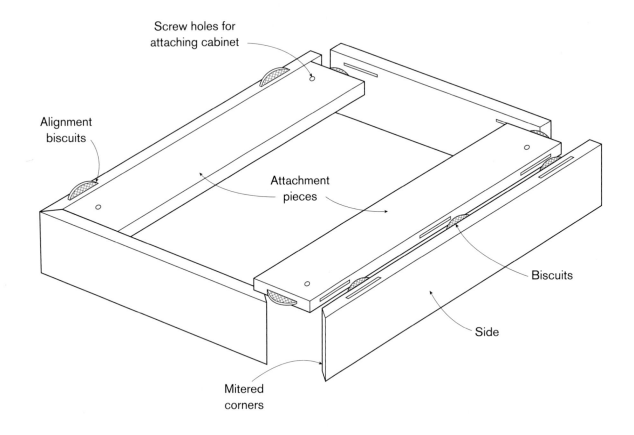

Screw holes for
attaching cabinet

Alignment
biscuits

Attachment
pieces

Biscuits

Side

Mitered
corners

SECTION THROUGH CABINET SIDE

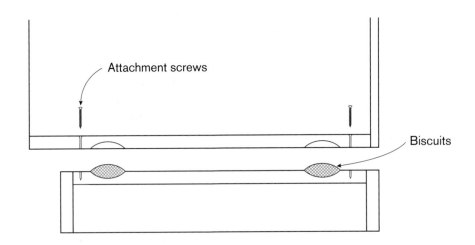

Attachment screws

Biscuits

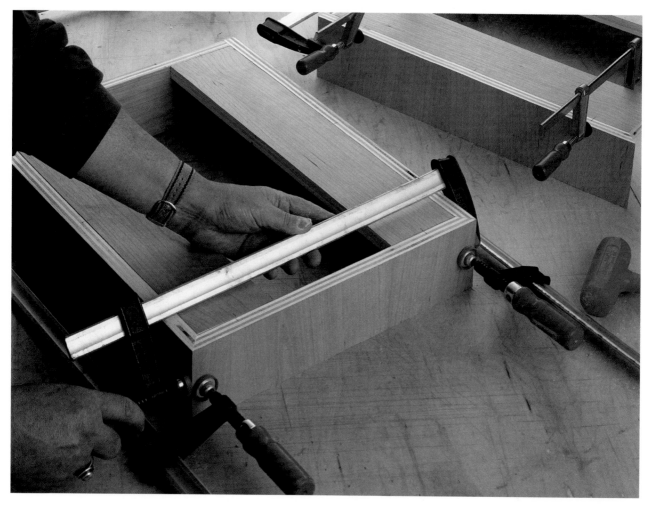

and divider, again making sure all of the front edges are flush, and press down firmly.

5. Clamp at each biscuit location. The clamps will go across the case at the top and bottom and across the front at the divider (see **photo G** on p. 215).

6. Check the cabinet box for square, adjust the clamps if necessary, and set the box aside to dry.

7. When the glue is dry, finish-sand the outside of the cabinet to 150 grit.

8. Cut two biscuit slots on the bottom edge of each side of the cabinet, positioned as shown in the illustration on the facing page. These will mate with slots cut in the base later.

9. Finish-sand the ½-in. plywood back, slip it into its rabbets, and screw it in place.

Making the Base

The base for this cabinet has front corners that are mitered together, which avoids the necessity of edge-banding raw plywood edges. Edgebanding wouldn't look attractive on the front of the base, and if it were placed on the sides its thickness would have to be factored into the construction.

1. After cutting the cherry plywood for the cabinet base to size, make two subassemblies of the two attachment pieces and the two sides. Glue, biscuit, and clamp these pieces together.

2. Once the glue is dry, complete the assembly by gluing, biscuiting, and clamping the front and back to the subassemblies. The mitered corners do not require any biscuits, just careful alignment and clamping (see **photo H**).

PHOTO H: The mitered corners must be aligned and clamped carefully, but they don't require any biscuits.

3. When the glue from the front and back pieces is dry, finish-sand the outside of the base to 150 grit.

4. Cut two biscuit slots in the top edge of each of the base sides to mate with the slots you cut in the bottom of the cabinet. Position the slots in the base so the back of the base will be flush with the back of the cabinet.

5. To attach the base, place biscuits into the slots in the top of the base. No glue is required, since these are for alignment only.

6. Position the cabinet onto these biscuits, making sure the back of the cabinet is flush with the back of the base, and push down until the cabinet sits flat on the base. Use clamps if necessary.

7. Lay out and drill a hole in each corner through the bottom of the cabinets and into the attachment pieces of the base. The fasteners you choose will determine the size of the holes. I used Confirmat or Euro screws, shown in **photo I**.

8. Screw the cabinet to the base.

File Drawers

While the details of constructing and installing the file drawers are not covered in this section, the importance of considering drawer design is as follows: Since the file drawers affected other elements of the design, I thought it would be interesting to use them as an example of how design decisions are interrelated.

Whenever you design a cabinet to house a particular object, start with that object and design around it. In this case, the object is a hanging file folder, which is 11¾ in. wide with metal hanging bars extending ½ in. on each side. The bars are notched to fit over rails that are attached to the drawer tops. To give the file folders a little wiggle room, the inside of the file drawer should be about 12 in. wide. (Actually, the rails, which extend upward from the inside edges of the drawer sides, can be spaced apart anywhere from 12 in. to 12⅜ in., but 12 in. is the easiest measurement to work with.) Since the sides are ½ in. thick, the drawer box should be 13 in. wide on the outside.

Hanging file folders are 9⅛ in. high. They extend over the top of the rail by ⅜ in., but they're raised off the drawer bottom ⅛ in., so the drawer sides need to be 8⅞ in. high on the inside. Adding the thickness of the drawer bottom (¼ in.) and the amount of material needed under the drawer bottom to support it (⅜ in.) gives a total of 9½ in. outside height.

The depth of the drawer box is based on the length of a standard drawer glide. Drawer glides come in several sizes, but the most appropriate size for this purpose is 20 in., which becomes the depth of my drawer box. You'll see later why I couldn't use a longer drawer glide.

Once you have the outside dimensions of the drawer box, you can design the cabinet itself. The drawer glides add ½ in. to the width on each side, and the cabinet sides are each ¾ in. thick, so the total outside width of the cabinet is 15½ in.

To calculate height, take the drawer heights (9½ in. each) and add the ¾-in. thicknesses of the cabinet's top, bottom, and divider boards. In addition, each of the two drawers needs clearance inside the cabinet—⅜ in. for the folder rails, ⅞ in. for folder tabs, and ¼ in. at the bottom. Adding all these numbers gives us a cabinet box that is 24¼ in. high.

To the 20-in. drawer depth, add ½ in. for the cabinet back and ¾ in. for the inset drawer fronts to obtain a depth of at least 21¼ in. However, you also have to take the desktop into account. The desktop is 24 in. deep, a dimension I chose mainly to save material, since I used 4x8 plywood. The

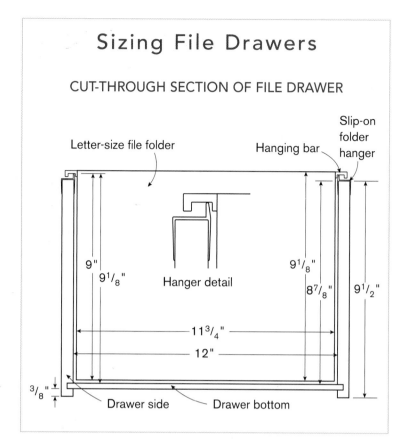

Sizing File Drawers

CUT-THROUGH SECTION OF FILE DRAWER

Letter-size file folder

Hanging bar

Slip-on folder hanger

9"

9¹⁄₈"

Hanger detail

9¹⁄₈"

8⁷⁄₈"

9¹⁄₂"

11³⁄₄"

12"

³⁄₈"

Drawer side

Drawer bottom

cabinet can't take up all the space under the desk; it needs at least 1¼ in. of clearance behind it for baseboard as well as wiring, and it's more attractive with a ¾-in. overhang in front. Thus, the cabinet can't be more than 22 in. deep. I could have made the cabinet any depth from 21¼ in. to 22 in. I chose 22 in.

I've also sized the cabinet base so that the cabinet will fit snugly under the desktop. The desktop is 30 in. high—a height most people find comfortable—and 2 in. thick, with a space of 28 in. underneath. Since the cabinet box is 24¼ in. high, this leaves 3¾ in. for the height of the base.

PEDESTAL CABINET

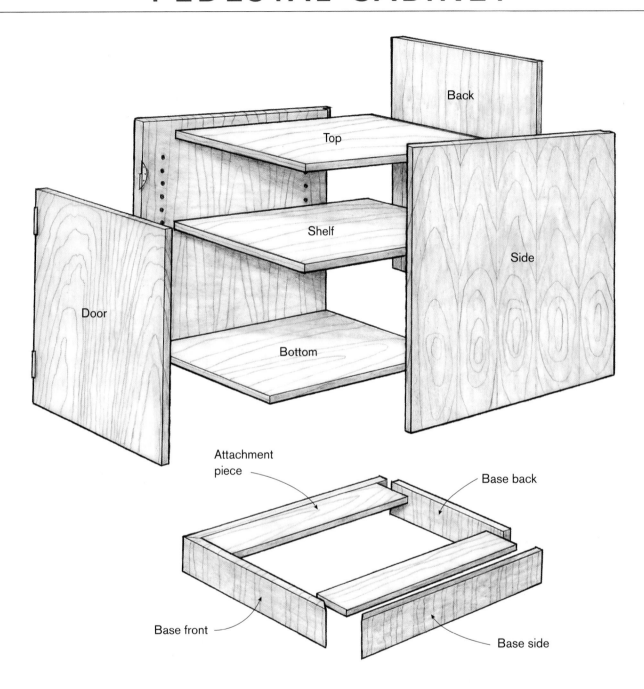

Back

Top

Shelf

Side

Door

Bottom

Attachment
piece

Base back

Base front

Base side

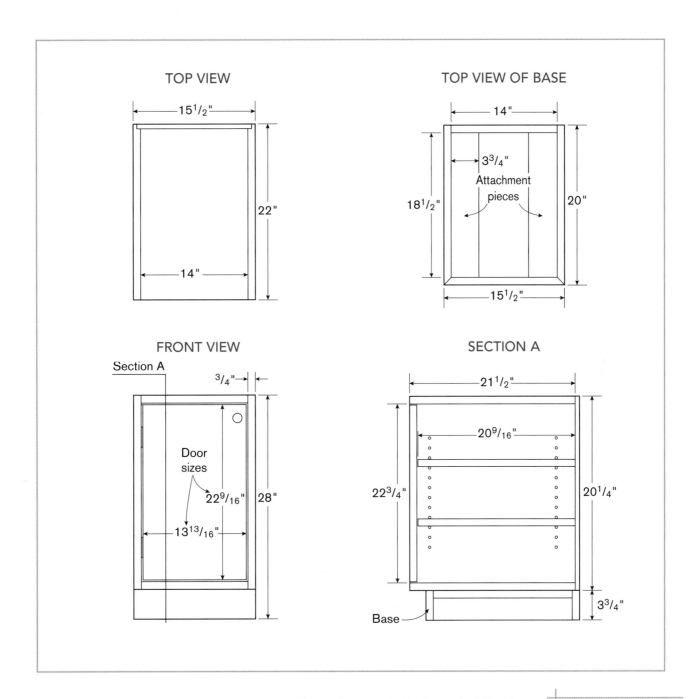

TOP VIEW

15½"

22"

14"

TOP VIEW OF BASE

14"

3¾"

Attachment
pieces

18½"

20"

15½"

FRONT VIEW

Section A

¾"

Door
sizes

22⁹/₁₆"   28"

13¹³/₁₆"

SECTION A

21½"

20⁹/₁₆"

22¾"

20¼"

Base

3¾"

Construction and Assembly

ALTHOUGH THIS CABINET and base are identical to that used in the file cabinet pedestal, the drawers have been replaced with a door and adjustable shelves.

1. Following the detailed instructions on pp. 208–213, lay out and cut all of the parts for the cabinet and base, omitting the drawers,

drawer fronts, and dividers and adding the door and as many shelves as you need. The door should be about ³⁄₃₂ in. smaller all around than the opening it fits into. (Remember that these dimensions include edgebanding, so take into account the thickness of the tape when you size the doors.) Shelves should be about ³⁄₃₂ in. less than the width of the inside of the cabinet and ⅛ in. shorter front to back.

2. Cut all of the biscuit slots as described on p. 214.

TIP

A good rule of thumb for locating shelf pin holes is to measure one-sixth the total depth in from the front and back edges.

CUT LIST FOR PEDESTAL CABINET

Base

1 Front	15½" x 3¾"	¾" cherry plywood
1 Back	14" x 3¾"	¾" cherry plywood
2 Sides	20" x 3¾"	¾" cherry plywood
2 Attachment pieces	18½" x 3¾"	¾" cherry plywood

Cabinet Box

1 Top	21½" x 14"	¾" cherry plywood
1 Bottom	21½" x 14"	¾" cherry plywood
2 Sides	24¼" x 22"	¾" cherry plywood
2 Shelves	20⁹⁄₁₆" x 13⅞"	¾" cherry plywood
1 Back	24¼" x 14¾"	½" cherry plywood

Door

1 Door	22⁹⁄₁₆" x 14¹³⁄₁₆"	¾" cherry plywood

Other Materials

Approximately 20 linear ft. edge tape	cherry
1 Door knob	
4 Confirmat screws	
8 Shelf pins	
2 Duplex hinges	
#20 biscuits	
Finish	

3. Using iron-on edgebanding, edge-band the exposed raw plywood edges on the front of the sides, top, and bottom, and on all of the edges of the door.

Shelf pin holes

Before continuing with the assembly, drill holes for the shelf pins that will be used to support the adjustable shelf or shelves. Since shelf pins come in various sizes—the most common fit into 5mm or ¼-in. holes—you should select your pins before you drill the holes.

Drill two rows of holes in the sides, one about 4 in. in from the front of the cabinet and the other about 3½ in. in from the back (see **photo A**). I use a commercial jig made by Festool, but many other jigs are available, and you can easily make your own by drilling a series of holes in a piece of plywood that fits the space. Even if the holes are not perfectly spaced, your shelves will lie flat as long as each row is the same (see **photo B**). Make sure you always register the jig from the same edge.

After drilling the holes for the shelf pins, finish assembling the cabinet and base, then attach the cabinet to the base.

PHOTO A: This commercial jig makes accurate shelf pin holes quickly.

PHOTO B: This simple straight pin is just one of many types of shelf supports available.

The Door

The two most common styles of cabinet door are inset and overlay. These names refer to the position of the door relative to the cabinet opening. Overlay doors, which are common on European cabinetry, overlay or cover the front of the cabinet. This is a very forgiving arrangement, since the door hides small, out-of-square errors in the cabinet. Inset doors have a more traditional look. They fit within the sides of the cabinet. The cabinet frames the door, and the gap between the door and the cabinet sides is small. Any irregularity or out-of-square construction in the cabinet is emphasized, and in severe cases a door may rub against the frame.

Since all the doors in this office are inset doors, pay particular attention to squareness when you cut and assemble your cabinets as well as when you cut and size the doors (see **photo C**). The stout, ½-in. backs will help square up the cabinets, but you can't rely on this alone.

Installing the hinges

Another difference between overlay and inset doors is the type of hinge used. Overlay doors are typically hung on European or

PHOTO C: The use of inset doors requires an absolutely square cabinet.

Door Installation

HINGE INSTALLATION DETAIL

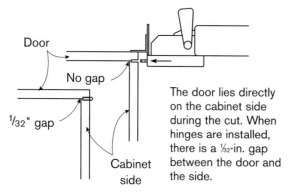

Door

No gap

$^1\!/_{32}$" gap

Cabinet side

The door lies directly on the cabinet side during the cut. When hinges are installed, there is a $^1\!/_{32}$-in. gap between the door and the side.

OVERLAY DOOR INSTALLATION

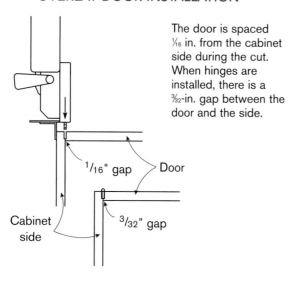

The door is spaced $^1\!/_{16}$ in. from the cabinet side during the cut. When hinges are installed, there is a $^3\!/_{32}$-in. gap between the door and the side.

$^1\!/_{16}$" gap   Door

Cabinet side

$^3\!/_{32}$" gap

concealed hinges, which have the advantage of being adjustable in four directions. Not only does this make the fit of the door less critical, but it also makes the installation of the hinge easier. Inset doors are typically hung with straight butt hinges, which are more difficult to install. These hinges must be fitted into mortises in the case as well as in the door. The mating of the two mortise locations and the fit of the hinge in its mortise is critical to the fit of the door.

For these cabinets, I chose a type of butt hinge called Duplex (see **photo D**) manufactured by Lamello, which fits into a biscuit slot. Interestingly, Duplex hinges are designed to be used with overlay doors and are very easy to install on those doors. Installing them on inset doors is a little trickier but is still much easier than installing regular butt hinges. However, I strongly recommend that you test this installation on some scrap pieces before you try it on a finished cabinet.

1. After laying the cabinet on its back, use some scrap plywood as temporary supports to prop up the door in its opening while you lay out and install the hinges. Cut a few pieces of scrap long enough to support the door in place, inset about $^1\!/_{16}$ in. from the front of the cabinet, and place them upright in the cabinet near the top and bottom.

PHOTO D: Lamello Duplex hinges are designed to fit into biscuit slots.

PHOTO E: Wedges temporarily align the door for laying out and cutting slots for the hinges.

Place the door on the supports in the cabinet opening.

2. Place wedges in the spaces around the door so that the door is centered top to bottom and is just slightly closer to the hinge side of the cabinet (see **photo E**).

3. Mark the centerlines for the locations of the hinges.

4. Next, set the depth of the biscuit joiner to 15mm (approximately ⁹⁄₁₆ in.), and set the joiner's fence so the cutter will plunge equally into the cabinet side and the door edge.

5. Line up the centerline of the biscuit joiner with the hinge centerline and cut a biscuit slot for each hinge, as shown in **photo F**.

6. Separate the hinges and screw the leaves with the pins to the cabinet and the other leaves to the door.

PHOTO F: The biscuit joiner cutter is positioned to cut an equal amount from the door and cabinet.

PHOTO G: These two-part hinges make hanging the door simple.

Hanging the door and installing the catch

Since these hinges separate, you don't have to hold the door in place while you screw on the hinges. Hanging the door is simply a matter of dropping the door with its hinge parts over the pin on the cabinet hinge parts (see **photo G.**)

To latch the door, I used Bull Dog catches (see **photo H**). These may not be the most elegant catches on the market, but they latch so solidly and install so easily that I've gotten hooked on them.

1. Start by standing the cabinet upright again. Holding the door closed, reach in through the back of the cabinet (which has not yet been attached) and mark the location on the inside of the cabinet top where it meets the corner of the swing (unhinged) side of the door.

2. Line up the front of the bracket portion of the catch with the line you've just made, and mark the locations of the slotted holes in the bracket. Drill pilot holes in the center of these marks, then screw the bracket in place.

3. Insert the pin portion of the catch into the bracket and close the door firmly. The pin has a screw inserted in it, which will mark its location.

4. Drill a pilot hole on the mark made where the screw hits the door, and screw on the pin. You can microadjust the catch by sliding the bracket in or out.

PHOTO H: These Bull Dog catches latch firmly.

LOW CABINET

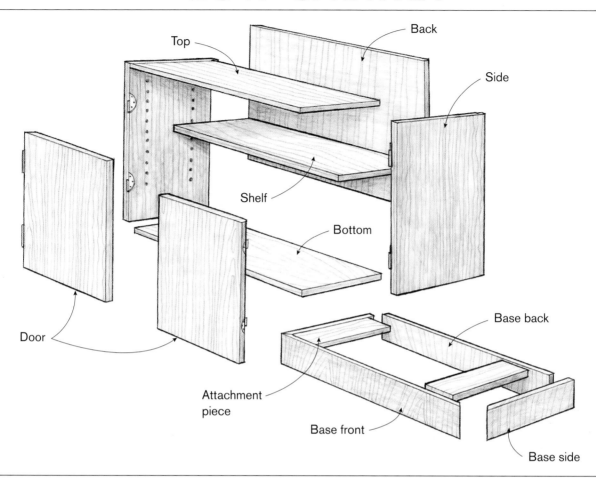

Top

Back

Side

Shelf

Bottom

Base back

Door

Attachment piece

Base front

Base side

Construction and Assembly

THIS CABINET IS SMALLER than the pedestal cabinet but since the construction is virtually identical, I've described it in less detail. For a fuller explanation of construction methods, refer to pp. 208–218.

1. Begin by laying out and rough-cutting all of the cherry plywood for the cabinet boxes.

2. Using a tablesaw and then a radial-arm saw, rip and crosscut the parts to their finished dimensions.

3. Cut the rabbets in the side pieces.

Low Cabinet Views

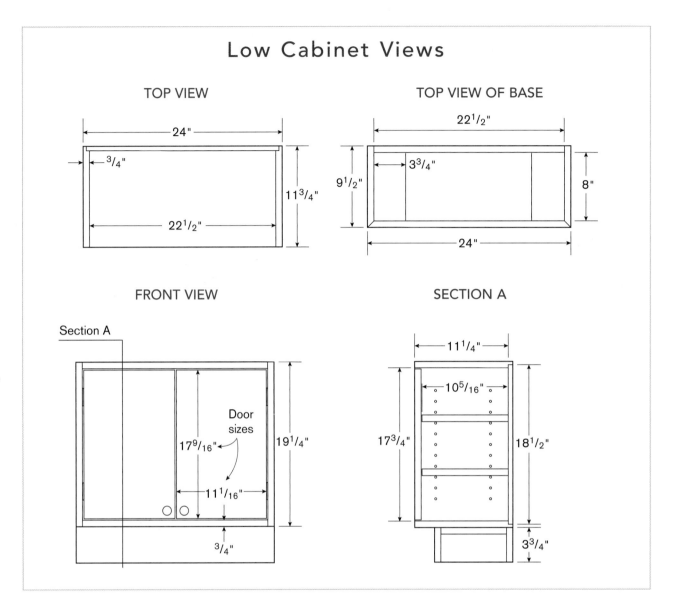

TOP VIEW

24"

³/₄"

11³/₄"

22¹/₂"

TOP VIEW OF BASE

22¹/₂"

3³/₄"

9¹/₂"

8"

24"

FRONT VIEW

Section A

Door sizes

17⁹/₁₆"

19¹/₄"

11¹/₁₆"

³/₄"

SECTION A

11¹/₄"

10⁵/₁₆"

17³/₄"

18¹/₂"

3³/₄"

4. Cut biscuit slots for the corner joints so that the top and bottom will be between the sides and so that the front edges of all of the parts are flush.

5. In the sides of the cabinet, drill shelf pin holes. Since this cabinet is shallower than the pedestal cabinet, the rows of holes will be closer to the front and back edges of the sides. Remember that the rule of thumb is to measure one-sixth of the cabinet's depth in from the front and back.

6. Edge-band the front edges of all of the cabinet parts.

7. Cut, size, and edge-band the doors. Since this cabinet has two doors, you have to size

the doors to leave room for the space around and between the doors, as well as for the edgebanding around the outside of the doors. The space between the doors (after edgebanding is applied) should be ³/₃₂ in., just like the space around the doors.

8. Finish-sand the inside faces of all of the parts to 150 grit.

9. Glue, biscuit, and clamp the cabinet together.

10. When the glue is dry, finish-sand the outside of the cabinet.

11. Cut two biscuit slots on the bottom edge of each side of the cabinet in the

CUT LIST FOR LOW CABINET

Base

1	Front	24" x 3¾"	¾" cherry plywood
1	Back	22½" x 3¾"	¾" cherry plywood
2	Sides	9½" x 3¾"	¾" cherry plywood
2	Attachment pieces	8" x 3¾"	¾" cherry plywood

Cabinet Box

1	Top	22½" x 11¼"	¾" cherry plywood
1	Bottom	22½" x 11¼"	¾" cherry plywood
2	Sides	19¼" x 11¾"	¾" cherry plywood
2	Shelves	22⅜" x 10⁵⁄₁₆"	¾" cherry plywood
1	Back	23¼" x 18½"	½" cherry plywood

Doors

2	Doors	17⁹⁄₁₆" x 11¹⁄₁₆"	¾" cherry plywood

Top

1	Panel	74½" x 12"	¾" cherry plywood
1	Edge strip	76" x ¾" x ¾"	solid cherry
2	Edge strips	12¾" x ¾" x ¾"	solid cherry

Other Materials

	Approximately 20 linear ft. cherry edge tape
2	Door knobs
8	Shelf pins
4	Duplex hinges
	#20 biscuits
20	Hex-drive connector bolts and threaded sleeves
	Finish

Base Construction

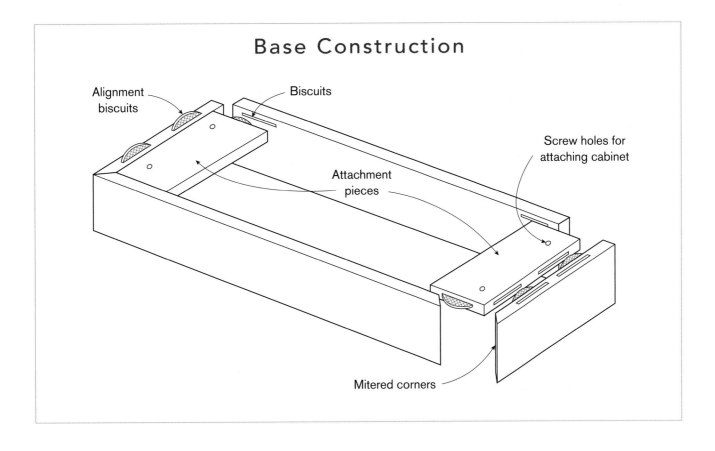

Alignment biscuits

Biscuits

Screw holes for attaching cabinet

Attachment pieces

Mitered corners

PHOTO I: Dry-fitted biscuits align the base and cabinet.

gle, freestanding piece of furniture.

If you knew for certain that you would connect multiple modules, you might be better off building a single base to support all three pieces. However, you would then be locked into this arrangement, which could be a problem if you had to move your office. If you do decide to build a single base, you will have to change the grain orientation. The wood grain on the bases in all of these pedestal projects runs vertically, which is impossible to achieve with plywood construction if the base is more than 48 in. wide.

1. Lay out and cut to size all of the cherry plywood for the cabinet base.

2. Glue, biscuit, and clamp the base together.

3. When the glue is dry, finish-sand the outside of the base to 150 grit.

4. Cut two biscuit slots in the top edge of each of the base sides to mate with the slots you cut in the bottom of the cabinet. Position the slots so the base will be flush with the back of the cabinet (see **photo I**).

Don't screw the base to the cabinet yet. The shelving modules that will be joined to this cabinet are open, so any screws used to attach their bases would be visible. For this reason, their bases will be attached from underneath.

Making the Top

Like the pedestal cabinets, this cabinet has a top that is less than attractive. In this case, however, there is no desktop to slide the cabinet under. I could have built the cabinet in such a way that the top looked better but not without compromising the modular nature of the construction. The solution is to add a long top that covers the cabinet and two low shelf units of the same height. This will improve the appearance of all of these pieces and integrate them visually. This may seem contradictory to my reason for building separate bases, but if you changed the configuration of these cabinets in the future it would be relatively simple to make a new top. Alternatively, you could build a separate

positions marked in the illustration on p. 229. These will mate with slots cut in the base later.

12. Finish-sand the ½-in. plywood back, slide it into its rabbet, and screw it in place.

Making the Base

Although the base for the low cabinet is a different size, it is constructed like the base of the pedestal cabinet. However, unlike the pedestal cabinet, which is simply placed under a desktop, this cabinet is designed to become a module. By combining this module with other shelving modules of the same height, you can create what looks like a sin-

top for the low cabinet, but this might look less attractive. The top is constructed of the same plywood as the rest of the furniture, but for durability the front and sides are edged with solid wood rather than edge tape.

1. To make the top, cut a piece of ¾-in. cherry plywood 74½ in. long and 12 in. wide.

2. For the edging, mill solid cherry strips ¾ in. wide by approximately $^{13}/_{16}$ in. thick. Cut one length of approximately 78 in. and two lengths of approximately 15 in. each. These pieces are thicker and longer than you need but will be cut down. The $^{13}/_{16}$-in. face will be attached to the edge of the plywood and sanded down to the thickness of the plywood later.

3. Carefully miter one end of each of the three strips at 45 degrees across the ¾-in. face.

4. Line up the miter on the long strip at one end of the long edge of the plywood, using one of the short pieces as a guide to align it.

5. Next, clamp the strip in place and mark the other end where it extends past the plywood, then unclamp it and miter the marked end.

6. Apply glue to the strip, then carefully realign it and clamp it again to the edge of the plywood. Make sure the strip stands proud of the top and bottom faces of the plywood (see **photo J**).

7. Glue and carefully align the short strips and clamp them to the ends of the plywood.

8. After the glue dries, scrape off any excess and plane the edging flush with the face of the plywood using a sharp handplane, as shown in **photo K**. You could use a router but it would be difficult to control on the thin edge of the plywood.

9. Using a sharp handsaw, trim off the back ends of the edging, then finish-sand the top to 150 grit.

PHOTO J: A strip of solid cherry edge (above) hides the raw plywood edge of the top.

PHOTO K: The cherry edging is quickly and easily planed flush using a sharp handplane.

STORAGE SHELF

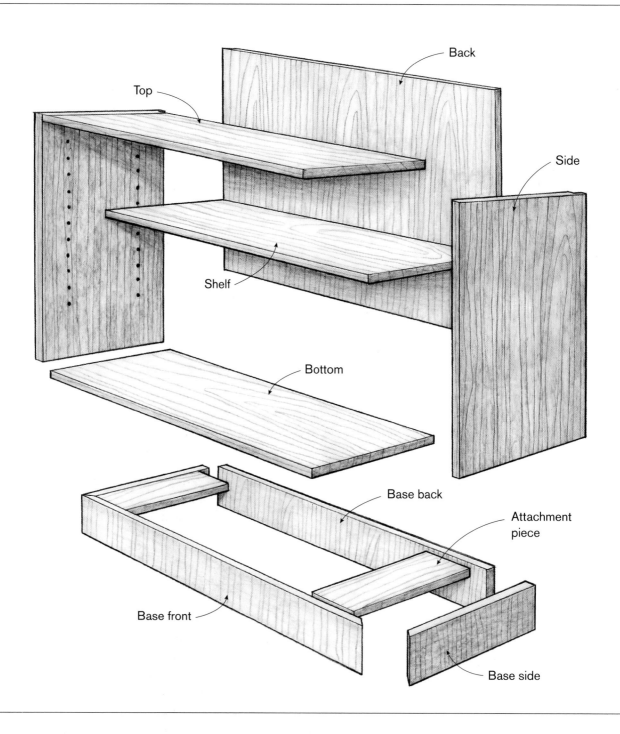

Back

Top

Side

Shelf

Bottom

Base back

Attachment
piece

Base front

Base side

Shelf Unit Dimensions

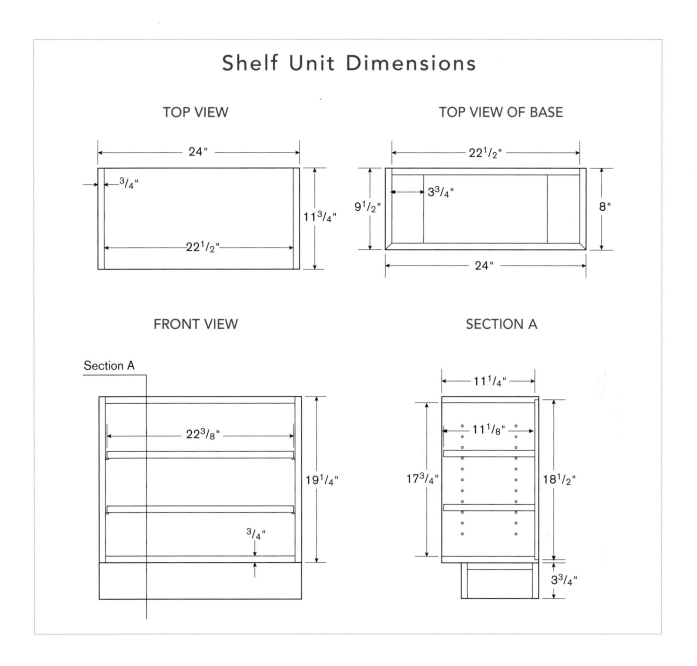

TOP VIEW

24"

³/₄"

22¹/₂"

11³/₄"

TOP VIEW OF BASE

22¹/₂"

3³/₄"

9¹/₂"

8"

24"

FRONT VIEW

Section A

22³/₈"

19¹/₄"

³/₄"

SECTION A

11¹/₄"

11¹/₈"

17³/₄"

18¹/₂"

3³/₄"

Construction and Assembly

THIS UNIT AND THE WALL-HUNG unit described after it are by far the simplest projects in this book. By now you should be able to build this type of plywood cabinet, top, and base without any problem, so I won't repeat the basic instructions (but see pp. 208–218 for details if you're building the shelves before tackling the cabinets). However, I do want to discuss a few issues related to connecting units together.

Connecting the units

The two low shelves and the low unit discussed at the beginning of this section make up a single piece of furniture, so they will need to be fastened together securely. At the same time, since they are modular, you wouldn't want to give up the possibility of changing or adding to their arrangement. Also, it is handy to be able to break down larger pieces when you need to move them.

Various kinds of knockdown fasteners are available for exactly this purpose. Some are difficult to install, others require special tools, and many are just hard to find. For the

CUT LIST FOR LOW SHELF UNIT

Base

1	Front	24" x 3¾"	¾" cherry plywood
1	Back	22½" x 3¾"	¾" cherry plywood
2	Sides	9½" x 3¾"	¾" cherry plywood
2	Attachment pieces	8" x 3¾"	¾" cherry plywood

Cabinet Box

1	Top	22½" x 11¾"	¾" cherry plywood
1	Bottom	22½" x 11¾"	¾" cherry plywood
2	Sides	19¼" x 11¾"	¾" cherry plywood
2	Shelves	22⅜" x 11⅛"	¾" cherry plywood
1	Back	23½" x 18½"	½" cherry plywood

Other Materials

Approximately 20 linear ft. edge tape		cherry
8	Shelf pins	
#20 biscuits		
20	Hex-drive connector bolts and threaded sleeves	
Finish		

projects in this section, I used special flat-head bolts, driven with a hex driver, that screw into threaded inserts. These are easy to install and use and are readily available. The disadvantage of these fasteners, unlike some of the more specialized fasteners on the market, is that they show on the surface. I think they look nice in the right situation, but in this project you will be keeping them out of sight when necessary and practical.

In this office, you can connect two low shelf units on either side of a closed cabinet unit discussed in the "Low Shelf Unit" section. The fasteners only have to show on one side of the walls they join together, so you'll keep the part that shows on the inside of the closed cabinet.

To install and use the knockdown fasteners, follow these steps:

1. Start by lining up the cabinets to be joined and clamping them together. Mark the locations of the holes for the fasteners, placing one at each corner of the inside of the sides of the center cabinet (in this case, the closed cabinet).

PHOTO A:
Threaded fasteners are installed to accept connector bolts.

Hole-Drilling Sequence for Fasteners

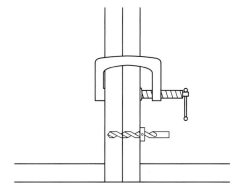

Drill a ¼" hole.

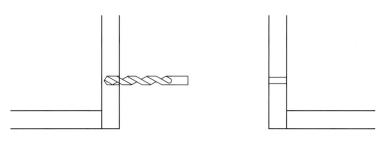

Enlarge the hole to $\frac{11}{32}$"

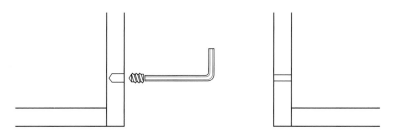

Install a threaded insert.

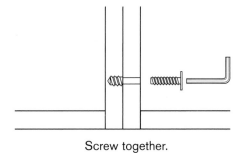

Screw together.

2. Drill a ¼-in. hole 1⅜ in. deep at each location (drilling through one cabinet and partly into the adjacent cabinet). To avoid drilling completely through and into the adjoining cabinet, use a depth stop on your drill bit.

3. Separate the cabinets and enlarge the holes in the outside cabinets using an ¹¹⁄₃₂-in. drill bit. (These are the holes that don't go all the way through.)

4. Install the threaded inserts into these holes. The drivers for installing the inserts are available from the suppliers of the inserts (see **photo A** on p. 234).

5. Line up the cabinets again (you don't need clamps this time) and screw the bolts through the ¼-in. holes and into the inserts, as shown in **photo B**. That's all there is to it.

PHOTO B: Once the threaded fasteners are installed, simply bolt the cabinets together.

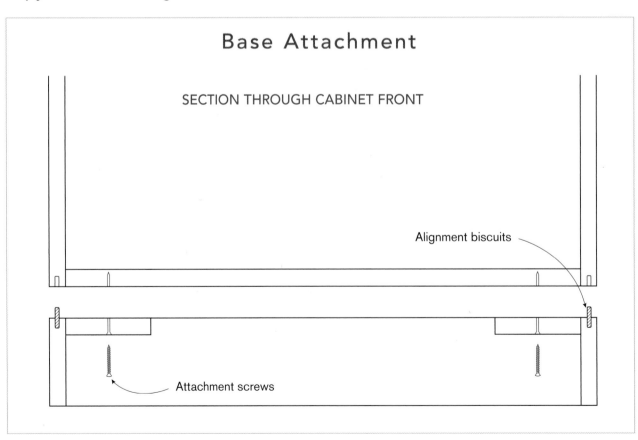

Base Attachment

SECTION THROUGH CABINET FRONT

Alignment biscuits

Attachment screws

Attaching the base

To hide the attachment fasteners, the base is attached from the underside.

1. Place the attached cabinets upside down on the floor and insert the alignment biscuits (without glue) into the bottoms.

2. One at a time, place the bases on the cabinet bottoms, aligning the biscuit slots so that the backs of the bases are flush with the backs of the cabinets. Press down until the bases are tight against the cabinets (see **photo C**).

3. Following the sequence described in "Connecting the Units" on pp. 233–236, install one fastener in each corner of each base, then attach the bases (see **photo D**).

PHOTO C: The bases are positioned on their alignment biscuits prior to drilling holes for fasteners.

PHOTO D: The bases are firmly fastened to the undersides of the cabinets.

PHOTO E: The top is fastened to the cabinet just as the base was.

Attaching the top

The top is attached using the same fasteners used to attach the base. The fasteners are inserted from inside the cabinets, so technically they show, but you won't see them unless you are lying on the floor.

1. Place the top upside down on a bench, using a blanket so you won't scratch the top.

2. Place the cabinet/base assembly you just created upside down on the top.

3. Aligning the backs of the cabinets flush with the back edge of the top, center the cabinets on the top. There should be a 2-in. overhang on each end and a 1-in. overhang in front.

4. Following the same sequence as when you attached the bases, install one fastener in each corner of the underside of the cabinet top and attach the top (see **photo E**).

TALL BOOKCASE

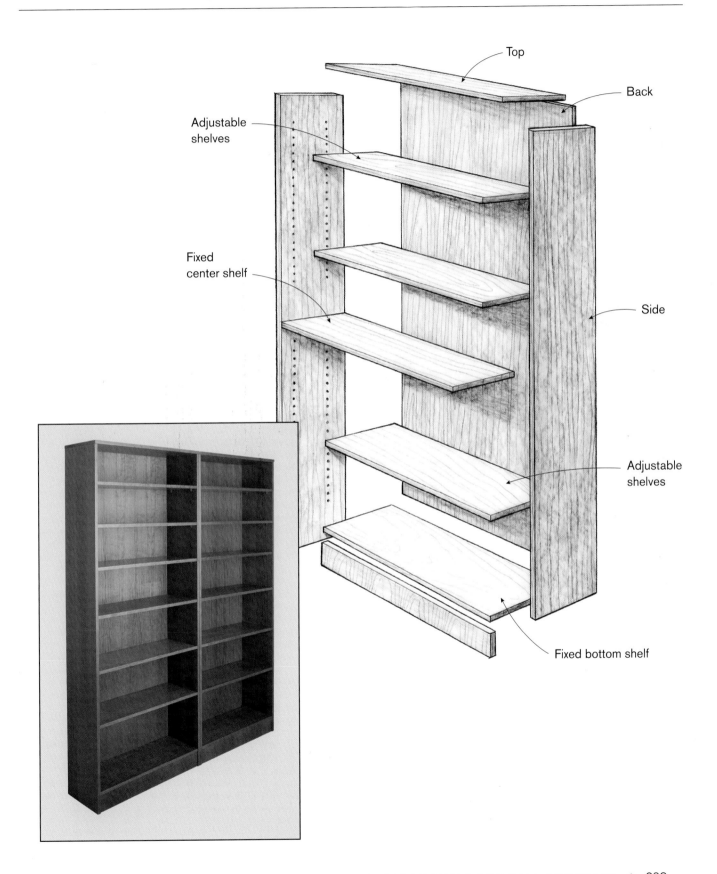

Top

Back

Adjustable shelves

Side

Fixed center shelf

Adjustable shelves

Fixed bottom shelf

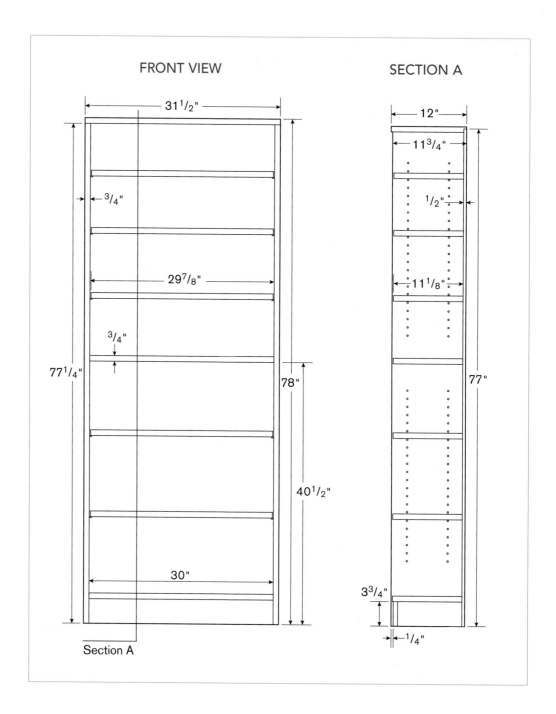

FRONT VIEW

SECTION A

Construction and Assembly

ALTHOUGH THE CONSTRUC-TION of this case is similar to the rest of the cabinets in this section, there are important differences. Most if not all of which involve the relationship between its size and what it is destined to hold: Books, or to put it simply, heavy stuff!

The weight-bearing capacity of shelves depends on the material of which they are constructed. For the ¾-in. plywood being used here, 30 in. is about the maximum length for an unsupported span. Longer spans risk sagging over time if they're loaded with heavy objects—and books are heavy. While softcover books can weigh as little as a few ounces apiece, a row of hardcover novels can easily weigh a pound per inch. Some large art books can weigh four times this amount.

The sides of the bookcase also need support to avoid the risk of the sides bowing. The maximum unsupported height for the materials you'll be using is about 36 in., so the center shelf of this bookcase has to be fixed in place.

This bookshelf is designed around these maximum spans for ¾-in. plywood. The vertical span, or the distance between supports (top of piece, fixed center shelf, and bottom shelf), is 36 in. and the horizontal span (shelf length) is 30 in. The depth is sized to be efficiently cut from sheets of plywood, but you'll find that all but the largest books will fit comfortably in this bookcase. Working from these spans and adding in the thickness of the material, I arrived at a bookcase 31½ in. wide by 78 in. high by 11¾ in. deep.

Layout

You should be able to cut both sides of the bookcase and six shelves from a single sheet of plywood without difficulty. You'll probably find you can cut the top and any additional shelves from the plywood left over from other projects. If you don't need more than five shelves, you can squeeze the whole bookcase, including the kick, out of one sheet of plywood. Keeping in mind that the top is deeper and wider than the shelves, lay out the pieces carefully, leaving enough room between them for the saw kerf, and pay attention to your cut sequence (see "Plywood Layout" on p. 242 and **photo G**). You will have to cut some of the parts very close to their finished size, so there won't be much waste left for trimming.

Cutting the rabbets

After you have cut all the plywood for the case to size, cut rabbets at the inside back edges of the sides and the top using a router fitted with a ½-in. piloted rabbeting bit. Because the top is positioned over the sides, rather than between them, the rabbet in the top must be a stopped rabbet, as shown in **photo H** on p. 243. The rabbets in the side pieces can run from end to end.

CUT LIST FOR TALL BOOKCASE

Case

1	Top	31½" x 12"	¾" cherry plywood
1	Bottom fixed shelf	30" x 11⅛"	¾" cherry plywood
1	Center fixed shelf	30" x 11⅛"	¾" cherry plywood
2	Sides	76½" x 11¾"	¾" cherry plywood
5	Adjustable shelves	29⅞" x 11⅛"	¾" cherry plywood
1	Back	77" x 31"	½" cherry plywood
1	Kick	30" x 3¾"	¾" cherry plywood

Other Materials

Approximately 50 linear ft. edge tape	cherry
24 Shelf pins	
#20 biscuits	
Finish	

PHOTO G: Marking out both sides at the same time ensures that they will be identical.

Plywood Layout

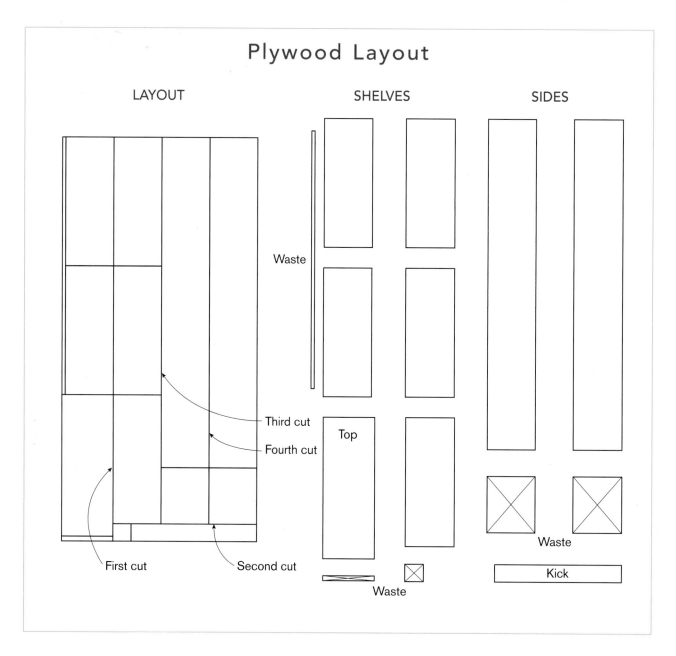

LAYOUT

SHELVES

SIDES

Waste

Third cut

Fourth cut

Top

First cut

Second cut

Waste

Waste

Kick

Cutting the biscuit slots

Lay out and cut the biscuit slots for the case joints, as shown in **photo I** on p. 243. The slots should be cut so that the top of the bookcase lies over the sides and so that the center shelf and bottom shelf are between the sides. When you lay out the slots for the center and bottom shelves, pay attention to how you orient the biscuit joiner for the cuts. This is also the time to cut the slots that you will use to join the kick to the bottom shelf. You don't need to cut biscuit slots

to join the ends of the kick to the case sides. A little glue on these edges when you clamp the case is all that's needed.

Once the slots are cut, dry-fit the piece together to make sure everything is located correctly.

Edgebanding

Edge-band the front edges of the sides and shelves and also the side edges and front edge of the top (see **photo J** on p. 244). Because the top is edge-banded after the biscuit slots are cut, the edge tape will be proud of the side of the bookcase. If you position two of these units side by side, they will have a space between them twice the thickness of the edge tape. To attach the units, you would have to add spacers between them at the locations of the fasteners. A washer or two will probably do the job. If you don't like the look of the space, or if you don't want to deal with spacers, factor in the thickness of the edge tape when you cut the top and edge-band the sides of the top before cutting the biscuit slots.

Shelf pin holes

Before continuing with the assembly of the bookcase, drill the shelf pin holes for the adjustable shelves. Two sets of holes are needed on each side, one above and one below the center shelf. It is best to drill the entire row at once, referencing your jig from the same edge for each row. The Festool jig shown in **photo K** on p. 244 has long enough guides to accommodate the whole

PHOTO H: Rabbets in the sides can run from end to end, but the rabbet in the top should stop short of the ends so it won't be seen.

PHOTO I: Cutting biscuit slots at the end of a board is easier if the piece is held in a vise.

PHOTO J: Edge-banding can be easily trimmed by scoring it in back with a sharp knife and breaking it off.

PHOTO K: A long jig is ideal for drilling shelf pin holes in the sides of this bookcase.

row, but if your jig is shorter you will have to pay close attention when you move positions. Alternatively, you can make your own jig sized for this operation. I prefer jigs that use a router rather than a hand drill since routers generally cut cleaner holes, but with a little extra care hand drill-based jigs work fine.

All that's really important is being able to drill a row of evenly spaced holes that lines up properly—not only with the other row on the same side of the case but also with the rows on the opposing side. You need to find a way to locate the jig repeatedly at a specific distance from the front and back edges as well as from the top and bottom edges.

Preassembly

To make the final glue-up easier, preassemble the kick and bottom shelf. This reduces

PHOTO L:
Rounded corners
left by a router
can be quickly
squared up using
a sharp chisel.

the time for the final glue-up and the number of clamps you will need.

Make sure the ends of the kick are perfectly flush with the shelf during the first glue-up; there is no way to fix it after the fact, since sanding or trimming it to flush it up will change the size of the assembly.

Assembly

Assembling a case this size can be tricky. It pays to prepare the space and gather all of the clamps, glue, and biscuits you will need so you don't have to go looking for something in the middle of a glue-up.

1. Remove the clamps from the bottom shelf/kick assembly and finish-sand the top of the shelf and the face of the kick to 150 grit. Sand the insides of the top, center shelf, and sides to 150 grit.

2. Glue biscuits into the slots in the face of the sides and the top.

3. Lay one long side down on a couple of sawhorses with the inside face up, then glue and position the bottom shelf/kick assembly and the center shelf on their mating biscuits. Glue and place the other long side on top of this assembly.

4. Clamp across the case at the front and back of both shelf locations. Check for square and adjust the clamps if necessary.

5. Glue and position the top on its biscuits and clamp it in place front and back on both sides.

6. When the glue is dry, remove the clamps and finish-sand the outside of the case to 150 grit.

Installing the back

1. With the case lying on its face, use a sharp chisel to square up the corners of the stopped rabbet in the top (see **photo L**).

TIP

Gluing and clamping a large piece can be a real juggling act, so simplify by creating subassemblies whenever possible.

The routing you did earlier will have left rounded ends.

2. Measure the opening created by the rabbets and cut your ½-in. plywood back to fit snugly. Fitting the back as tightly as possible gives stability to the case and also helps keep it square.

3. Finish-sand the back to 150 grit and fit it into the rabbets.

4. Mark out and drill pilot holes for small screws around the perimeter of the back and across the backs of the shelves, then insert the screws as shown in **photo M**. (I use 1-in. trim-head screws.)

Finishing

I finished these pieces using a spray-on lacquer, but there are several other finishing methods to choose from.

PHOTO M: To make the bookcase strong, fasten the back not only around the perimeter but also to the backs of the fixed shelves.

DESKTOPS

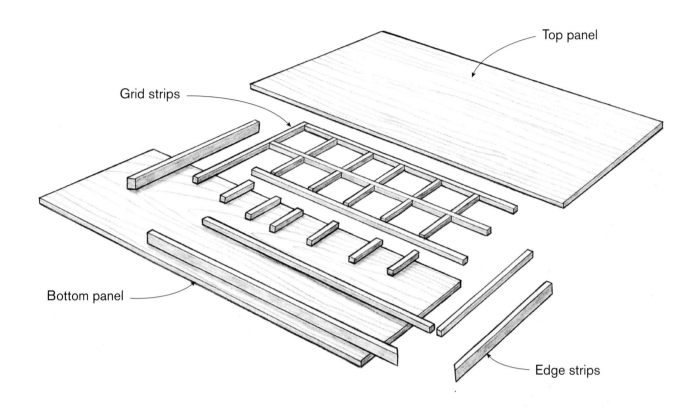

Top panel

Grid strips

Bottom panel

Edge strips

Construction and Assembly

THE THREE DESKTOPS in the example office (8 ft., 5 ft., and 4 ft.) meet the needs I just mentioned elegantly and simply. You can build them in whatever lengths you need. Regardless of length, they are all built using torsion-box construction, a type of hollow-core construction that is very strong and rigid. There are other ways to construct this type of top, but most of them, like the honeycomb core in **photo A** on p. 251, require special materials and machinery. Even torsion-box construction is easier to do if you have a veneer press, but the method used here doesn't require any special tools or machinery.

The tops shown in this chapter are possibly a bit overbuilt. In retrospect, the smaller tops probably could have been made with more widely spaced grids. Still, it won't hurt the top to be too strong, and the project offers good practice in a valuable technique.

TOP VIEW (4-FT. DESKTOP)

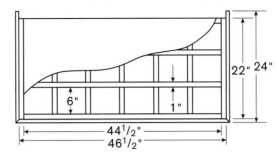

22" 24"

6"

1"

44¹/₂"

46¹/₂"

FRONT VIEW (4-FT. DESKTOP)

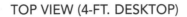

48"

1" ¹/₂" 2"

TOP VIEW (5-FT. DESKTOP)

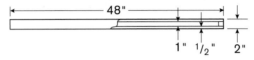

22" 24"

6"

1"

56¹/₂"

58¹/₂"

FRONT VIEW (5-FT. DESKTOP)

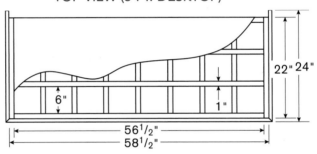

60"

1" ¹/₂" 2"

TOP VIEW (8-FT. DESKTOP)

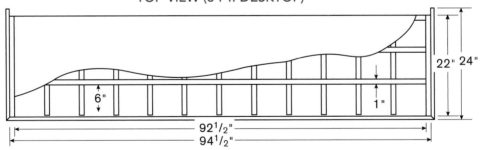

22" 24"

6"

1"

92¹/₂"

94¹/₂"

FRONT VIEW (8-FT. DESKTOP)

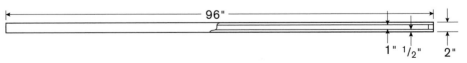

96"

1" ¹/₂" 2"

Torsion-Box Construction

A torsion box consists of two skins of plywood glued to a core grid of thin wooden strips. In essence, you are creating many small I-beams within the box. The resulting structure is stronger than either the skin or the core alone and has tremendous resistance to twisting and bending forces. The engineering of the torsion box converts any applied force into shearing stress on the glue lines between the skin and core grid.

To make the core, you could use nearly any clear species of wood, from poplar (which is used in this chapter) to maple. Just make sure that the wood is stable and all of the same species—if you use different types of wood, differences in seasonal movement could eventually distort the finished panel. Because you are building 2-in.-thick desktops and using ½-in. plywood as the skins, the thickness of the core strips must be exactly 1 in. The width of the strips is not

CUT LIST FOR 8-FT. DESKTOP

Top and Bottom Faces

2	Faces	94½" x 22"	½" cherry plywood

Core

4	Grid strips	92½" x 1" x 1"	solid poplar
2	Grid strips	22" x 1" x 1"	solid poplar
33	Grid strips	6" x 1" x 1"	solid poplar

Edging

1	Edge strip	96" x 2" x ¾"	solid cherry
2	Edge strips	22" x 2" x ¾"	solid cherry

Desktop Connectors

2	Blocks	3" x 1½" x 1½"	solid cherry
2	Blocks	3" x ¾" x 1½"	solid cherry

Other Materials

2	Carriage bolts, with nuts and washers	3" x ⅜"
Approximately 200 screws		#8 x 1¼"
Finish		

CUT LIST FOR 5-FT. DESKTOP

Top and Bottom Faces

2	Faces	58½" x 22"	½" cherry plywood

Core

4	Grid strips	56½" x 1" x 1"	solid poplar
2	Grid strips	22" x 1" x 1"	solid poplar
21	Grid strips	6" x 1" x 1"	solid poplar

Edging

1	Edge strip	60" x 2" x ¾"	solid cherry
2	Edge strips	22" x 2" x ¾"	solid cherry

Other Materials

Approximately 130 screws	#8 x 1¼"
Finish	

CUT LIST FOR 4-FT. DESKTOP

Top and Bottom Faces

2	Faces	46½" x 22"	½" cherry plywood

Core

4	Grid strips	44½" x 1" x 1"	solid poplar
2	Grid strips	22" x 1" x 1"	solid poplar
15	Grid strips	6" x 1" x 1"	solid poplar

Edging

1	Edge strip	48" x 2" x ¾"	solid cherry
2	Edge strips	22" x 2" x ¾"	solid cherry

Other Materials

Approximately 100 screws	#8 x 1¼"
Finish	

critical, but you don't want to make them too thin. Thin strips would be difficult to work with and could compromise the strength of the structure, which comes from the gluelines. For convenience, the strips you will use here are 1 in. square. Whatever dimension you choose, all of the core material must be accurately prepared: It must be flat, uniformly thick, and cut off squarely.

Cutting and laying out the grid

1. Cut to size two pieces of ½-in. plywood for each of the desktops you are building.
2. Rip, joint, and plane as many feet of 1-in. by 1-in. poplar as you need for your desktops, as shown in **photo B** on p. 251. (Refer to "Core Grid Layout" on p. 252 to calculate the length of material you need for the grid.)

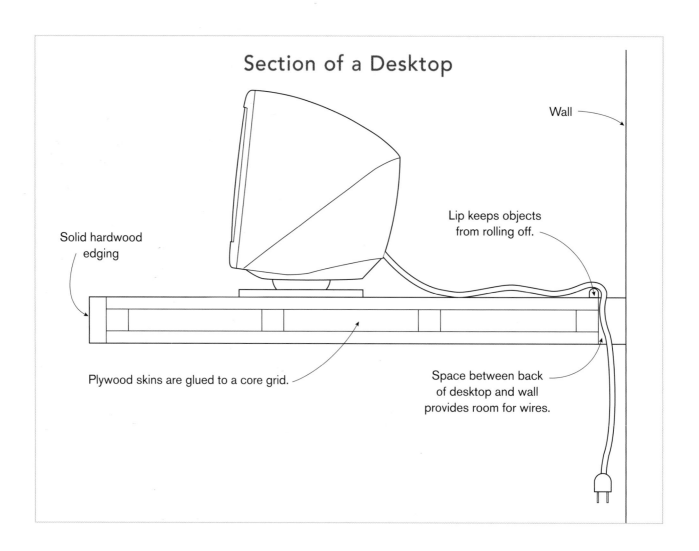

Section of a Desktop

Wall

Lip keeps objects from rolling off.

Solid hardwood edging

Plywood skins are glued to a core grid.

Space between back of desktop and wall provides room for wires.

PHOTO A: Torsion boxes can be constructed using various cores. On the left is an example of a shop-built core and on the right is an example of a manufactured core.

PHOTO B: Ripping all the material for the core at the same time will ensure consistency.

Core Grid Layout

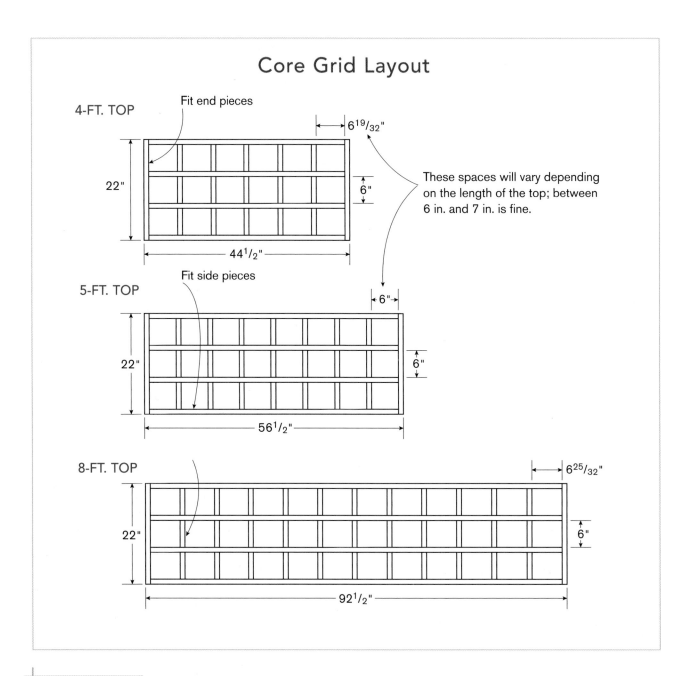

4-FT. TOP

Fit end pieces

6¹⁹/₃₂"

22"

6"

44½"

These spaces will vary depending on the length of the top; between 6 in. and 7 in. is fine.

5-FT. TOP

Fit side pieces

6"

22"

6"

56½"

8-FT. TOP

6²⁵/₃₂"

22"

6"

92½"

TIP

The interior pieces of the grid should all fit snugly, but you don't have to be fanatical about the fit; the strength of this construction comes from the gluelines and not from how well the core is joined.

3. Lay the top piece of plywood face down on a flat surface. The flatness of the surface is important, since the top will take on the properties of the surface it is assembled on and clamped to. If you assemble the top on a surface that is bowed or twisted, the finished top will also be bowed or twisted.

4. Lay out the two end pieces of the core grid, and clamp them in place temporarily.

5. Cut and fit the four interior pieces that run lengthwise end to end, as shown in **photo C** on p. 253.

6. Temporarily clamp the two outside lengthwise pieces in place.

7. Cut and fit the short crosspieces.

Attaching the core to the top

As I mentioned earlier, a veneer press would certainly make the rest of this process easier—if you have one, by all means use it. If you are using a press, you must first prepare the grid by hot-gluing or stapling the four outside pieces of the grid together so they will contain the inner parts when you assemble the torsion box in the press.

PHOTO C: Fit and lay out all the core components before beginning glue-up.

PHOTO D: Bearing down forcefully on the parts when installing the screws will help seat them properly.

If you don't have a veneer press, use the glue and screw method described here. It is very low tech and requires a lot of screws, but it works just fine.

1. When all of the core grid pieces are fitted, remove them, then drill and countersink pilot holes for #8 by 1¼-in. screws in all of the grid parts.

2. Glue and screw the parts in place in the same order you used to fit them, as shown in **photo D**. Be careful not to drive the screws in too deep—you don't want them going through the top.

Attaching the bottom to the core

You can either leave the screws in place (they won't harm anything) or remove them before you attach the bottom. If you choose to remove them, wait until the glue dries before continuing.

1. Place the bottom piece of plywood over the grid and mark the locations of the strips

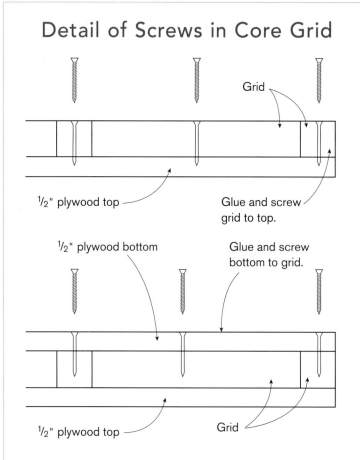

Detail of Screws in Core Grid

Grid

½" plywood top

Glue and screw grid to top.

½" plywood bottom

Glue and screw bottom to grid.

½" plywood top

Grid

on it so you will know where to place the screws (see **photo E**). Regardless of whether the first set of screws is still in place, mark the locations of those screws (or of the empty screw holes) so you don't screw into the same places when you attach the bottom. Then mark the new screw locations.

2. Spread glue on the top of the grid and carefully position the bottom piece of plywood over it, making sure its edges are flush with the side pieces. Clamp the bottom in place.

3. Drill and countersink pilot holes at all of your location marks, and screw the bottom to the grid.

4. If you don't like the idea of having these screws visible under your desktop, remove them after the glue is dry and plug the holes.

Attaching the edging

The torsion-box edge, which is now a sandwich of plywood edge and poplar, needs to be finished to match the desktop. The most straightforward solution is to glue a solid cherry edge to the core. The instructions given here are for the 8-ft. desktop.

1. Cut, joint, and plane some solid cherry 2⅛ in. wide by ¾ in. thick, and cut one length to approximately 98 in. and two lengths to approximately 26 in. each. These pieces are slightly oversize; the 2⅛-in. face will be attached later to the edge of the torsion box and planed flush with the faces of the top.

2. Carefully miter one end of each of the three cherry strips at 45 degrees across the ¾-in. face.

3. Line up the mitered end of the long strip at one end of the long edge of the top, using one of the short pieces as a guide to align it.

Clamp in it place temporarily and mark the other end of the piece where it extends past the top (see **photo F**).

4. Miter the other end of the strip at the location you've marked.

5. Next, spread glue on the strip, carefully realign it, and clamp it to the edge of the top, making sure it is about ¹⁄₁₆ in. proud of the top and bottom faces of the top.

6. Spread glue on the short strips and at the miters, align them carefully, and clamp them to the ends of the top.

7. When the glue is dry, scrape off any excess and plane the edging flush with the face of the top using a handplane.

PHOTO F: Solid cherry edging hides the exposed plywood and poplar sandwich.

TIP

When two desktops meet, one of them will have to be supported by the other, so the support underneath them has to be very strong.

8. With your table saw fence set to 24 in. from the blade, run the top through the saw with the front edge against the fence. This will trim off the excess edging on the ends of the top, leaving it protruding 2 in. beyond the back edge. The 2-in. space allows you to feed wires down the back of the desktop.

9. Finish-sand the top to 150 grit.

Attaching the lip

The ⅜-in. bullnose lip glued to the back edge of the desktop keeps pencils and other small objects from rolling into the 2-in. gap behind the desktop and ending up on the floor (see **photo G**).

1. To attach the lip, cut, joint, and plane a strip of solid cherry 94½ in. by ⅜ in. by ⅜ in.

2. Sand the top edges of the strip aggressively until they are quite round.

3. Carefully glue and clamp the strip to the back top edge of the desktop.

Supporting the Top

Depending on how you configure your office, the desktop may or may not need some additional support. If you've made a single desktop that rests on cabinets at both ends, you don't need any further support. However, if your desktop ends at a wall, you will need a way to support the top. This is especially important if you have two desktops meeting in a corner with no cabinet underneath to support them.

One approach is to screw ledgers to the wall. On inside corners, such as the corner where the two longest tops come together, ledgers are all but invisible. However, in other places, such as where the 4-ft. desktop hits the wall, they are quite visible and don't look very elegant. More important, ledgers have to be anchored securely, which in practice usually means they must be lagged to the wall into the wall studs. Anchoring them can be a difficult and frustrating process.

A better solution is to build a side panel

Desktop Support Panel

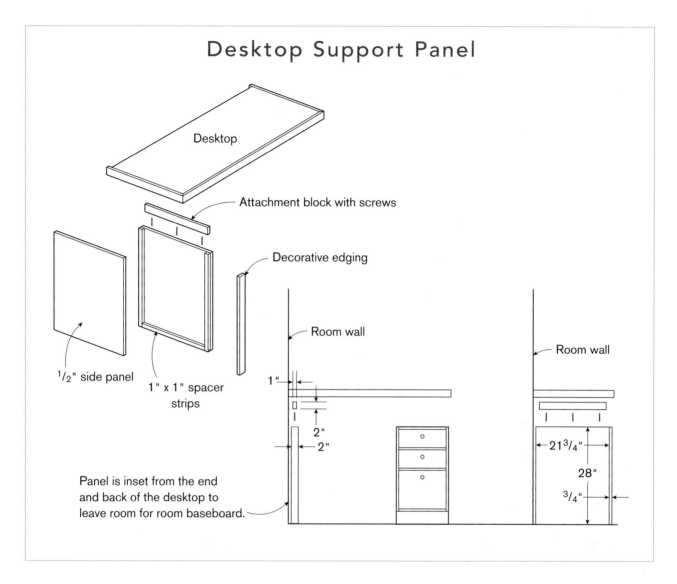

Desktop

Attachment block with screws

Decorative edging

Room wall

Room wall

1/2" side panel

1" x 1" spacer strips

1"

2"
2"

21³/₄"

28"

³/₄"

Panel is inset from the end and back of the desktop to leave room for room baseboard.

high enough to support the top and transfer its weight directly to the floor. The panel is constructed similarly to the desktop but without the inside grid core structure. Also, the outside edging goes around only three sides of the panel. The top of the panel is left open to form a pocket into which a strip glued to the desktop will fit.

1. Start by cutting two ½-in. plywood panels each 28 in. by 21¼ in.

2. Cut, joint, and plane solid poplar 1 in. by 1 in. (the same size used in the core grid), and cut one 19¾-in. strip and two 28-in. strips.

3. Glue and clamp the two 28-in. pieces to the front and back of one of the plywood panels, placing each flush with the edge.

4. Glue and clamp the 19¾-in. piece to the bottom of the panel between the other two pieces.

5. When the glue is dry, remove the clamps and glue on the other panel, making sure the edges line up perfectly. Allow the glue to dry again, then clean up any excess and remove the clamps.

6. Cut, joint, and plane a piece of solid cherry 28 in. by 2⅛ in. by ¾ in. This is the same stock used for the desktop edging.

7. Glue and carefully align this piece onto the front edge of the assembly and clamp it in place, making sure it is approximately ¹⁄₁₆ in. proud of the plywood faces.

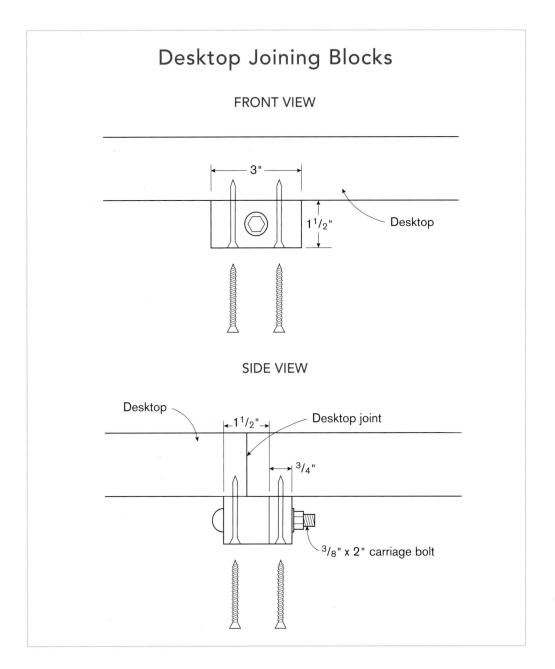

Desktop Joining Blocks

FRONT VIEW

3"

1¹/₂"

Desktop

SIDE VIEW

Desktop

Desktop joint

1¹/₂"

³/₄"

³/₈" x 2" carriage bolt

8. When the glue is dry, scrape off any excess and use a handplane to plane the edging flush with the faces of the panel.

9. Finish-sand the assembly to 150 grit.

10. To attach the side panel to the desktop, cut, joint, and plane a piece of solid poplar 21⅝ in. by 2 in. by 1 in. After chamfering the edges slightly, screw this piece to the underside of the desktop along the side that needs to be supported. It will fit into the pocket created in the top of the support panel assembly. Since you've made it ⅛ in. shorter

than the pocket, which is 21¾ in. long, it can be inserted easily.

Attaching Two Tops

Where two tops come together at right angles, they must be connected in some way. This connection must not only join the top surfaces flush but also must firmly support the free edge of the long top. I didn't want to use a connection that required cutting or screwing anything into the edges of the desktops, which might make the edges unsightly if you rearranged the desktops in the future.

Since I couldn't find any hardware that met all of these requirements, I designed the connectors shown in **photo H**. The solution turned out to be very simple.

1. Cut two solid cherry blocks each 3 in. by 1½ in. by 1½ in. and two blocks each 3 in. by 1½ in. by ¾ in. Clamp each larger block to a smaller block. You should now have two block assemblies that are each 3 in. by 2¼ in. by 1½ in.

2. Drill a ⅜-in. hole into the center of one 3-in. by 1½-in. face and all the way through both blocks. Repeat the process for the second pair of blocks.

3. Separate the parts and drill two countersunk pilot holes into each block at right angles to the ⅜-in. holes. Locate the pilot holes ¾ in. from the ends of the blocks and ¾ in. from the outside faces.

PHOTO H: This side panel provides elegant support for the top.

PHOTO I: Spacers fitted during the installation of the blocks ensure that the tops will pull tightly together.

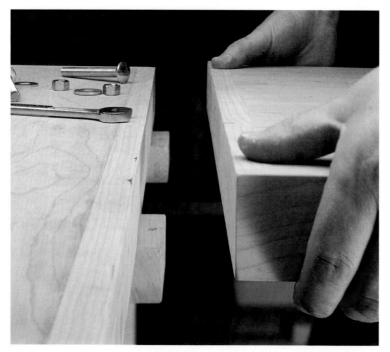

PHOTO J: The extending portions of the larger blocks support the second top.

4. Turning the two desktops to be joined upside down, clamp them together in the position they will be when joined.

5. Center the larger blocks on the seam, 4½ in. in from the front and back edges of the larger top with the bolt holes perpendicular to the seam, and mark their locations.

6. Glue and screw the blocks in place, making sure to glue them only to the smaller top. The larger top will rest on the protruding portions of the blocks.

7. Insert ⅜-in. by 3-in. carriage bolts from the sides of the blocks that are not protruding, then spread glue on the bottoms of the smaller blocks and carefully (so as not to smear the glue) slide them onto the bolts. The smaller blocks should be glued to the larger tops as shown in **photo I** on p. 259.

8. Place a 1⁄16-in. spacer (a small piece of edge tape is perfect) between each set of blocks, install a washer and nut on each bolt, and tighten.

9. Screw the smaller blocks in place. When the glue is dry, remove the clamps, bolts, and spacers, and turn the tops over.

When you're ready to connect the tops, rest the larger top on the protruding portion of the blocks as shown in **photo J**, line up the holes in the blocks, install the bolts (without the spacers), and tighten. The small gap left by the spacers will ensure that the joint between the tops will close up tightly (see **photo K**).

Finishing

I finished these pieces using a spray-on lacquer, but there are several other finishing methods to choose from.

PHOTO K: The tops fit together tightly and flat.

PRINTER STAND

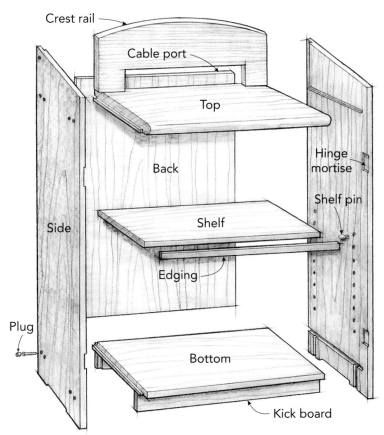

Crest rail

Cable port

Top

Back

Hinge mortise

Shelf pin

Side

Shelf

Edging

Plug

Bottom

Kick board

The case joinery consists primarily of tongues on the horizontal pieces that fit into dadoes and grooves in the case sides. The crest rail and back simply fit into rabbets cut into the rear edges of the case sides. The large cable port allows room for projecting cable plugs. The raised kick boards and lower cutouts on the sides allow the case to sit on four "feet" for good stability.

The door frames are joined with loose tenons. The solid-wood panels are rabbeted to create tongues that fit into grooves cut in the door frames.

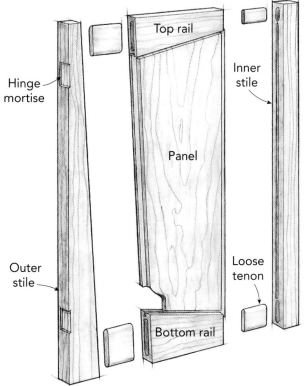

Hinge mortise

Top rail

Inner stile

Panel

Outer stile

Loose tenon

Bottom rail

DESIGN OPTIONS

- ✦ Outfit the inside of the cabinet with custom dividers and pigeonholes.

- ✦ Design the door stiles and rails to match existing cabinetry.

- ✦ Incorporate a drawer into the cabinet.

- ✦ Use hardwood plywood for the case and door panels.

Top, Side, and Front Views of Printer Stand

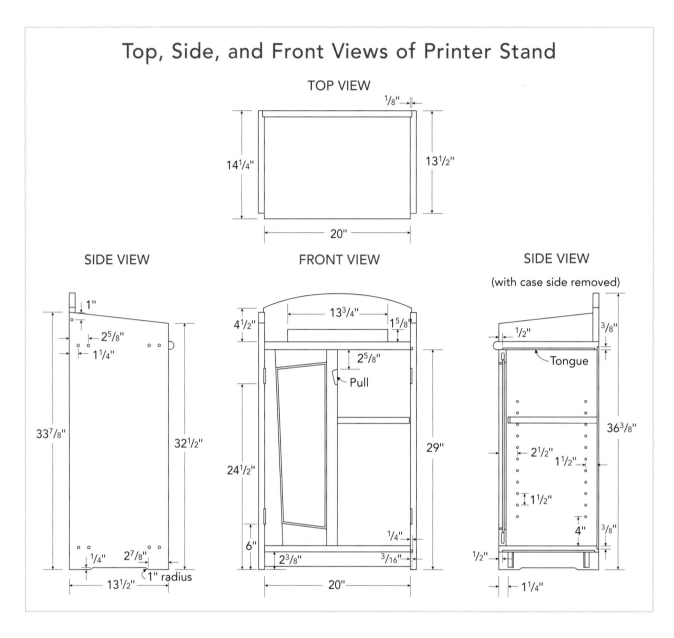

TOP VIEW

SIDE VIEW

FRONT VIEW

SIDE VIEW
(with case side removed)

A

S WHEN MAKING ANY cabinet with inset doors, it's necessary to make the case first so that the doors can be fit precisely into their openings.

Constructing the Case

This cabinet is made from solid wood, so the first step is to make the panels for the parts. After that, you'll cut the joints, drill the shelf holes, and assemble the case.

Prepare the parts

1. Make the solid-wood panels for the sides, top, and bottom. Pick attractive boards for the sides. If you have to edge-join narrower boards to make the panels, lay them out for consistent grain and color match.

2. Plane and rip the stock for the kick boards and crest rail. Leave the pieces slightly oversize in length for now. You'll crosscut them for a perfect fit after assembling the case.

3. After flattening and smoothing any joined-up panels, lay out the angle at the top of each side and the profile at the bottom.

4. Cut the angle at the top of each side. Remember that there's a left and a right, and that you'll want to keep the good sides facing outward. You can use a commercial after-

Front and Side Views of Doors

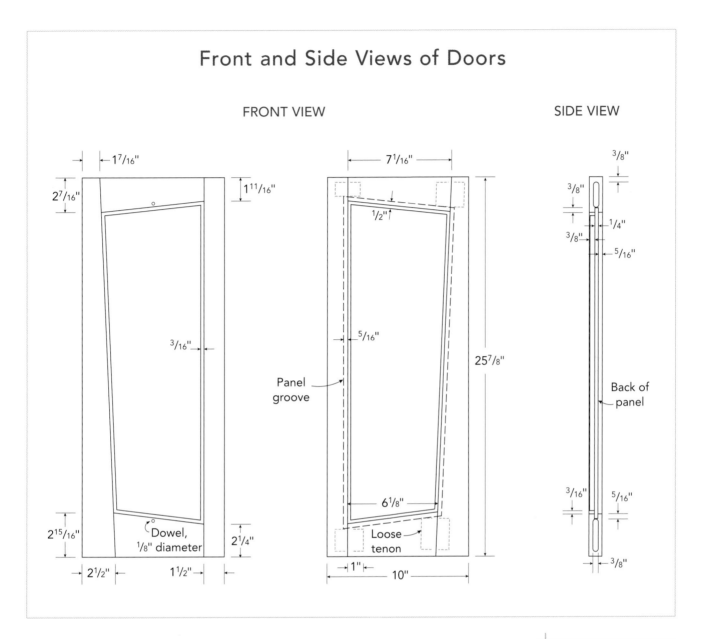

FRONT VIEW

SIDE VIEW

1⁷/₁₆"

2⁷/₁₆"

1¹¹/₁₆"

3/16"

2¹⁵/₁₆"

Dowel, 1/8" diameter

2¼"

2½"

1½"

7¹/₁₆"

1/2"

5/16"

Panel groove

25⁷/₈"

6¹/₈"

Loose tenon

1"

10"

3/8"

3/8"

1/4"

3/8"

5/16"

Back of panel

3/16"

5/16"

3/8"

market miter gauge with a long extension fence to make the cut. Alternatively, you could tack a temporary fence onto a crosscut sled or cut the angle with a jigsaw or portable circular saw guided by a wood fence clamped to the workpiece.

5. Cut the profile at the bottom of each side that creates the "feet." First shape the ends using a 1-in.-dia. drill bit. Then cut the remaining straight section with a jigsaw. You could also make a hardboard template of the shape and use it to guide a router outfitted with a template guide. Chamfer the bottom

edges of the feet slightly to prevent tearout when dragging the cabinet.

6. Lay out the curve on the crest rail. To get a fair curve, spring a thin strip of straight-grained wood to the proper curvature.

7. Cut the curve with a jigsaw or bandsaw or use a router guided by a custom template. Then sand the curve smooth.

8. Cut the plywood shelves to size; then make the solid-wood edging strips and apply them to the front edge of each shelf.

TIP

When laying out parts, select the nicest-looking boards for the most prominent surfaces. Consider how a piece of furniture will be viewed in place. For the typical base cabinet, the front and top are the most prominent, followed by the sides.

CUT LIST FOR PRINTER STAND

Case		
2 Sides	¾" x 13½" x 33⅞"	solid wood
1 Top	1" x 14¼" x 20½"	solid wood
1 Bottom	¾" x 13½" x 20½"	solid wood
2 Kick boards	¾" x 2" x 20⅜"	solid wood
1 Crest rail	¾" x 6⅜" x 20¼"	solid wood
1 Back	¼" x 20¾" x 26⅝"	hardwood plywood
4 Shelves	¾" x 11¾" x 19⅞"	hardwood plywood
4 Shelf	¼" x ¾" x 19⅞"	solid wood edgings
Doors		
2 Outer stiles	1" x 2½" x 25⅞"	solid wood
2 Inner stiles	1" x 1½" x 25⅞"	solid wood
2 Top rails	1" x 2 7/16" x 7 3/16"	solid wood
2 Bottom rails	1" x 2 15/16" x 6¼"	solid wood
2 Panels	⅝" x 7¾" x 22 11/16"	solid wood
2 Pulls	¾" x ¾" x 2"	solid wood
Other materials		
4 Butt hinges	2" x ⅞"	from Rockler; item #32926
16 Shelf support pins	¼"	from Rockler; item #30437
2 Brass ball catches	1¾" x 5/16"	from Rockler; item #28613

Make the joints

1. Lay out the ¼-in.-wide dadoes in the sides to accept the tongues you'll cut on the ends of the top and bottom. The bottom groove is 2⅜ in. up from the bottom, and the top groove is 29 in. up from the bottom.

2. Rout the dadoes 5/16 in. deep, guiding the router with a straightedge.

3. Lay out the ⅝-in.-wide grooves in the sides to accept the kick boards. The grooves run all the way to the bottom of each side, although the kick board doesn't. Then rout the 3/16-in.-deep grooves, again guiding the router with a straightedge.

4. Cut the rabbets on the ends of the top and bottom pieces to create the ¼-in.-thick by ¼-in.-long tongues. This is easily done on the router table, feeding the workpiece on end against the fence (see **photo A** on p. 265). Instead, you could make the cuts on the tablesaw. Aim for a snug fit in the dadoes.

5. Use a handsaw to trim away the front section of each tongue to match the length of the stopped dado. Clean up the sawn surface with a chisel if necessary.

6. Rout the ¼-in.-wide by ⅜-in.-deep rabbets in the rear edges of the sides and top and bottom to accept the ¼-in.-thick back panel. Dry-assemble the case pieces to determine where to stop the rabbets on the case sides.

7. Lay out and rout the ¾-in.-wide by ⅛-in.-deep rabbets in the rear edges of the sides to accept the ends of the crest rail.

Cut the hinge mortises in the case

An attractive, well-hung door depends on good-quality hinges that fit well in properly cut mortises. With a bit of careful work, you can install hinges that fit sweetly in their mortises and create perfect planar alignment of a door with its frame. Before you mortise your project, it's wise to cut two mating mortises in scrap, then temporarily join them with a hinge to check the gap between the two pieces.

1. Position the hinge so that its pin projects just beyond the case front.

2. Hold the hinge down firmly and scribe around the perimeter of the leaf with a sharp knife (see **photo B** on p. 265). Make your first pass a light one to prevent shoving the hinge. Deepen the outline on the second pass.

3. Adjust a your router so a straight bit projects 1/32 in. below the center of the hinge pin (see "Bit Adjustment for Routing a Hinge Mortise" on p. 267). This will create a 1/16-in. gap between the door and its frame. For less of a gap, increase the bit projection accordingly.

4. Rout the majority of the waste from the mortise, staying 1/16 in. or so inside the scribed lines (see **photo C** on p. 266).

5. Using a very sharp chisel, pare back to your scribed outline, cutting downward to the depth of the mortise bottom (see **photo D** on p. 266). Remove the waste by paring it away from the bottom of the mortise, moving toward the edges (see **photo E** on p. 266).

6. After you slice away all bits of remaining wood inside the scribed outline, the hinge should fit perfectly (see **photo F** on p. 266).

Assemble the case

1. Dry-clamp the top and bottom between the sides to make sure the joints draw up tightly and the pieces all properly align.

2. With the case still clamped, measure for the back and cut it to fit snugly within its rabbets.

3. Drill and counterbore the holes in the case sides for securing the top and bottom into their dadoes with #10 by 2½-in. flat-head screws.

4. Glue the case sides to the top and bottom. Place the unglued back into its rabbets to help hold the case square while drying. Lay the case on its back on a flat surface and compare the diagonal measurements across the front. If necessary, pull the case into square by applying clamp pressure diagonally across the front.

5. Measure between the kick board grooves and cut the kick boards to length. Then glue and clamp the pieces to the case bottom and sides.

6. Trim the crest rail to fit within its rabbets, then saw the cable port.

7. Attach the crest rail, gluing it to the top and screwing it to the sides.

TIP

Good-quality extruded brass hinges are more expensive than the stamped hinges typically found in hardware stores, but they look and work much better. They're beefier, stronger, and the pins won't slop around in the knuckle like in the stamped steel jobs.

PHOTO A: Cut the rabbet on each end of the top and bottom piece to create the ¼-in. by ¼-in. tongue. Cutting the rabbets on the router table as shown here ensures a tongue of consistent thickness.

PHOTO B: Hold the hinge down firmly and scribe around the perimeter of the leaf with a sharp knife. Make your first pass a light one to prevent shoving the hinge. Deepen the outline on the second pass.

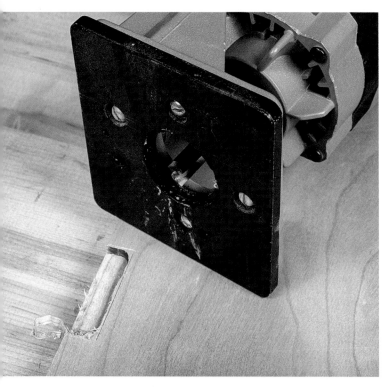

PHOTO C: When routing the waste from the mortise, stay ⅟₁₆ in. or so inside the scribed lines.

PHOTO D: With a chisel, pare back to the scribed outline and then cut down to the full depth of the mortise.

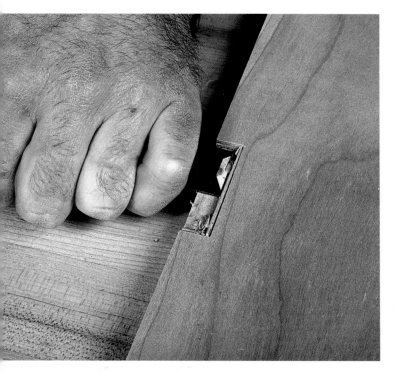

PHOTO E: Pare the waste from the bottom of the mortise.

PHOTO F: The hinge should fit perfectly.

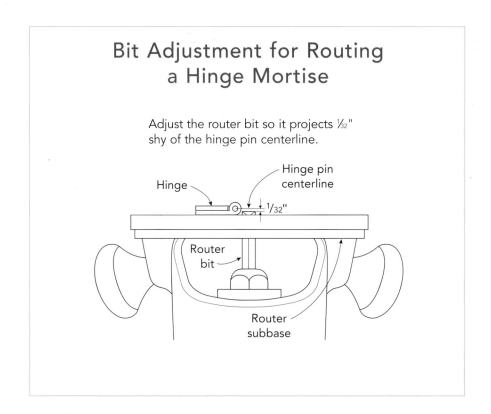

Bit Adjustment for Routing a Hinge Mortise

Adjust the router bit so it projects $\frac{1}{32}$" shy of the hinge pin centerline.

Hinge

Hinge pin centerline

$\frac{1}{32}$"

Router bit

Router subbase

PHOTO G: After assembling the case, glue the ebony plugs into the counterbored screw holes.

PHOTO H: You can use a shopmade drilling template to save layout time and ensure that the shelf support holes are spaced accurately.

TIP

When installing wood plugs, be sure to orient the grain of the plugs parallel to the grain of the workpiece so that the wood of both will move in the same direction. This also helps disguise plugs that aren't of a contrasting wood.

8. Make the plugs for filling the counter-bored screw holes. Although Burton used plugs made of ebony, you could use any contrasting or matching wood. Glue the plugs into their holes (see **photo G** on p. 267). After the glue dries, trim the plugs flush.
9. Drill the holes for the shelf supports. A shopmade template makes quick work of this and ensures accurate spacing (see **photo H**).
10. Make the shelves. Burton used ¾-in.-thick birch plywood edged with solid wood.

Constructing the Doors

Now that the case is built, you can make the doors for an exact fit. If you like, you could forego making the tapered frame doors in favor of doors that match your existing office cabinetry. But if you want to give it

a try, you'll find the tapered stiles and rails aren't all that difficult to make. The technique provides a method to account for small errors in the rail angles so that the doors still come together correctly. You'll cut the rail angles, do the joinery, and then glue the rails onto the straight stiles before attaching the angled stiles. You'll cancel out any small errors in that assembly by passing it lightly by the sawblade so that the rail faces are cut parallel to the door sides. The final stile is not tapered, so the assembly ends up being very similar to any other door.

Make the parts
1. Begin by making a full-size drawing of the door so you'll be able to take direct measurements from it for the various angles and tapers.

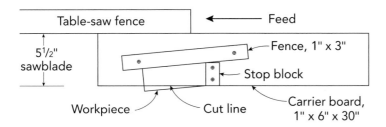

Tapering Jig

Table-saw fence

← Feed

$5\frac{1}{2}$" sawblade

Fence, 1" x 3"

Stop block

Workpiece — Cut line

Carrier board, 1" x 6" x 30"

This three-piece jig consists of a fence, a stop block, and a carrier board with straight, parallel sides. To use it, set your fence to the width of the carrier board and align your cut line to the edge of the carrier board, as shown. Screw the fence and stop block against the workpiece and you're ready to cut.

2. Mill the square blanks for the rails and stiles. Leave the rails about ¼-in. oversize in length for now. Mill the panels to ⅝ in. thick, but leave them oversize in width and length.

3. Lay out the rails and stiles for a pleasing grain pattern and mark them for orientation (see "Triangle Marking System" on p. 18).

4. Trimming away as little as possible, square the end of each rail that abuts the center stile.

5. Referring to your full-size plans, lay out the tapers on the rails and outer stiles.

6. Saw the tapers. Burton uses a simple, shopmade tapering jig for the job (see "Tapering Jig"). You'll need to reset the jig for each pair of top and bottom rails, because their tapers differ.

7. Again using your full-size pattern, lay out the tapered ends on the rails, then crosscut at that angle, about ⅛ in. outside of your cut line. You'll do the final trimming after assembling the rails to the inner stiles.

Cut the joints and assemble the doors

1. Lay out the ⅜-in.-wide mortises on the stiles and rails. The length of each rail mortise extends to within ⅜ in. from the edge of the rail.

2. Rout the mortises to a depth of 1 in. Use a router edge guide to center the mortises across the thickness of the stock. A jig can be very helpful when routing mortises in the ends of rails (see "Router Mortising Jig" on p. 278).

3. Mill lengths of stock from which to crosscut the individual tenons. Rip the stock to a width about ⅛ in. less than the length of its mortise. Then plane the tenon stock so it slides into the mortise with just a bit of finger pressure. After routing or planing a bullnose profile on both edges of the stock, crosscut the individual tenons to length.

4. Rout the ⁵⁄₁₆-in.-deep by ¼-in.-wide grooves in all of the rails and stiles to accept the door panels (see **photo I** on p. 270).

Space the groove ⁵⁄₁₆ in. away from the rear face of each rail or stile and stop it just short of each frame mortise.

5. Dry-assemble each rail to its outermost stile to make sure that the corners of the frame are square and that the tenons aren't too long. If necessary, trim the rail ends or tenons.

6. Glue and clamp each top and bottom rail to its outermost stile. Make sure the outer edge of each rail aligns with the end of its stile and that the joints are pulled fully home along their length. Let the glue dry thoroughly after wiping off any excess.

7. Set your tablesaw rip fence for an 8½-in. cut, then trim the inner ends of the rails to perfect length by feeding the frame assembly through the tablesaw (see **photo J**). This will reduce the depth of the mortise a bit, but you'll cut the length of your loose tenon to suit.

8. Saw the door panels to shape and size, taking measurements directly from the frame. When ripping them to width,

PHOTO I: Rout the ¼-in.-wide by ⁵⁄₁₆-in.-deep door panel grooves using a slotting cutter on the router table.

PHOTO J: After gluing the rails to the tapered outer stiles, feed the door frame assembly through the tablesaw to trim the innermost ends of the rails, creating a perfect fit against the edges of the inner stile.

remember to allow for wood movement across the grain.

9. Saw or rout the ⅜-in.-deep by ½-in.-wide rabbets in the front edges of the panels. This will create a ¼-in.-thick by ½-in.-wide tongue on the edges of the panels to fit into the grooves in the door frame.

10. Slip the panels into their grooves and dry-assemble the innermost stiles to their rails to check the fit of the joints and panel.

11. Prefinish the panels to prevent bare wood from showing when the panels shrink. Sand the inside edges of the stiles and rails through 220 grit.

12. Place the unglued panels in their grooves, then glue and clamp the stiles to the rails. Make sure the assemblies lie flat while under clamp pressure to prevent twisting the doors. To keep each panel centered in its frame, Burton pins them with two ⅛-in.-dia. dowels through the rear of the frame into the panel.

13. Sand the front and rear faces of the doors through 220 grit. Don't worry about the edges for now.

Attach the doors and pulls

Flush-mounted doors are one of the emblems of quality cabinetry. Although more difficult to install than overlay doors, they impart much more elegance to a piece. Here's how to correctly install them flush to the case with a small gap of consistent width between the doors and the cabinet opening.

1. Begin by cutting the hinge mortises in the case. (This is often done before case

PHOTO K: Replace the door in its opening, straddling a couple of ¾₄-in.-thick shims. Use a sharp knife to lay out each hinge into the front edge of the stile.

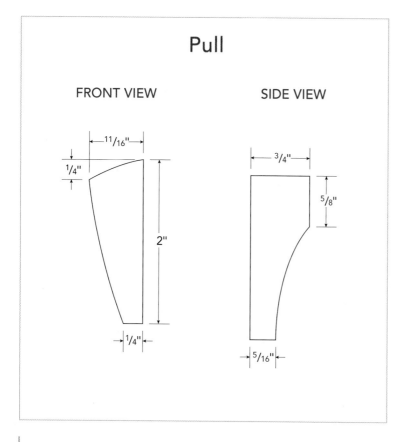

Pull

FRONT VIEW

11/16"

1/4"

2"

1/4"

SIDE VIEW

3/4"

5/8"

5/16"

5. Remove the door and align a hinge to your knife mark with the axis of the hinge pin projecting just beyond the case front. Trace around the hinge leaf with a sharp knife; then rout and chisel the mortises.

6. Install the door with one center screw per hinge, again offsetting the screws slightly to draw the hinge leaf against the rear wall of the mortise.

7. To establish the trim line at the top of the door, make a mark at each upper corner of the door ³⁄₃₂ in. away from the case top. Remove the door, connect the marks using a ruler, and then plane to the trim line.

8. Reattach the doors and check the gaps for consistency. Use a handplane to make any corrections.

9. Sand the edges of the doors through 220 grit and ease all of the corners slightly.

10. Make the pulls. Draw each front profile on ¾-in.-thick stock, then bandsaw and sand to the lines. Next, draw the side profile on the outermost edge of each pull and bandsaw to the line, laying the flat edge of the pull on the bandsaw table. Finish up by sanding the rear of the pulls.

11. Glue and screw the pulls to the doors, positioning them 2⅝ in. down from the tops of the doors.

Finishing Up

1. Remove the doors and hinges. Do any necessary touchup sanding to all exposed surfaces.

2. If you like, stain the birch plywood shelves to match the color of your case wood.

3. Apply the finish of your choice. Burton wiped on three coats of an antique oil finish, scuffing with 0000 steel wool between coats.

4. Attach the hinges and reinstall the doors, using all the hinge screws this time.

5. Install the brass ball catches to the case top and center stile of each door.

6. Install the shelf support pins and shelves. Then load up the cabinet and click "print"!

TIP

Avoid using magnetic catches of any sort near computer disks. The magnetic field can harm digital data.

assembly because the case top and bottom can impede router access afterward.)

2. Trim the door to fit the dimensions of the case opening minus ¹⁄₁₆ in. in length and width. Set the door into its opening, resting on the case bottom but pressed against the case side. Note any gaps along the bottom edge, then plane the bottom of the door until the stile and bottom rail sit entirely flush against the case side and bottom.

3. Install the hinges into their case mortises with one center screw per hinge. Offset the screws very slightly to draw the hinge leaf against the rear wall of the mortise.

4. Replace the door in its opening, straddling a couple of dimes or other ³⁄₆₄-in.-thick shims. Press the door stile against the folded hinges and run a sharp knife along the top edge of each hinge and into the front edge of the stile (see **photo K** on p. 271).

FILE CABINET

This heavy-duty file cabinet is constructed of ¾"-thick hardwood plywood with a solid-wood face frame and edging. The face frame is constructed with loose tenon joints. The drawer slide shims allow mounting of commercial full-extension slides.

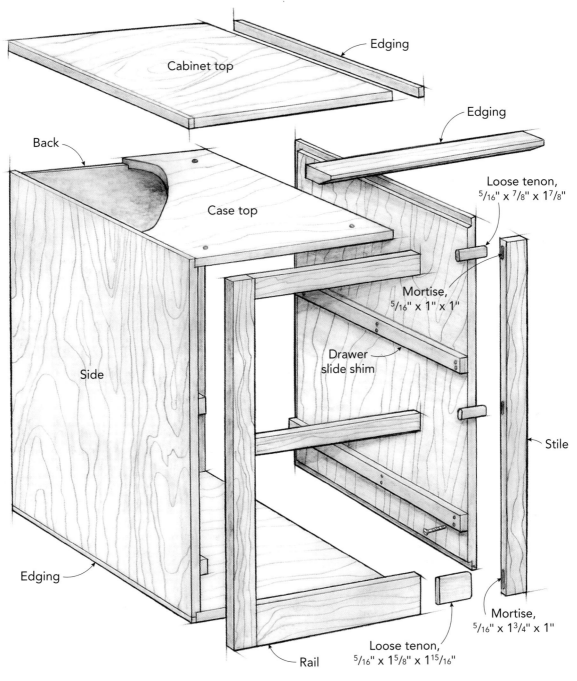

Edging

Cabinet top

Edging

Back

Case top

Loose tenon,
$5/16$" x $7/8$" x $1^7/8$"

Mortise,
$5/16$" x 1" x 1"

Drawer slide shim

Side

Stile

Edging

Mortise,
$5/16$" x $1^3/4$" x 1"

Rail

Loose tenon,
$5/16$" x $1^5/8$" x $1^{15}/16$"

Not to scale

Side and Front Views

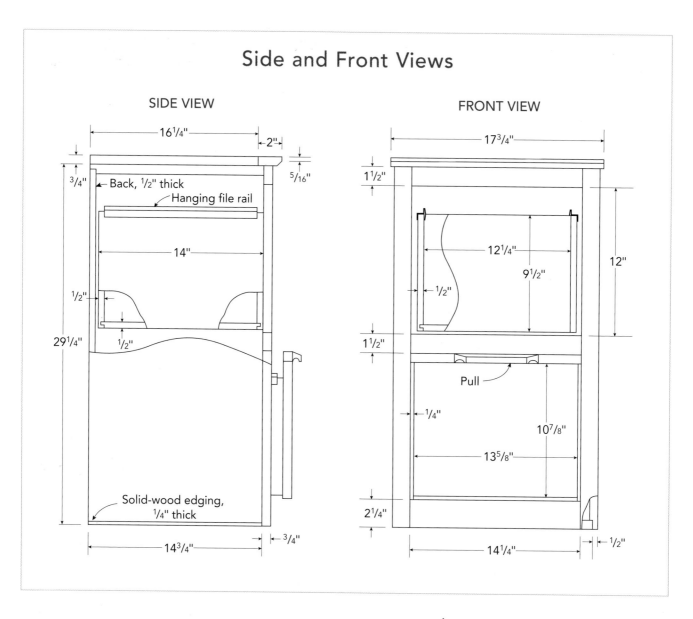

SIDE VIEW

FRONT VIEW

BUILD THE CASE and face frame first. Then make the drawer boxes and install them. Last, make and attach the drawer fronts and cabinet top.

Building the Case

Make the plywood box
1. Lay out and cut the cabinet top, case sides, case top, case bottom, and back to size.
2. Mark the pieces for orientation (see "Triangle Marking System" on p. 18).
3. Mill the ¼-in. by ¾-in. solid-wood edging for the bottoms of the sides. The edging protects the plywood from tearout when moving the cabinet.

DESIGN OPTIONS

✦ For a traditional look, make beveled, solid-wood drawer fronts, using commercially available brass pulls and card holders.

✦ For legal-size files, make the cabinet and drawers 3 in. wider than shown.

✦ Make an instant desk by placing a separate top across two file cabinets.

4. Glue the edging to the sides, then plane or scrape it flush to the plywood after the glue cures.

5. Cut the ¼ in. by ¾ in. rabbets in the top and bottom edges of the sides. I do this on the tablesaw using a dado head (see **photo A** on p. 276). Set up the cut using scrap from the same plywood sheet that yielded the sides.

6. Reset the rip fence for a ½-in.-wide cut, but leave the height of the dado head as is. Then cut the rabbets in the rear edges of all the case pieces to accept the ½-in.-thick plywood back.

7. Dry-clamp the case and make sure the back fits into its rabbets. The closer the fit, the better, as the back will help square up the case during glue-up.

8. Unclamp the case and apply glue to both halves of each joint. Clamp up the case using thick hardwood cauls to distribute pressure across the joints. Make sure the clamp screws align with the case top and bottom to prevent bowing in the case sides. Place the back unglued into its rabbets to hold the case square while the glue cures.

9. Mill the edging stock for the cabinet top. Rip the pieces from a board that you've planed to about ¹⁄₃₂ in. thicker than your plywood.

10. Glue the side edging on first, then plane or scrape it flush to the plywood after the glue cures. Next, glue on the front edging and plane it flush to the plywood.

11. Mark the 45-degree chamfer on the end of the front edging. Rip the chamfer on the tablesaw, then plane or sand off any saw marks.

Make and attach the face frame

1. Cut the stiles and rails to size. To ensure a flat, square face frame, joint the inside edges of the stiles square and crosscut the rails accurately. Mill extra stock for tool setup.

2. Lay out the pieces for a pleasing grain pattern and mark them for orientation.

3. Cut the face frame joints. I used loose tenon joinery, which consists of two mating mortises that accept a separately made tenon. I routed the mortises using a shop-made jig (see "Router Mortising Jig" on

CUT LIST FOR FILE CABINET

2	Sides	¾" x 14¾" x 29"	hardwood plywood
2	Case top and bottom	¾" x 14¾" x 29"	hardwood plywood
1	Top	¾" x 14¼" x 17¼"	hardwood plywood
1	Back	½" x 16¼" x 28¼"	hardwood plywood
2	Side/bottom edgings	¾" x ¼" x 14¾"	solid wood
1	Top edging	¾" x 2" x 17¾"	solid wood
2	Top edgings	¾" x ¼" x 14¼"	solid wood
2	Stiles	¾" x 11⁷⁄₃₂" x 29¼"	solid wood
2	Rails	¾" x 1½" x 14¼"	solid wood
1	Rail	¾" x 2¼" x 14¼"	solid wood
4	Drawer slide shims	¾" x 2½" x 14⅛"	solid wood
2	Drawer fronts	¾" x 10⅞" x 13⅝"	hardwood plywood
4	Drawer sides	½" x 9½" x 14"	hardwood plywood
4	Drawer fronts and backs	½" x 9½" x 12¾"	hardwood plywood
2	Drawer bottoms	½" x 13½" x 12¾"	hardwood plywood
2	Pulls	¾" x 1½" x 14⅛"	solid wood
2	Drawer front edgings	¾" x ¼" x 13⅝"	solid wood
4	Drawer front edgings	¾" x ¼" x 11⅛"	solid wood

Other materials

2 pairs Overtravel drawer slides	14"		from Woodworker's Hardware; item #KV8505 14
1 Hanging file rail	2.5m		from Woodworker's Hardware; item #CPF32500

TIP

Hardwood plywood often varies from its nominal thickness. To ensure accurate overall dimensions, measure the positive half of a cut joint, not the negative space. For example, when cutting the ¼-in.-deep rabbets in ¾-in.-thick case sides, make sure that the tongue is ½ in. thick, regardless of the depth.

PHOTO A: After applying protective solid-wood edging to the bottom of the side pieces, saw the rabbets in the top and bottom edges using a dado head and an auxiliary rip fence.

PHOTO B: To ease assembly, connect and align one half of the face frame before the glue sets up tack. Then glue on the other stile. The ¾-in.-diameter dowels center the clamp pressure on the stiles, preventing them from buckling under clamp pressure.

p. 278). Alternatively, you could join the face frame using biscuits, pocket screws, or dowels.

4. Rip long strips for the tenons from stock that you've planed to fit the mortises snugly. Round over the edges of the tenon stock on the router table to match approximately the radius of the mortises. Then cut the individual tenons to length.

5. Glue up the face frame on a flat surface, carefully aligning the rails with the ends of the stiles (see **photo B**). Make sure that the drawer openings are 12 in. high.

6. After the glue cures, plane or belt sand both faces of the frame. To ensure a good glue joint against the case, make certain that the rear face is very flat.

7. Make the drawer slide shims.

8. With the cabinet back sitting unglued in its rabbets and the drawer slide shims temporarily in place, attach the face frame. Make sure the drawer slide shims are equally aligned with the inside edges of the stiles before tightening the clamps.

Drawer

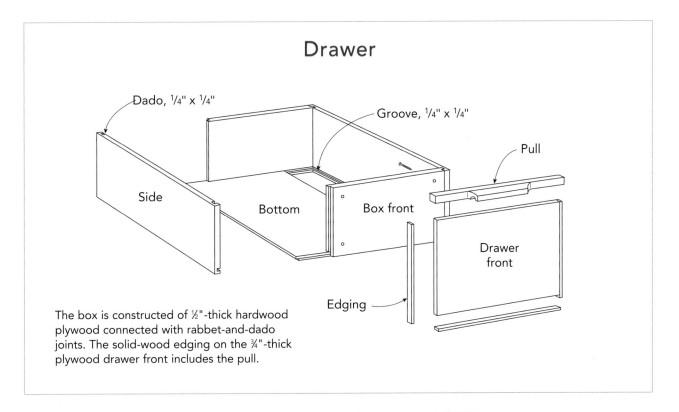

Dado, ¼" x ¼"

Groove, ¼" x ¼"

Pull

Side

Bottom

Box front

Drawer front

Edging

The box is constructed of ½"-thick hardwood plywood connected with rabbet-and-dado joints. The solid-wood edging on the ¾"-thick plywood drawer front includes the pull.

9. Using a flush-trimming bit, rout the stile overhang flush to the sides of the case.

Building the Drawers

The drawers are simple plywood boxes. The drawer fronts are made separately and then attached with screws after installing the drawer boxes into the case.

Make the boxes

1. Cut the plywood pieces for the drawer boxes. Accurate sawing here makes a big difference in the fit and installation of the drawers, so work carefully.

2. Mark the parts for orientation, then sand their inside faces. Sanding after cutting the joints can ruin the joint fit. Use a flat sanding block, being careful not to round over the edges.

3. Cut the drawer joints.

4. After doing a dry clamp-up to make sure all the parts fit well, glue up the drawer boxes on a flat surface (see **photo C**). I just spot glue the bottoms, applying a dab of glue in the center of each groove.

PHOTO C: Use hardwood cauls to distribute clamping pressure along the joints. Compare diagonal measurements to make sure the drawer box is square under clamp pressure. Cock the clamps a bit if necessary.

ROUTER MORTISING JIG

In a typical loose tenon joint, a mortise is routed into the edge of one member (in this case the stile) and a mating mortise is routed into the end of the other member (here, the rail). A separately made tenon is then glued into the mortises to create a very strong joint.

Edge mortises are easy to rout using a standard router edge guide. However, end mortises require a jig to hold the workpiece vertical and provide router support. The mortising jig shown here allows you to rout edge mortises and end mortises with the same edge guide setting. Router-travel stops ensure mortises of matching length. The vertical fence can be installed at an angle for routing mortises in the ends of mitered pieces. Here's how the jig works to cut face frame joints.

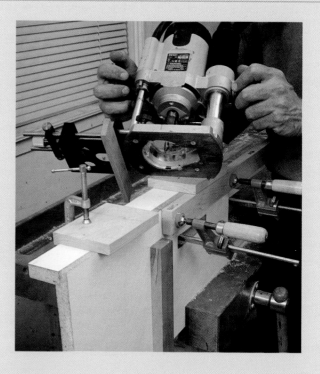

1. Mark the rail spacing on the inner edges of your face frame stiles. Then lay out one stile mortise.

2. Mount an upcut spiral bit of the proper diameter in the router.

3. Clamp the stile to the jig so the stile's inner edge is aligned with the top edge of the jig. (Important: To ensure flush joints, always place the inner face of a workpiece against the face of the jig.) Align the rail position mark (or end of the stile when appropriate) with a line drawn upward from the jig's fence (see photo above). Then clamp the router-travel stops in place.

4. Adjust the router edge guide to locate the bit over the marked-out mortise. Position the bit at one end of the mortise and clamp a stop against the appropriate side of the router base. Slide the router to the opposite end of the mortise and clamp the other stop in place.

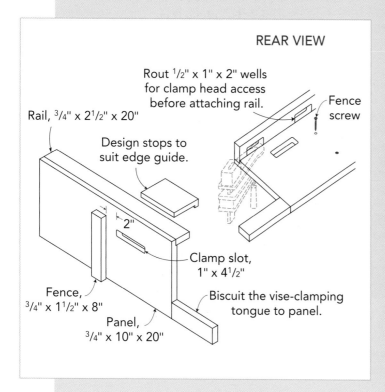

REAR VIEW

Rout $1/2$" x 1" x 2" wells for clamp head access before attaching rail.

Fence screw

Rail, $3/4$" x $2^1/2$" x 20"

Design stops to suit edge guide.

2"

Clamp slot, 1" x $4^1/2$"

Fence, $3/4$" x $1^1/2$" x 8"

Biscuit the vise-clamping tongue to panel.

Panel, $3/4$" x 10" x 20"

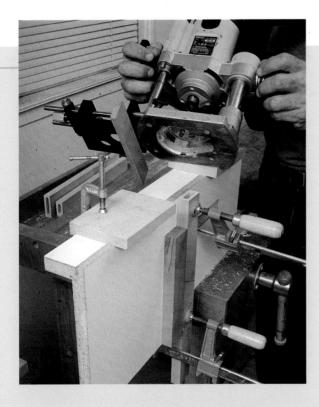

5. Rout the mortise in successive passes, pushing the router away from you with the edge guide to your right. Maintain firm downward pressure on the half of the router that rides on the jig.

6. Rout all other stile mortises of the same length in the same manner.

7. To set up to rout the mating mortises, clamp a rail in place against the jig's fence and flush to the top of the jig (see photo above). Without changing the position of the stops, rout the mortise. Repeat for all other rail mortises of the same length.

8. To rout mortises of a different length, simply adjust the position of the right-hand stop, then rout the matching stile and rail mortises in the same manner as above.

This process reads more complicated than it is. Once you've completed one set of joints using this jig, you'll find the process very efficient.

5. Sand the joints on the front of each box flush.

Make the drawer fronts

1. Working as accurately as possible, cut the plywood for the drawer fronts.

2. Make the edging pieces and the blanks for the pulls. I plane the stock for the edging about $\frac{1}{32}$ in. thicker than the plywood. Then I rip the strips slightly oversize, plane them to $\frac{1}{4}$ in., and crosscut them about $\frac{1}{16}$ in. oversize in length

3. Glue the bottom edging in place. I use bar clamps to pull both drawer fronts together with their bottom edges butting. After the glue cures, pare the ends flush with a very sharp chisel, and plane and scrape the faces flush.

4. Apply the side edging in a similar manner; then trim it flush to the plywood. Sand the face of the drawer front through 220 grit.

5. Lay out the shape of the pull on its blank (see "Drawer Pull" on p. 280). Then bandsaw to within $\frac{1}{16}$ in. of the cut line.

6. Rout, file, or sand to the cut line. I like template routing for this because of its accuracy and repeatability (see **photo D** on p. 280). I make the template from $\frac{1}{2}$-in.-thick hardwood plywood, cutting the shape with a jigsaw and then refining it with files and sandpaper.

7. Rout the recess on the underside of the pull using a $\frac{1}{2}$-in.-diameter corebox bit mounted in the router table.

8. Glue each pull to its drawer front. After the glue cures, scrape the edging flush to the drawer front, feathering back from the projecting area of the pull.

9. Tilt the tablesaw blade about 14 degrees and rip the bevel on the pull, with the drawer front lying on its back on the saw. The rear edge of the bevel should meet the plane of the drawer front after smoothing, so saw a bit shy of the final shape.

10. Smooth the bevel with a block plane, then sand the pull through 220 grit.

Drawer Pull

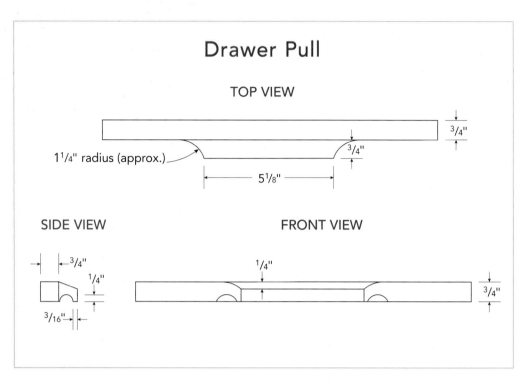

TOP VIEW

1 1/4" radius (approx.)   3/4"   5 1/8"   3/4"

SIDE VIEW   FRONT VIEW

3/4"   1/4"   3/16"   1/4"   3/4"

PHOTO D: A template guides a flush-trimming bit for routing the pull to final shape. The wooden fence registers the pull blank and supports the router. Double-sided tape holds the blank to the template.

Installing the Drawers

Commercial drawer slides typically consist of two parts: One that attaches to the case and one that attaches to the drawer box. With the slides that I used, you mount the sliding rail assembly on the case and a quick-disconnect rail on the drawer box. If you use a different style of slide, refer to its installation instructions.

Attach the slides

1. Screw the drawer shims to the case sides. Align the bottom edge of each shim with the bottom of the drawer opening. The exposed faces of the shims must be flush to the face frame. Plane or shim them as necessary to accomplish this.

2. Screw each sliding rail assembly to its drawer shim. Make sure the slides are square to the face frame and set back ⅛ in. from it. Install just a front and a rear screw into the vertical slots for now.

3. Screw the rails to the drawer boxes. I used a 2¹⁵⁄₁₆-in.-wide spacer to locate each rail the proper distance from the bottom edge of the drawer side (see **photo E**).

4. Install the drawer boxes and adjust the slides as necessary to bring the drawer box front flush with the rear face of the face frame. There should be about ⅛ in. of space between the box bottom and the drawer opening.

Attach the drawer fronts and file rails

1. Remove the drawer boxes, and bore a ³⁄₁₆-in.-dia. hole through the box front near each lower inside corner (see "Drawer" on p. 277). Drill from the inside of the box.

2. Drill a ⁹⁄₆₄-in.-diameter hole through the box front near each top corner. Then countersink these holes from the inside of the box.

3. Reinstall the drawer boxes. Then apply a piece of thin double-sided tape to the outside of the drawer box front near each corner.

4. Place ¹⁄₁₆-in.-thick shims at the bottom of each drawer opening. Stand the drawer fronts on top of the shims and center them in their openings.

5. Press each drawer front firmly against the tape, then remove the drawers without shifting the fronts. Attach each drawer front using #6 by 1-in. pan-head screws driven through the ³⁄₁₆-in.-dia. lower holes.

6. Reinsert the drawers, then recheck the drawer opening gaps for consistency. If necessary, shift the drawer fronts using small bar clamps pulling against the drawer box on one end. When you're happy with the fit, drive a #6 by 1-in. drywall screw through each of the upper drawer box holes.

7. Replace the pan-head screws with drywall screws, countersinking the holes first. Any remaining inconsistencies in the gap can be corrected by handplaning the drawer edging.

8. Drive the rest of the screws into the drawer slides to secure the adjustments.

9. Cut the plastic file rails to length and snap them onto the drawer sides (see **photo F**).

Finishing Up

1. Touch-up sand all of the exposed surfaces. Then apply the finish of your choice. Sometimes I lacquer these cabinets, but I applied four coats of wiping varnish to this

PHOTO E: After installing the sliding rail assemblies to the case, attach the quick-disconnect rails to the drawer box sides. A plywood spacer quickly and accurately positions the rails.

PHOTO F: Plastic file rails slip tightly over the drawer sides to carry hanging file folders. No nails or screws are required.

one, sanding between coats with successively finer grits. (see the section "A Favorite Finish" on p. 19). Don't finish the drawer interiors unless you want to honestly complain about all of your "stinkin' bills."

2. Attach the cabinet top with six screws from inside.

SOURCES

FLAMINGO

Flamingo Specialty Veneer
Company Inc.
356 Glenwood Ave.
East Orange, NJ 07017
Phone: (973) 672-7600
Fax: (973) 675-7778
Veneer and veneering supplies

GARRETT WADE

161 Avenue of the Americas
New York, NY 10013
(800) 221-2942
www.garrettwade.com
Woodworking tools and supplies

HIGHLAND HARDWARE

1045 N. Highland Ave. NE
Atlanta, GA 30306
(800) 241-6748
www.tools-for-
woodworking.com/index
*Tools, woodworking supplies,
and finishes*

LEE VALLEY

P.O. Box 1780
Ogdensburg, NY 13669
(800) 871-8158
www.leevalley.com
*Cupboard locks, knife hinges, hardware,
tools, and woodworking supplies*

LIE-NIELSEN TOOLWORKS

P.O. Box 9, Route 1
Warren, ME 04864
(800) 327-2520
www.lie-nielsen.com
Exceptional handplanes

ROCKLER

4365 Willow Dr.
Medina, MN 55340
(800) 279-4441
www.rockler.com
*Hardware, casters, tools, and
woodworking supplies*

WOODCRAFT

P.O. Box 1686
560 Airport Industrial Rd.
Parkersburg, WV 26102
(800) 225-1135
www.woodcraft.com

WOODWORKER'S HARDWARE

P.O. Box 180
Sauk Rapids, MN 56379
(800) 383-0130
www.wwhardware.com
*Drawer slides, hanging files, rails,
casters, hinges, clothes rods, locks,
catches, pulls, etc.*

WOODWORKER'S SUPPLY

1108 N. Glen Rd.
Casper, WY 82601
(800) 645-9292
www.woodworker.com
*Large dowels, General Finishes
Seal-A-Cell and Arm-R-Seal, hardware,
tools, and woodworking supplies*